PERSONS AN[

VIBS

Volume 77

Robert Ginsberg
Executive Editor

Associate Editors

a volume in
Natural Law Studies
NLS
Vincent L. Luizzi, Editor

PERSONS AND IMMORTALITY

Kenneth A. Bryson

Amsterdam - Atlanta, GA 1999

∞ The paper on which this book is printed meets the requirements of "ISO 9706:1994, Information and documentation - Paper for documents - Requirements for permanence".

ISBN: 90-420-0485-1
©Editions Rodopi B.V., Amsterdam - Atlanta, GA 1999
Printed in The Netherlands

DEDICATION

This book is dedicated to the goals and objectives of value inquiry, a task made urgent by the pressing relativism of the age.

CONTENTS

EDITORIAL FOREWORD

Kenneth A. Bryson's thesis in *Persons and Immortality* confronts some ponderous questions and formidable realities. They are intriguing. He argues that there is reasonable hope for immortality. His arguments deviate from traditional views, and so they will invite the reader to re-spur his own desultory thoughts about (1) mind-body dualism, (2) God's nature, (3) our identity. These are the big three that, in my judgment, will draw the reader into Bryson's text. The careful reader will agree, I think, that Bryson has handled adroitly these difficult topics that link into his thesis about immortality. This is not a book to buzz through. His prose and arguments are weighty.

In his corner, no longer an antimony but an ally, is the fact that religion and science these days are more often, and with greater ingenuity, discovering where they can agree. From E.O. Wilson's acceptance of God as a possible explanation of creation, to Stephen Jay Gould's naturalistic articulation of science\religion common denominators and Stephen Hawking's stalwart willingness to say that it is within the purview of science at least *to consider* the question of God, it is no longer clever to dispute the partialities of science or denigrate the ontological story spawned by religion. Bryson knows this, and so he draws without reserve from the wells of atomic physics to help support his thesis.

Bryson's approach to the huge question of immortality is ignited by our monumental after-death curiosity and fear, and the latter are ignited, in turn, by our obstinate clinging to the idea of God and what He wants of us. Bryson's labors on behalf of these "permanent things" make no sacrifice in philosophical acuity, critical scholarship, and courageous insight in abandoning familiar paths of inquiry he thinks untrue. He does not leave us empty; he fills their place with positive replacements that make sense. We recognize in ourselves a "psychological addiction to God." Are we to abandon this addiction, or shall we try to account for it as reasonably as we can? Perhaps the biblical James is wrong: "For what is your life? It is even a vapor that appeareth for a little time, and then vanisheth away" (*James* 4:4).

Four interrelated central lines of thought, in my judgment, affix the argument as Bryson sees it. These lines of thought are really different from what we are used to, and they are what make Bryson's book fascinating for the reader and a mark of excellence in scholarship.

(1) Immortality means nothing to us if we abandon our individuality and merge, as Buddhists believe, into an inchoate, impersonal, cosmic whole. Since we are embodied in this life, therefore, we need our bodies to survive our death.

(2) Our personal identity no longer can be understood through an abstract definition of "human nature," which rests on the old "essence definition." (It led also to the disembodied self through a dismantling dualism. This does us no good in our afterlife addiction.) Rather, personal identity is defined through our relationships: to ourselves, to others, to nature (God's creation).

(3) Accordingly, mind-body dualism has to be abandoned. The Cartesian split is false. What takes its place? Matter (body) reduces to mind (soul) in Bryson's account. Now we can more clearly see our way toward a meaningful personal immortality.

(4) What about the inexplicable mystery of God's goodness and the existence of evil in the world? God has two aspects from which to view His being. There is God the creator (this aspect of God is indirectly responsible for evil in the world). There is also God the perfect and divine being to whom we pray and, importantly, to whom we reach out for moral direction. In making choices to be moral (to avoid evil), we show the teleological nature of our spiritual needs and inspiration. These two aspects of God merge into one comprehensive Being. And our capacity to choose good over evil makes sense of the reason why both we and God the Creator would want to be immortal.

Of course we have free will. Through choice and reflection, we make ourselves (the person-making process Bryson alludes to). Hence our existence captures an entelechy that is distinctly human and spiritual. Becoming immortal is becoming God-like, that is, continuing in the afterlife to strive for the morally perfect.

Along the way, Bryson criticizes several key figures in the broad philosophical tradition that have a bearing on what we can reasonably believe about our survival after death. His criticisms are necessary in order to shift our understanding both from secular epistemology and from the usual theologically embroidered story of our immortality that is founded in Greek philosophy (overly rationalistic) and stresses only our soul as surviving. The shift moves us toward Bryson's alternative that he thinks makes sense to our modern mind.

(1) Aquinas does not have it quite right. Body and soul are separated in what is implied in Christian theology about an afterlife. We need our bodies to be complete individuals or persons. (2) Descartes's mind-body dualism, too, does not comport with science; we know, for example, that we need our bodies to think. Nor does it relieve our desire to know who we are after our death. Our bodies help to define our personalities. (3) Kant's moral philosophy, which, for Bryson, makes little sense when only secular, that is, godless and not tied to what we believe God wants of us, is incomplete. (4) Hume's "bundle theory" of perception has no unified "self" at all. What can immortality mean to us if we have no self?

Natural law. What makes Bryson's book a natural law study is its take on this age-old moral tradition. It goes like this: Traditional rationalism in definition of natural law is abstract and does not come to grips with the local and particularistic nature of our moral choices. We may "have a nature," but (1) we create it, and (2) it is defined by relationships, not by an essence. (3) Moreover, *we* create this nature by our choices. Hence through a few tidy conceptual linkages, Bryson acknowledges personal freedom; redefines our nature as essentially relational; indicates how evil got here in the first place; and makes a large place for our desire to continue to live.

Essences as the prototype for limitations of meaning and hence as prototypes for "human nature" (rational animal) as the basis of teleological natural law no longer suit the scope of what we know. Essences are out of step with science and modern culture. The belief that human nature reflects certain constants or universals is probably true, as evinced by current social, anthropological, and genetic studies. But the definition need no longer base itself on a stoney set of necessary and sufficient features, of which "rational" has philosophically been determinative of what ought to be our moral quest and values. For Bryson's purposes, "rational animal" also provides no grounds–indeed, it repudiates those grounds–that preserve the value of our bodies as essential components in idiosyncratic survival.

As an alternative to this disembodied, socially isolated, and overly rational concept of our nature (silent, as well, on our vital capability to choose), Bryson proposes three relationships that constitute the perspectives through which our nature is defined and which account for both the self that lives now, at this moment, and the person that self-presents in the afterlife. "The natural law is expressed in human relationships rather than in human nature" (p. 80). He thinks these relationships are not only obviously evident but they clarify, as well, the natural orders, patterns, and laws of the universe as we know them–in particular, those familiar to our social experience. Importantly, unlike an abstract "human nature," they identify our unique personalities that go with us after death. These important relationships, central to Bryson's immortality thesis and its logic, are our relations to ourselves, to others, and to nature and the world around us.

Some years ago, I too came to see the shortcomings of "rational animal" in a number of respects. It fails, for one, a vigorous and widely ranging applicability of the moral life as we know it, which comprises far more than the obligation to fulfill our rational nature. Aristotle's "social animal" seemed a sturdier ground for a definition of our nature. Tentatively, I posited "human being-in-society" as a more useful idea for the way in which we evolve toward a higher moral self; for all of our social morality rests on our relations to other persons. Bryson has spelled out and extended these social bonds.

Technology and nature. Bryson greatly respects science. But he is critical of unexamined technological changes when they seem to damage nature or our spiritual interests (for instance, direct themselves toward the worst excesses of materialism). Skeptical myself of political intervention in the culture and greatly dubious of the capacity of central governments to foresee cultural consequences, I doubt most technological changes can be examined with sufficient prevision to thwart socially destructive results. The history of wise political forethought is dim. Bryson fears technological fixes to social problems. I fear political fixes because they are coerced, not freely chosen. Do we have to fish between the devil and the deep blue sea? I wonder whether Bryson is overly harsh in believing technology robs our significant relationships, especially those with nature, of their natural ends toward self, others, and the world.

Our technocratic mentality, he thinks, downgrades and alienates our humanness, setting us further from goodness. By materializing everything, it degrades the richness of our lives. It invades and alters nature, that most precious relationship we have to the world which the creator God put us in. Bryson says, "the psychology of modern technology [is] the incessant addiction to power and control..." (p. 147). Sometimes by innuendo, the stereotypes of exploitation, oppression, domination, and economic inequality creep into Bryson's text regarding his negative view of technology. Thus, it would be easy for him to fall into the worst excesses of communitarianism, which is statism. But he does not bite this poison apple. His "spiritual change of heart" and emphasis on personal freedom, our choice of relationships, and our individuality save him from the falsehoods of crude economic determinism. *We* make our soul. And it is our soul, not our economic condition, that defines the person-making process that, engaged in with moral sensitivity, admits us to heaven.

I have noticed that technology-bashing is most often done by people who emphasize only its dark side: its (1) frequently mechanistic modes of application; (2) sometimes foolish waste and disutilities; (3) unintelligent, dangerous, and sometimes criminal atrocities like torture, terror, and war. Yet the same nuclear discoveries that manufacture bombs also manufacture energy–our lifesaving possibility to abandon the waste and pollution of fossil fuels. Technological genius works both ways. The weaving loom and the home arts do nothing, it is true, to destroy nature; but they kept India in poverty until she discovered the computer, leaving time for play and leisure, innovation, and the astonishing market system that spells economic betterment.

A too lavish love of nature's ways (romanticism) is as pernicious a philosophy as too slavish a love of technology. What is technology anyway? We can only define the extreme cases. The hard cases blend the simple into the complex: fire? the flint knife? the well or the aquaduct? the sun window or the agriculturalist's greenhouse? the hybrid seedcorn? How to place these innovations?

In his effort to preserve the integrity of our third relationship, that to nature, Bryson makes a beginning by differentiating between the mindless stockpiling of energy that may deplete a useful resource and benign intervention with benign purposes like skinning a fish or drawing water (for instance, the proposed new Israeli waterfall that will aerate water from the Dead Sea as it spills into the desert plains of northern Sinai and thence into the channels of the Nile). Bryson's formula is a useful distinction. But it is hard to make judgments that face the future with facts we do not have.

Nature is not always good: crop failure, property losses, drought and freeze, disease, floods, typhoons, tornados. It is putting technology to work–distribution of food, administration of medicine–that gets us out of nature's disasters. The buffalo plow never cured any society of starvation, but the resourceful technologies of water delivery can save a society from ruin.

Technology is not the villain. The villain, as Bryson recognizes, is disregard for effective, valuable, and humane applications of these useful means toward useful ends. It cannot be Bryson's object to defend another dualism. The technocratic mind-set faces in two directions: We can use it to express that singularly curative quality of hope. Or we can be careless and arrogant. It is certain that a sustaining arrogance can dispel all hope of spiritual recovery.

> Science and technology are preoccupied with results (technicism), but results can only be evaluated as ethical when they are aligned with a celebration of the divine telos within psyche (p. 147).

Bryson's *Persons and Immortality* should occupy shelf space in every divinity department, religious institution, theology school, and philosophy library. And it should be prominent on the shelves of medical schools and accessible to their ethical-counseling services regarding end-of-life decisions. What I have said should make clear that Bryson has worked hard and conscientiously at matters of life and death for their practical, moral, logical, and religious implications as they affect dying individuals. And indeed affect all of us who harbor hope for continuation. The teleological perspective on life bestows on us these difficult questions which our psyches, anyway, affirm as essential in thinking about the quality of human life, about each other, and about why anything exists at all. The greatest moral advance of all times, in my judgment (its origin in Judaism, continuation in Christianity, embodiment and emphasis in Locke and the American legal system), is that the individual is important and that the individual's own life counts as nothing less than an absolute good. If we can be convinced that our personal immortality is an essential plank in this irreproachable moral idea of the sanctity of the individual person, then a mature and comprehensive defense such as Bryson's should be taken very seriously.

Virginia Black
Founding Editor, Natural Law Studies (1992-1996)
Pace University, Pleasantville, N.Y.
August 1998

Dualism

~~P14~~ P10.

being a person + immortal   P11.

good life   P15

consciousness   P40

Sartre's play No Exit P46   + flower book P146

God   P49

What is death P57-58   P77-76.

against God's existence   P77.

Human being   P77

Human death is oxymoronic   P93.

PREFACE

The study of persons and immortality moves from thanatology to eschatology. My interest in thanatology grew out of my lectures in existential phenomenology during the early 1970s. At that time, the limitations of phenomenology prompted me to examine death from the perspective of being's unconcealment rather than consciousness. Thus, I view death, not as the absence of consciousness, but as the infolding of being's unconcealment. At human death, being asserts its final primacy by refusing to be for consciousness. Being does not stand outside consciousness, however. The traditional legacy of mind-body dualism is indefensible. Yet, it is reasonable to posit the existence of a mirror image of being's unconcealment in our *post-mortem* existence, raising the dialogue to new heights in the afterlife.

In the past twenty-five years of teaching, I have sought to introduce my students to an array of issues in the expanding universe of philosophy, but it has become increasingly difficult to document why we are ethical beings, or should care about our associations. The deconstruction of human nature undermines the traditional base of ethics. So, we need to look elsewhere, namely, to the possibility of entering into relationships as the base of ethics. The existence of an absolute is a hard pill to swallow in the age of emotivism, however, but how else can we sustain a meaningful dialogue in philosophy without foundation?

The first task is to investigate the insufficiencies of the traditional representation of being human. This prepares the way for a fuller account of being ethical. We become persons in three main perspectives, namely, in self, toward others, and in being's unconcealment. This view of being a person is panentheistic. Panentheism is not the identification of God and nature, but the belief that God is in all things, or that the whole of existence arises because of divine patterns, or laws. That view provides a fulcrum, not only for ethics, but for a defensible afterlife argument. Since our relationships define us, they must continue in the afterlife, if the principle of personal identity is to be safeguarded. Yet, if death is the end of my relationships, how can that be me in the afterlife?

The opening pages of the book invite the reader to join in a simple experiment. Imagine that in one stroke all your support systems are removed and you find yourself completely alone, without friends, spouse, family, or acquaintances. You are no longer part of any culture or belong to any society because all traces of the world have disappeared. To make matters worse, you are afflicted by a sudden acceleration in the loss of memory cells and all remembered experiences are vanishing in turn, leaving an overwhelming sense of anxiety. You search your heart for some sign of a greater good, but that too is gone. As you frantically look about to identify some familiar trace of reality, your central nervous system begins to fail; you cannot see, smell, hear, taste, or sense anything. All is gone. So this is death, you say, and this is what it feels like to die. But you are still conscious of the last strings of remembered experiences, how then is this death? The experience seems more like dying, a condition which although incompatible with the continuance of life is not irreversible. How, then, is the condition reversed? It is reversed through a process in which my stream of consciousness reconnects with God, the other, and being's unconcealment.

In this imaginary death world all relationships with self, others, and being have ceased. No rational agent or subject of experiences remains. The perspective of the person as a being in relationships provides a key to some of the psychological, ethical, epistemological, and metaphysical questions we have about the nature of persons and the afterlife.

Being human is not an event, but a process. The focal point of the book is to examine the process through the study of those relationships that make us persons. We begin our journey as belonging to the whole, only to enter into specific relationships that individuate us. We become individuals through a dialogical fusion of opposites when our tendency toward relationships meets the particulars of a given locale. The tendency is absolute while the particulars are relative to culture. The person-making process allows us to view certain ways we have of framing the world, and becoming human. The process of becoming human enlists the typology of entering into relationships with good and evil, other human beings, and reality, or being's unconcealment. Since the evidence suggests that the creator enters into personal relationships with us in this world, we expect that the creator will want to maintain us in the afterlife. The creator entering into personal relationships with us is another name for God.

So, the study moves from thanatology into eschatology as an explanation, not only of becoming human, but of continuing the process in the afterlife. The view of death from the perspective of being's unconcealment, as well as recent developments in quantum physics, characterize the afterlife state as a continuation of relationships begun on earth. The "nothing" surrounding the "Big Bang" origin of cosmos plays a focal role in physics, philosophy, and religion.

ACKNOWLEDGMENT

I wrote this book while a Visiting Fellow at the University of Wales, Lampeter, on sabbatical leave from the University College of Cape Breton, Nova Scotia. I would like to thank both institutions for their support. In particular, I wish to thank the following individuals from the Lampeter academic community: David Cockburn for his candid discussion of two papers I read at seminars in Lampeter, and for permission to quote from a special collection of papers he edited on *Death and the Value of Life* (Saint David's University: Trivium, 1992). I am grateful to Paul Badham of the Department of Theology, Religious Studies and Islamic Studies, Saint David's University, Lampeter, for permission to quote from his unpublished article, "Religion, Science, and Philosophy." I have found their work to be of great value in the preparation of my own text. I am grateful to James Robinson, intellectual at-large, for his commentary on my interpretation of Heidegger and Wittgenstein. He often set me straight. Thanks for his friendship while I was in Lampeter. I owe a debt of gratitude to Morland Beazley, who is pursuing his own work on angels at Lampeter, for arranging frequent meetings with doctoral students. We engaged in stimulating discussions of the afterlife, and on John Hick's *Evil and the God of Love* (1977), while sipping on a good cup of tea. These individuals exemplify the tradition of *Vera Lex* (Journal of the Natural Law Society) in action. My thanks to Virginia Black, Executive Editor, *Vera Lex,* for permission to quote from an article written by Robert Humphrey in *Vera Lex*, 14:1&2. I wish to express special thanks to Virginia Black for her role as my Editor. Since 1996, she has conscientiously been my partner in this project, suggesting in a soft, insightful voice not only the meaning of words, but the meaning of sentences. Her dedication to the rigors of natural law theory sharpened my own interest in the universal as transcultural experience. I thank my family for their love and support at those times when our relationship was reduced to an e-mail connection.

Grateful acknowledgment is extended to Bantam Doubleday Dell Publishing Group, Inc. for permission to quote a story from Anthony de Mello's *(1984) The Song of the Bird.* My thanks to ITP Nelson Canada for permission to quote from *People, Penguins, and Plastic Trees.* Second Edition. Christine Pierce and Donald Van De Veer eds. (1995). References to these and other quotations appearing in the book are noted in Works Cited.

INTRODUCTION

The success of the religious belief in immortality depends on the evidence for the existence of God, an immaterial soul or mind, and human nature. We also need to support the view that God will always want to maintain relationships with us in the afterlife. So, immortality is a hard sell.

The existence of God is not self-evident. What we might ascribe to the divinity is often of cultural origin. Further, contemporary literature is usually skeptical about the existence of an immaterial mind or soul. But even if the belief is proven true, the soul's separation from the body at death raises the troublesome problem of personal identity. How can a disembodied soul be me in the afterlife? Although the Christian and Islamic world expresses a belief in the resurrection of the body, this compounds the problem of personal identity, for now I must explain how I can be me with a different body. Finally, in our day of genetic engineering, being human is nothing special, even less is it a gift from God. The design of a nature for humans has become a technological issue, although it raises moral problems.

But the rejection of God, soul and human nature does more than throw out the case for immortality. It carries the objective ground of values in its wake, prompting moral relativism. Yet, the belief in immortality lingers.

If the present study was to focus on proofs for the actual existence of the afterlife state, it might never get off the ground. But if we can imagine the possibility of such a state, then, we can develop the sorts of arguments required to render the belief in its real existence more likely. So, my hunch is that the belief in immortality (and ethics) is supported by a paradigm shift in which we move away from the traditional representation of being human to focus on the relationships or associations that characterize us. In that event, we are immortal if the laws or patterns and other associations that individuate us in our *pre-mortem* existence continue to do so in our *post-mortem* state.

One

PERSONAL IDENTITY

1. Who Am I?

I am a string of relationship stories, remembered, and forgotten, acting out the many roles of being a person. I am nothing outside my relationships: parent, spouse, worker, researcher, teacher, committee member, consumer, statistic, advocate, and someone the dog recognizes at night. I get involved in social action and attend church. I sleep and eat, wash, shave, and bleed. I love, hate, fight, withdraw, and pay taxes. I have a fifty-six-year history of being human, one too long to be told or of much interest to anyone except my family and a few friends. I am a typical human being. But other human beings have similar stories. What individuates me? My daughter's dog also has relationships. How does she know I am not the dog? It is not enough to say that I am a rational animal, or have no whiskers, since we both enter into relationship with her. What else makes me who I am rather than the dog, or some other human being?

I do not have a problem with my identity until I begin to look for the fundamental element of being human. The problem is that I am not anything outside my experiences. Where is the illusive subject, or self, in the absence of experiences and associations? I seem to be no more and no less than the sum of my relationships. In quantum physics, the properties of the part can only be understood from the dynamics of the whole. The term Fritjof Capra (1992) uses to denote this phenomenon is systemic thinking, or systems theory, although this does not describe it completely. Structure is the manifestation of underlying processes. Being human, then, is an outcome of a movement from the whole to the part. I am born out of relationships that individuate me.

Since I also believe in the existence of an afterlife condition (originating in my participation in church relationships), will my relationships accompany me in the afterlife? If that is me that survives death, then, the whole of my relationships must accompany me in death. But how is that possible? Nothing of my relationships survives death. My human body, for instance, is reduced to particles. The goal of this book is to undertake that inquiry.

2. Some Focal Points

The study of persons and immortality enlists a number of interdependent topics, such as God, soul, survival, personal identity, relationships, being's unconcealment (including my empirical or natural existence), and dualism. The reference to "unconcealment" corresponds to Heidegger's use of the term "*Unverborgenheit*" as an opening out from protective concealing, a harboring forth. Being is equivalent to presence and is dependent on *Dasein* (person). *Dasein* is the being for whom entities are made present or manifest. Thus, being's unconcealment is a condition in which the real shows itself, sending us on an errand, so that truth or "*aletheia*" happens. However, concealment is the source and foundation of all unconcealment. Our "*Gestell*" or enframing is a calling-forth, a demanding summons that "gathers" so as to reveal or unveil what is concealed (truth).

The three main lines of argument for immortality are the religious, or metaphysical, the psychological, and the epistemological. But the arguments fail to convince the skeptic that a belief in personal immortality is a true belief. So it is fitting that we should raise anew the problem of immortality. Our aim is to do so in the perspective of the person as a being in relationships. This occasions a shift in the interpretation of natural law theory from the conception of human nature as universal essence toward an assessment of the particulars of our relationships. In order to legitimate that shift, however, the tendency to enter into relationships must be seen to be absolute. This moves the ground of ethics toward kinds of relationships and away from fixed essences. But before we can examine the arguments in detail, we must recognize what is deficient about the traditional representation of being human. One of the major difficulties–carried into our own day–is the problem of dualism.

The view of the disembodied soul generates the problem of personal identity: if the afterlife exists, there must be continuity between the *pre-mortem* and *post-mortem* states of the person. But the human body does not leave the natural order at death. The tradition tries to solve the problem by identifying the person with the soul. Thus, dualism carries the problem of personal identity.

Saint Thomas Aquinas (1225-1274) seats the divine telos within human nature. He says in the *Summa Theologica* that "knowledge of the eternal law is imprinted in us" (1-2, Q. 93, a 2). We perfect ourselves by following the basic moral principles of human nature. These principles are objective. They are accessible to the speculative intellect. Although the human essence is universal, we act as a dynamic unit of body and soul in concrete circumstances. We are individuated entities. Once the human project is complete, the soul separates from the body to rejoin God in the afterlife. The incomplete status of the person as disembodied soul raises questions about being human. The body is an essential part of a human life. Ask anyone confined to a wheelchair, or seriously disabled. So, something is fundamentally wrong with the Thomistic view. Since my body does not immediately follow me in the afterlife, that cannot be me that survives death, or accomplishes the divine telos.

Perhaps being human is a process rather than an event. The person as process becomes human through relationships rather than through an appeal to eternal essences. Person-making processes take place at three fundamental levels: in self, with other human beings, and in the world. This view provides a solution to the problem of personal identity. It also lays a dynamic foundation for ethics and morality. The shift moves on the arms of being's unconcealment.

The focal place Martin Heidegger (1884-1976) assigns to being's unconcealment serves in the study of both thanatology and eschatology. It provides a principle of continuity from our *pre-mortem* to our *post-mortem* existence. Heidegger does not venture beyond the natural order, however. In order to move beyond him, the text maintains a new distinction between being's unconcealment and the horizon surrounding it. The study of being is the object of metaphysics or the theory of reality in general. The horizon, or the possibility of the nothing surrounding being is the creator, possibly God. The horizon points beyond itself to the root of the possibility of doing metaphysics. Heidegger hints that this is the case, but refuses to move beyond the natural order. But a study of the principles that accompany scientific inductions reveals that the psychology of thought moves us beyond the natural order to wait for an explanation of that order. This might not be God, but it is at least the creator. The belief in a loving creator, however, does not lead to a belief in personal immortality. Yet, it makes our continued existence more likely, if the creator is God. If it can be shown that God as loving creator interacts with us in the temporal order, it becomes more reasonable to expect that God might wish to maintain relationships with us after death. This is a big gulp to take in a small book. But the shift toward relationships is a beginning.

The study of the person as a being in relationships points beyond itself to the root of the possibility of entering into relationships. Is God the objective ground of that possibility here and in the afterlife? In order for that to be the case, God must be seen to interact with us at two levels; the natural and the supernatural. In that event, God is revealed in the natural order (as creator), although hidden in the supernatural order. But if it can be shown that God's transcendence is the ground of the creator's immanence, as containing the possibility of the person's dialogue, the possibility of doing metaphysics is explained. The God postulate will make sense. But we need a focal point. The person as correlate of being's unconcealment provides a bridge between both orders of existence. Metaphysics has to be rehabilitated to accomplish this stretch. How is this possible? Frederick Ferré (1996) suggests that the merger of religion and quantum mechanics is a first step toward that goal. This study also takes that path.

First, we need to examine the meaning of being a person, and how that connects to being's unconcealment. The view of the person as a rational soul or "subject of experiences" is unsatisfactory, as René Descartes's (1596-1650) mind-body problem demonstrates. Some cartesian philosophers, or string-theorists, then added that being a person only has a linguistic meaning. David Hume (1711-1776) and Derek Parfit (1984) maintain that nothing real corresponds to being a person, since we are not anything in the absence of our associations. The independent subject of experiences does not exist. They provide good insight, although they do not go far enough into the process of delineating relationships, or rising above their own associations. Perhaps we can begin from systems theory rather than from the part. It seems more likely that the part obtains from the whole rather than the whole from the part. My view is panentheistic (God is present in the part). It fills the perceived deficiencies of traditional metaphysics while avoiding the extremes of the no-person theory. It explains God's immanence and transcendence.

We need to connect being's unconcealment and being human with the immortality propositions of religion. The religious argument is a non-starter without immortality. Belief in the afterlife is carried on the assumption that the divine telos includes us in the afterlife. The legitimacy of this claim is secured in the role being plays in a human life. How does the divine telos unfold in history? The study of being's unconcealment suggests that the divine telos postulates unconcealment on both sides of being, in our *pre-mortem* life as well as in our *post-mortem* existence. Human death, then, must occasion a mirror image in being's unconcealment, one in which human dialogue continues, and possibly emerges to absolute unconcealment at the meta space-time level of intelligibility. The realization of the divine telos orders an end to the struggle between good and evil. This cannot happen here, so it must happen beyond the natural order where evil ends. However, the problem of evil remains a difficult challenge in theodicy. Two connected issues arise: The first, how can a loving God allow the suffering of innocent victims? The second, can that be me in the absence of the struggle between good and evil?

3. Some Dead Ends

The study of persons and immortality introduces us to a large number of interdependent issues. Paul Edwards's work *Immortality* (1992) contains an excellent introduction to the major problem areas as well as a comprehensive bibliographic guide to the issues. One of the major problems with the work in this area, however, is that immortality seems to be a non-starter without dualism. So, the problems are many. Dualism and materialism are two of the main problems. Dualism begets the problem of personal identity (can I be me as a disembodied soul) while materialism contradicts the belief many of us have about personal immortality. Materialism cannot even account for the meaning—or the truth—of its own assertion. The belief in immortality does not even get off the ground in materialism. It reduces our desire for immortality to a relativism of context. Yet, we have reason to believe that the absolute exists within us. Transcultural standards exist in human relationships. They enable us to proceed process-like toward our ultimate end, thereby avoiding the global chaos of cultural relativism and contextual determinism, or historicism.

Whatever else critics say about René Descartes, he cannot be faulted for method. He advises in his *Rules for the Direction of the Mind* that whenever we encounter the complex, we ought: "in the case of every series in which we have deduced certain facts the one from the other, to notice which fact is simple, and to mark the interval, greater, less, or equal, which separates all the others from this" (Rule vi).

This is good advice, as Descartes says; "no rule is more useful than this" (*ibid.*). We open our own study with some distinctions, and two views on being a person. The simple view on being persons is that we are a non-physical substance or subject of experiences (S). The complex view is that we are a mixture of physical and non-physical characteristics (SB). What is the connection between being a person and being immortal? The three main types of arguments for immortality are the metaphysical or religious, the epistemological and the psychological. The psychological argument is a subset of the metaphysical argument. The religious argument is based on the fundamental assumption that God exists (G). It expresses the belief that God will seek to maintain relationships with us in the afterlife. That belief corresponds to the psychological desire we express for immortality. The epistemological argument is based on the nature of human understanding. If reasoning uses immaterial processes, then, we can argue that the person, or at least the rational characteristic of being a person, does not come to an end at death. The metaphysical argument is based on the existence of a necessary, universal law of human nature. It affirms that we are created to enact the divine telos. Thus, if persons are immortal, it is because of one of the following configurations between the divine telos (G), the human soul (S), and the human body (B), namely, (GS), (GB), (SB), or (GSB). At the risk of oversimplifying the issue, the main arguments for immortality in the tradition from Plato (427-347 B.C.E.) to Descartes can be identified as follows: Plato (GS), Aristotle (384-322 B.C.E.) (SB), Aquinas (GSB), and Descartes (GS) or (GB).

Two main problems arise out of these models: dualism and personal identity. While the Thomistic argument (GSB) appears to avoid these problems, it does not. The reason it fails is found in his metaphysics where person appears primarily as being an (S). His theistic metaphysics overlaps his epistemology (and natural law philosophy). Aquinas's ethics is also based on the existence of eternal law in human nature, or soul. From the point of view of personal immortality, all of the above views lead to dead ends. This explains, in part, why contemporary philosophers have rejected both the simple and the complex view of the person. The skepticism of our age has (paradoxically) added support for a belief in the string-theory of the person, namely, that we are not anything in the absence of our associations, or remembered experiences.

And now for some definitions: According to Reese's *Dictionary of Philosophy and Religion* (1980), the immortality of the soul is "the infinitely prolonged existence of that center of awareness to which the term 'I' refers." The reference suggests that the soul or subject of experience is the essential characteristic of being human. The Oxford English *Dictionary* views the self as being "that which a person is really and intrinsically; the ego; a permanent subject of successive and varying states of consciousness." Descartes is the first to give the soul an epistemological spin toward mind. But the intent is the same: the thinking substance is unextended. The term person as an "I," "self," or "ego" also suggests the representation of the human as a substance or center of activity. It is not known when the sense of "I" as subject came into being or why we use it to refer to who we are. But in the tradition, the essential "I" is a soul or subject of experiences.

The view of the person as a soul or subject is carried in both the simple and the complex view. According to John Foster (1991), the simple theory views the person as being a basic subject or non-physical substance (p. 238). The subject as center of activity appropriates actions such as sensing, thinking, willing, and doubting, under the stewardship of the soul. The complex view is that a person has two natures, the one corporeal, the other incorporeal. What happens at human death? Both views generate a vision of an afterlife populated by disembodied souls. An added problem is that the complex view is based on dualism. Foster supports dualism, as do most proponents of immortality. In the life of a person, the interaction between mind and body is seen to generate increasingly comprehensive stages of maturity. For instance, in the early stages of development, infants are less than persons. They do not have the same rights as persons. They cannot marry, run for public office, or vote. This suggests that something happens to infants when in ordinary language we say they become adults. They learn to act responsibly. But adults are not necessarily responsible individuals. Some incompetent adults are not held criminally responsible for their actions. We seek to help them. In the tradition, the ability to anticipate and solve problems is the essential thing about being a person. This suggests that thinking is central to both the simple and the complex view of the person. What is thinking? Not every philosopher agrees that thinking is the activity of a non-physical substance, however. Materialists would not make such a claim. Identity theorists express the belief that physical events explain mental events. Paul Edwards (1992), expresses an interest in behaviorism since it preserves what is interesting about dualism while avoiding what is objectionable, such as having to explain the interaction between the physical and the non-physical (p. 44). So, the choices facing us reduce to the view of the person as non-physical substance and dualism, or else materialism. Materialism explain the intricacies of the non-physical self by explaining it away.

The "I" remains an elusive entity. We can use "I" to point to the self that underlies experiences. But it is not that subject. The "I" that is currently thinking exists beyond what is brought to mind. The subject enlists the "I" in pointing to itself. The expression "self," or "ego," also fails in that regard. Hume's objection is that the "self" is not itself a subject of experiences. He concludes that no person exists in the absence of experiences. This is a good case for materialism. But his work ends in skepticism. Why is that? Hume represents the metaphysical self through epistemology. Is that legitimate? The self can also be expressed through the characteristic property of intentionality. At that level, the self exists in body-soul relationships. But is it the same self without the body? What is the soul? Reese's

Dictionary describes soul as the vital principle of being human. The equivalent Greek term is *"psyche"* or *"pneuma."* The pre-Socratics derive the sense of soul from breath and air, a phenomenon associated with life. The Latin term is *"anima."* Soul is a valuing, somewhat pious name for self. It does not include the body. The modern epistemological sense of soul as mind is equally elusive. We cannot grasp it except in relationships. Franz Brentano's (1838-1917) characterization of consciousness as intentional deals a devastating blow to cartesianism in that regard. The separate existence of soul or mind is based on dualism. But since no self exists outside the body, dualism is difficult to defend. The soul cannot represent both itself and the body. Thus, soul and body must be seen to survive the death of a person in order to preserve personal identity. But that is manifestly impossible. The body is seen to die and rot. But can we imagine personal survival if the body operates under different laws in the afterlife?

Some philosophers think that the problem of personal identity is exaggerated. Thomas Reid (1710-1796), for instance, says that the conviction we have about our personal identity needs no philosophy to strengthen it. His definition of identity appears in John Perry (1975), where he says it expresses "a relation between a thing which is known to exist at one time, and a thing which is known to have existed at another time" (p. 108). That being the case, only an insane person doubts his identity. But the problem is that it relies on memory, which can be faulty. Although identity expresses a fundamental law of reason, the question remains: Am I the same individual when I am not reasoning or remembering? Emile Meyerson (1859-1933), a French philosopher, falls into the trap of seating identity in reasoning. To think is to identify. The problem is that when reason completes the task of identifying, it ceases to exist. What am I when I do not identify, or remember identifying anything? I usually do not think or identify when I sleep. Do I continue to exist as myself? Perhaps God keeps me in existence in the absence of my perception of myself (GS). This view was maintained by George Berkeley (1685-1753). Although Meyerson does not use God to maintain identity, his dilemma is equally profound. If we imagine a world of total identifications, one emptied of all diversity, reason posits itself into non-being. Reid also follows the Rationalist path. He says that a person is something indivisible, or "what Leibniz calls a monad" (ibid., p. 109). It turns out that a person's identity is not self-evident as he makes it out to be, or that a person exists as a "monad" in the absence of a remembered identification.

The problem of personal identity requires an identification between the states of life of the individual. That same state is expected to be maintained in the afterlife, if survival is personal. The resurrection theory establishes identity between the *pre-mortem* and *post-mortem* states of the person. But it too poses a serious problem for memory. How can I remember being me during the interval I exist without my brain? If God maintains my existence, a belief which is no doubt emotionally rewarding, can I remember that I am being maintained in the absence of my body? The possibility of personal survival is rooted in dualism. Unless I hold the (GS) view that I am essentially an immaterial mind or soul, (or monad), that is not me in the afterlife. Being a soul has a certain appeal. The belief was held by Plato and is continued in the tradition ending in Descartes. Thomas Aquinas is a Realist, that is, he claims the primacy of reality over the thought of reality, but the operations he ascribes to the speculative intellect present a conception of the person as more angelic or divine than human. Aquinas is a mystical philosopher. His view on death, for instance, as the departure of the soul from the body, raises doubts about the intimacy of the mind-body connection on earth. It satisfies his metaphysical ambition, but double-crosses the epistemology. In a discussion of the condition of the resurrected, the *Summa Theologica* reads: it is "identically the same man that shall rise again" (3, Q. 79, a 2). Although the belief is emotionally rewarding, it is deficient or leaves the shift from (GS) to the (GSB) model without justification.

The metaphysical foundation of Aquinas's difficulty is expressed in his (GS) theory of human nature and natural law. We are made in the image of God. Yet, his epistemology leaves no doubt that the body is important to being a person. The human is a dynamic union of body and soul (GSB). Consequently, the disembodied individual is diminished by death. Still, our metaphysical telos (our divinity) triumphs at the end times. The resurrection theory is riddled with difficulties. Aquinas struggles with these problems throughout the *Summa Theologica,* especially in the treatise on the resurrection (3, QQ. 69-86). The metaphysical belief that the person is primarily a soul was first expressed by Plato. While Aquinas strives to avoid Plato's idealism and dualism, he does not completely succeed. The Thomistic soul remains the essential part of the knowing process; it is primarily an intuiting thing. Descartes' s view of reason as the product of an incorporeal substance repeats the theme. It results in dualism: mental events happen to a human being because of a soul, whereas bodily events happen because of the body. Somehow both events happen to the same person. Since dualism is difficult to maintain in the face of the evidence that mind and body are joined, it usually reduces itself to materialism or its contrary idealism. Materialism explains mental events through the activity of the physical body. In that case, death is the end of the organism. In brief, the choices facing us lie between the conception of an afterlife populated by disembodied souls, or no afterlife at all.

The most influential representative of the Materialist camp is Aristotle. He suggests that body and soul are materialist principles of the person. The soul as form of the body reduces to the potentiality of matter at death. He believes in the existence of God but not in the afterlife, since God does not care about human affairs. Yet, his metaphysical biology is unclear. The *De Anima* suggests that the soul is incorporeal, or irreducible to matter, but the *Physics* views soul as being ultimately reducible to matter. His explanation of change rests on the distinction he establishes between being in act and being in potency. The union of body and soul provides an instance of act and potency. Soul is the perfecting principle of the human, while body limits it. The key to his materialism is that act and potency can only exist as co-principles. They constitute the fundamental unity of things. We read in the *Physics* that motion is "the fulfillment of what exists potentially, in so far as it exists potentially" (3, 201a, 10). It rests on the activity of three co-principles; privation, potentiality, and act. In this model, privation and potentiality function as limiting principles. Act is a perfecting principle, signifying the determination of the potentiality of matter, thereby filling privation. But act can go no further than the potentiality of matter allows. Thus, matter is an intrinsic limitation of act. The activity of the human is finite because human potential is finite. We cannot venture beyond experience. On the occasion of human death, the perfecting principle or soul of the human collapses into the potentiality governed by the limiting principle. Death returns act to prime matter. In death as in life, potentiality determines outcomes. Although the human soul is reduced to the potentiality of matter at death, it is not thereby annihilated. His refutation of Heraclitus (540-475 B.C.E.) rests on the perdurability of a substantial core of matter in time, although death marks the end of the human process. Aristotle expresses the belief that the gods appear to be indifferent to what happens to us.

The interplay between act and potency explains the continuity of bodily states from birth to death, while safeguarding the differences that arise in the human being. This view generates two aspects of human personality, one changing, the other fixed. At birth, human life is educed from the potentiality of matter, only to be reduced to it at death. The lifeless form maintains personal identity by returning to the reservoir of divine reason from which all things come. Aristotle's metaphysical biology provides the foundation for his ethics. Since human beings have a specific potential, they realize their aims or goals through a process of movement toward the divine telos or final cause. The good life is one in which the individual develops a lifestyle that is in harmony with the common good of the citizenry. Individuals are brought together under the rule of the polity as it directs the flow of events toward their natural end. Thus the good life is both local and cosmic. All things actualize a potential toward a final end. The tension between the individual and the state is felt throughout the argument of the *Nicomachean Ethics* as a tension between the particular and the universal. Aristotle introduces his doctrine of the means or "middle ground" as an enticement to avoid excesses in the development of a human life. The process of avoiding extremes in coping with harms, dangers, temptations, leads to the good life. It also leads to the development of virtues and happiness. While Aristotle's materialism is an attractive alternative to dualism, several things are wrong with it. For instance, the state of potentiality is not real. Aristotle's metaphysical biology is not accepted today.

Thomas Aquinas is deeply influenced by Aristotle but raises that philosophy beyond materialism. There can be no authentic religious belief without immortality. The union of body and soul provides an instance of act and potency. In the process, however, the human form or soul being immaterial raises the person into immortality. At human death, Thomistic metaphysics raises the soul beyond Aristotle's metaphysical biology. We are not reduced to matter. But since we require body and soul to operate, the activities of the disembodied soul remain a mystery. The resurrection theory does not explain how the soul functions in the interim state of disembodied existence. The theory belies a fundamental schism between body and soul. The seeds of division are contained in the metaphysical ground of being a soul. The epistemological processes of a human life rest on a dynamic configuration between God, soul, and body (GSB), while the metaphysical life is direct (GS). The union with God provides a sufficient and necessary reason for the person's existence. God's imprint in us is discerned through reason. Speculative reason generates intuited insights into how to self-perfect by following the law of God within our hearts. Aquinas's natural law philosophy assigns to the speculative intellect the primary responsibility for decoding God's message. It intuits universal truths about the human condition. This is what gets him into trouble. Thomistic ethics is based on a metaphysics of human nature as objective fact. But what we observe about human nature has to accord with the ethics. Experience always provides us with particular instances. We always encounter the person as an individual, not as universal essence. When we meet other humans, we do not see God. We see the external manifestation of other human beings. Contemporary thought rejects Aquinas's conception of human nature. In particular, the analytical school of philosophy disclaims the possibility of absolute or universal knowledge.

Aquinas's distinction between the concept and the idea guarantees the objectivity of knowledge, but it places the agent intellect in existence prior to the reception of the form of the other. The person is a soul-in-waiting. I am an "inside" waiting for the "outside" to make itself manifest. Death means that I am no longer in waiting. I can leave. Aquinas's claim that the person is a dynamic unit of body and soul is weakened by this conception. The die is cast in his theory of knowledge once he downloads the metaphysical primacy assigned to the intuitive ways of the speculative intellect. The particulars of experience are snapped out of their concreteness and turned into universal essences from the first moment the speculative intellect is awakened. But perhaps this is a forced choice. The divine telos invites the human to a beatific vision at death. The accomplishment of that goal is what Aquinas is most desirous to unpack. Aristotle could not deliver it, although we expect no less from a mystic.

Aquinas's argument for immortality fails without dualism. Other philosophers, notably Paul Edwards, H.D. Lewis, and Richard Swinburne, endorse dualism as the gateway to immortality. Yet, because we need a body to be human, their view is problematic. The disembodied soul introduces an incomplete human in immortality. It must lie in wait for the body, which never appears. This generates the problem of personal identity. Aquinas's view is more comfortable in the Platonic world of eternal forms than in the familiar world. Aquinas's dualism is repeated in the work of the neo-Thomist philosopher Jacques Maritain (1882-1973), when he writes in *Approaches to God* (1954), "since we cannot imagine our inexistence, we must have existed in God before receiving our biological beginning" (p. 72). The sentiment is compatible with the eternal existence of the soul in God's timeless world. Although the human being has a temporal beginning, the soul existed in the Divine Mind, or exemplar plan of creation, before coming into real existence. Since God is timeless, the human soul is also timeless or eternal. Maritain says the intuition is clearest when we are "immersed in the fire of knowing" (*ibid.*).

Plato is an unabashed dualist. The *Phaedo* claims that the philosopher does not fear death because it is an opportunity to (finally) rid ourselves of the body. The soul attains eternal truths while the body only generates shadows or illusions. Plato's "Allegory of the Cave" reminds us that the philosopher's apprenticeship is preparation for death. Once separated from the body, the soul contemplates the world of eternal truth, unhindered. We become God-like. Plato tells us that the philosopher aims at detachment from the body in order to secure a vision of eternal truth. But he does not tell us why this is so, or how the soul comes to play the principal role in the life of a person.

John Hick (1976), a Presbyterian minister and theologian, traces the metaphysical foundations of dualism to a belief in the existence of an immaterial God (p. 178). The conception of the person as a soul reflects the belief that we are made in the immaterial likeness of God. That view is at the heart of the Thomistic synthesis, as Aquinas "baptizes" Aristotle, transforming his metaphysics of essence into a metaphysics of creation, or existence. We are created to follow a divinely ordered telos. In final analysis, because the human body is ill-suited for spiritual visions, it plays a minor role in Thomistic eschatology, however. His view carries over into modern philosophy except that Descartes, like Plato, gives soul an epistemological spin toward mind. But mind is fundamentally soul-stuff, which, in turn, is God-stuff.

Descartes's philosophy collapses without God, as the divine guarantees the perdurability of truth, and the laws of physics, in the absence of the thinking thing. Cartesian physics collapses without God. To be rational is to be assured of divine corroboration. The God connection continues to play a central role in modern science up to Isaac Newton (1642-1727) where God is implicated in preserving the mechanics of motion. However, contemporary thought grew increasingly weary of the functional representation of God. In our day, the progressive elimination of God contributes to the growing interest in materialism. This is evident in the seminal influence of Bertrand Russell's (1872-1970) logical atomism and atheism on contemporary beliefs. Secularism comes to full expression in Derek Parfit's important work *Reasons and Persons* (1984). His work completes the shift from theistic metaphysics to non-theistic epistemology. All absolutes (God, soul, and the thinking thing) have given way to the development of non-religious ethics. The critique of the tradition is completed. According to Parfit, and Heidegger before him, having rid ourselves of absolutes we can begin anew. Unfortunately, now that the base of ethics is deconstructed, values are relative to culture. We have no global agreement on how to bridge heterogeneous cultural values. In rejecting the tradition, morality has lost its transcultural foundation. Our world is in moral chaos. Parfit is understandably impatient to secure global support for the development of ethics, although the challenge is to do so without norms.

But the belief in immortality lingers in the age of materialism. It offers solid evidence that our values depend on objective ground. We are witnesses to a psychological thirst to enter into objective relationship, not only with God and other human beings, but also with the material world. We cry out in the ethical desert that the transcendent order is not an illusion. It provides a source of order in the chaos of global disunity. It offers positive law the secure moral foundation required to maintain the order of the planet. Pockets of "resistance fighters," to borrow a term from Neil Postman's *Technopoly* (1993), rebel against the materialism of the age. The person as a being toward good and evil is struggling to be heard. Materialism is attractive, but the voice of the sacred is equally vivid even within the secular. The desire for immortality totally engulfs us, enlisting the realm of feelings and emotions as well as reason and logic in the struggle toward the absolute. Resistance fighters are passionate. They cannot be silenced, since the drive is imbedded in the psychology of thought.

The desire to survive the materialism of death is not new with us. It dates back to the earliest beginnings of civilization. Civilization demands immortality. Søren Kierkegaard (1813-1855) uses the desire as a (subjective) proof that the state of immortality exists. The world religions guide us toward it. Yet, religion is affected by the secularism of the faithful. No ethical agreement exists among the religious voices, no concert master to bring us together in the age of relativism. Something is amiss.

We need a fresh base for ethics, a new foundation on which to build toward the realization of our common telos. Since we need to work together toward that goal, the new ethics can only arise out of the ashes of human relationships. It cannot return to the metaphysical view of the person as abstract essence. We need to govern international behavior. However, in our day, the standard is not religion, but economics. Economic realities shape human choices. But the profit motive can lead to the exploitation of people and the planet. We often draw on the evil within us to dis-empower other human beings. The result is a cultural relativism where each power group supports cultural ideology with military might. We celebrate fiscal responsibility, but do not share a unifying vision of the divine telos. The economic mentality is pervasive. Yet, the massive problems facing society serve notice that something is askew. Promising new developments in science and religion herald the return to objective values, however. Of this, more later.

Personal survival after death is for the Hebrew, Islamic, and Christian community a matter of profound belief, one that is not challenged by the faithful. But it is underdescribed. We must move beyond feelings and emotions to inquire into the logic of that belief. Why do we need ethics to shore up the belief in immortality? There must be something about us that can be shown to survive death for the belief in ethics and eternal life to be true. Further, that surviving human nucleus must be seen to individuate the person. The soul does not complete our mission statement. It is an intangible, immaterial entity that is difficult to locate. It does not have any physical properties to individuate the person. Intangible characteristics such as habit and virtue cannot be observed in the soul since it cannot act without the body. Nothing about the soul distinguishes one soul from another. My body not only characterizes me as an individual, it distinguishes me from everyone else. Yet, the body does not survive human death. The problem of personal identity is the biggest obstacle to personal survival. How do we shore up the belief in eternal life? To paraphrase Plato's *Euthyphro* dilemma: Is immortality what the gods want of us or is there some independent standard against which the gods find us immortal? The tradition harbors both views. The metaphysical argument depends on God's will for us, but the epistemology fixes on the immateriality of the human soul. According to Aquinas's classic argument, after Plato, the human soul is indestructible because it is not composed of parts. Still, we can come to an end in other ways. The bronze statue that is melted comes to an end. The death of the body is the death of the person. But the will of God prevails: the person is immortal, not *in se,* but *in alio.* God's will saves us from annihilation (GS) but we do not survive as persons. The traditional belief that an All Powerful God can do this is not contradictory, but why does God chose to maintain the soul and not the body? If God wishes to maintain a personal relationship with us, shouldn't that include our body? Aquinas's resurrection theory is inadequate. The (GSB) model accomplishes too little too late. Does God intervene to correct poor workmanship; the first time to save us from the annihilation of death, the second time to restore the body, and possibly a third time to reconnect soul and body? What if God made other mistakes such as joining the wrong body to the wrong soul, or became tired of maintaining us in the afterlife? If the epistemology of the immaterial substance is to survive, we need a better fit with the metaphysics. Perhaps the "immaterial substance" is not our essential feature?

Does reincarnation theory provide a simpler solution to survival? Death continues a cycle of re-births begun in this life, providing an opportunity to progress toward total enlightenment. But since a key feature of the belief lies in self-effacement, survival is impersonal. The reincarnation belief is similar to materialism. Materialists claim nothing exists after death. But if my survival is unknown to me, is that not the same as not surviving at all? The prevailing Western view is that survival is personal. It takes many forms depending on culture. It is a matter of chance that I was born in one culture rather than another. Thus, my beliefs are relative. Although cultural differences promote a certain blindness between us,

I must confess my own preference for personal survival. Where is the incentive to survive as an impersonal entity? We need to survive as persons, if the issue of immortality is to hold our interest. Yet, not every Western philosopher shares my belief in personal survival. Anthony Flew and John Wisdom, for instance, declare the absurdity of surviving death. Flew says in *The Logic of Mortality* (1987) that while I can imagine my own funeral, the belief that I can survive it is absurd (pp. 110-118). The possibility of disembodied existence is equally incoherent to Alfred Ayer, Peter Strawson, and Bernard Williams. They make a good point, but for the wrong reason. Ayer, for instance, claims in an article "What I Saw When I Was Dead" (Paul Edwards, 1992), to have had an out-of-body experience providing him with fresh evidence of the separate existence of the mind. But he recently recanted the view, attributing his vision of disembodied entities to the ramblings of a brain starving for oxygen (pp. 269-275).

Furthermore, individuals who share a common belief in the afterlife do not necessarily agree that life after death lasts forever. Some survivalists maintain that the soul endures for a time after death, although it might disappear at some point in time. Coming to an end is a characteristic of finitude. No Western philosophy maintains the temporality of the soul in the (GS) configuration, although some forms of Eastern philosophy express belief in immortality and atheism. My view of immortality is not supported by the conception of the person as eternal essence. If God maintains us in timelessness, God does so because of the primacy of the divine relation. Our ethical choices are made in that context rather than out of a fixed human essence. So, I have answered my own question: we are immortal because the Gods enter into relations with us. However, I have yet to argue how divine relationships individuate persons, and why that process presents fewer problems than the conception of the human as eternal essence, or soul.

At first blush, it seems wrong to think of Aquinas as oscillating between (GS) and (GSB). One of the strengths of his philosophy is the tight knit he weaves between ethics, metaphysics, and theory of knowledge. His case for the immateriality of the human soul explains how the speculative intellect arrives at the intuition of first principles. That view is necessary to unpack universals. But the problem with the metaphysics arises at human death. What is the status of the disembodied soul?

Aquinas's (GS) configuration follows closely on the heels of Plato's belief that the body imprisons the soul. Death liberates us from the bondage of the body. This is supported by the special status Aquinas confers on the agent intellect. It exists prior to the reception of form. One might object that temporal priority does not confer special status on anything since the brain also exists before the first act of human understanding begins. But the agent intellect is not a material organ, although the expressed species of sensation limits it. The agent intellect receives the form of the other as a perfecting principle receives a limiting principle. The form of the other limits the infinite appetition of the intellect to operate in a specified way. Its first operation is at the speculative level when the essence of things is grasped intuitively. One can only imagine the intuitive breakthrough the speculative intellect achieves when it leaves the body at death. But are we the metaphysical prisoners of the body? One of the deficiencies of the epistemology is seated in the metaphysics of being a person. Aquinas is primarily a theologian. He is also a mystic that appears impatient with things of the earth. For this reason, he anxiously pushes Aristotle's telos or final cause into the next world, to the breaking point beyond the limits of our present bodily existence. But he had to negotiate a fundamental departure from the Stagirite's metaphysical biology to accomplish that feat.

Aquinas accomplishes the goal in the *Summa Contra Gentiles* where we read that the human soul separates from the body at death (2 ch. 81 8). If the soul resists death it does so by being immaterial. Unlike corruptible things, the soul, not being composed of parts, is not reducible to parts. The soul is a simple substance, and therefore immortal. That view is criticized by Immanuel Kant (1724-1804) in the *Critique of Pure Reason*, "Refutation of Mendelssohn's Proof of the Permanence of the Soul." John Hick says in *Death and Eternal Life* (1976) that the view is criticized by Christians of the Protestant tradition as being unbiblical (p. 339).

Catholic doctrine suggests that the soul might be forced to undergo a period of purification in purgatory before seeing God. But exactly who is in purgatory? Either the soul is me or I am not in purgatory. And where am I in purgatory? One of the problems Paul Edwards (1992) unloads in *Immortality* is that the disembodied life is not actually seen to occur anywhere. "Pure minds do not occupy space and hence the next life cannot have any location" (p. 5). Finally, we can hardly expect God to accompany the disembodied soul into purgatory. In that event, Thomistic epistemology (GSB), not only deconstructs to a (GS) configuration at death, but becomes a simple (S) in purgatory. The (S) undergoes a period of purification by being removed from God. How to imagine (S)'s continued existence without (G)? Once purified, the soul rejoins God (GS). At the resurrection, the person becomes a (GSB~). The symbol ~ is added to distinguish between the resurrected body and the original body since they are different. The view gives rise to major difficulties: how does a foreign body restore my personal identity? If personal identity depends on brain states, where was I during the interval between death and resurrection? Perhaps consciousness and memory are not characteristic properties of personal identity. When I awaken each morning, I know myself to be the same person that went to bed, although I am not aware of what happens during the interval of sleep. But can I maintain personal identity in the absence of my brain? The theory is difficult to defend. What might it be like to be conscious without a body? Nothing in our experience as person allows us to imagine the nature of our disembodied existence. The disembodied soul is not only less of a person than the embodied person, it is not a person in any ordinary sense of things.

The Thomistic view of being a person is more angelic than human. Aquinas's epistemology tells the story: human nature is constituted in a few basic properties that can be summed up in a definition; the properties of intellect and will, as well as the properties of nutrition, growth, and reproduction, make us what we are, or give us our fundamental essence. We are rational animals. But our rationality participates in the divine light. The human act is ethical if it conforms to the human essence. Were our nature different, we would have different duties. The general principles of human nature are unchanging since they are divine like. They provide the ethical force necessary to make moral judgments. Our nature mirrors the eternal law, or God's plan for us. Universal principles of moral obligation are identical with the natural law. The basic principles of morals and legislation are objective, accessible to reason, and based on human nature. We act toward the ultimate end God intends for us, using reason to make the necessary choices facing us between good and evil. We self-perfect through our free choices of the good, and act toward the attainment of the ultimate good. But unlike Aristotle's telos, the Thomistic telos (*Summa Contra Gentiles,* 3, 1, ch. 37) moves beyond material goods to the contemplation of the divine essence. We attain the ultimate good through the activity of the speculative intellect contemplating the divine essence, a vision realized at death as soul separates from body. Although the separation is possible, as we said, it generates the problem of exact survival. The soul or speculative intellect's intuitive knowledge of essences introduces a mode of insight that is not characteristically human. It seems more appropriate to the divinity than humans, for how can we ever willingly do evil? In the attempt to depict the human essence as divine-like, Aquinas loses sight of the fact that we are not always good.

Although a belief in immortality does not necessarily follow from a belief in God, Aquinas says that the divine redemption offers us eternal life. His philosophy draws heavily on God's creative activity. The resurrection of Christ is a promise that we too shall rise from the dead. The argument for the existence of God appears in *The Summa Theologica* (1-1, Q. 2, a 3) where it opens with the rational need to discover the necessary causes and sufficient reasons of contingent existence. Aquinas develops five arguments corresponding to the five causes of being. What is the sufficient reason of contingent existence? Since it is not contained in the contingent, it must exist outside of it. Our quest for the discovery of an ultimate sufficient reason obviates the impossibility of rooting the explanation of contingency in an endless series of subordinate causes (or imaginary numbers). Reason ultimately posits the existence of an uncaused cause which we call God. God provides the explanation reason requires. The speculative intellect enters into a (GS) relationship with God. His theory of knowledge reveals that although the human is a unit of mind and body, the speculative intellect knows essences not through discursive processes but through an act of intuition. The act takes place high above the limitations of matter. For Aquinas, the intellect is a part of the soul that can operate without the body. It does so, for instance, in the intuition of essences and the intuitive understanding of first principles. The intellect also moves in a second way when it is rational. In that event, the connection to the body is clearer. Practical reason examines reality to advance from one thing to another. It directs our acceptance of a course of action. Thus "speculative reason," and "practical reason" are two ways reason operates (*Summa Theologica,* 2-2, Q. 83, a 1). While human death puts an abrupt end to the life of practical reason, it leaves speculative reason unfettered, finally able to ascend to a vision of God.

Aquinas's epistemology moves on the two arms of the metaphysics. We are divine-like and therefore spiritual substance. But we are finite, created entities. The dualism pours into the epistemology. He establishes a connection of dependence and independence between mind and body. The intellect cannot operate without the body, but the ideas it produces are irreducible to the body. This explains why the soul's departure from the body is possible, but also why the soul needs the body. The primacy of the soul is seen in the Catholic Church's teachings against abortion. The statement that life begins at conception means that the zygote is be-souled, or God-like in the undeveloped state. The speculative intellect sits in waiting for the developing body to begin the operations of human understanding. The process of knowing reality is one in which the intellect enters into union with its object. The speculative intellect cannot be material because its materiality would get in the way of the thing known (*Summa Theologica,* 1-1, Q. 25, a 2). How, then, is the union between an immaterial substance and the body possible? Aquinas explains it as follows: The union takes place at the level of form. The universal arises as a process of producing something to the likeness of the conceptual becoming the other. Knowledge seems to be an angelic process.

In his commentary on Boethius' *De Trinitate*, Aquinas specifies three levels of abstraction. At a first level, the intellect sets aside individual matter to retain common sensible matter. This operation is characteristic of the inductive sciences, including the philosophy of nature. Although philosophy of nature is deductive, it is included in the first degree of abstraction because verification of mentalistic events takes place in the world of sensory observations. The operations of the second degree of abstraction raise the distance between the speculative intellect and the body to even greater heights. In this case the intellect abstracts from common sensible matter to retain only the aspect of quantity, or size and number of things. Results are verified in the imagination. This is the world of mathematics, one in which Plato's eternal essences are most at home. The intellect's crowning victory over matter takes place in the final round where metaphysical thought is born. The study of metaphysics arises through a process in which the mind releases the aspect of being as both sensible and extended to concern itself with pure intelligibilities. Aquinas's Platonism is clearest here. The metaphysical abstraction separates from matter to grasp existence as a pure intelligibility, without reference to essence. The Aristotelian prime matter and privation are stripped away, layer by layer, to grasp the nature of act as act. The rarified focus is hardly human. It is not a vision of being as sensed, not even of being as extended, but of pure intelligibilities. Wisdom is given over to the contemplation of the divine essence. We have caught a glimpse of the first principle and highest cause of being.

But the insight is fleeting since we are embodied beings. We cannot achieve complete separation from matter in this life. The possibility of doing so only arises at death when the disembodied soul is totally freed from the corporeal world. The process of separating the incorporeal from the corporeal is repeated in modern philosophy. Descartes says in Rule Twelve (*Rules for the Direction of the Mind*) that we ought to strive as far as possible to divest the understanding from the phantasm or corporeal, since that world gets in the way of understanding the incorporeal. Descartes, like Aquinas, believes that sense perception contaminates the spiritual intellect's quest for the ultimate vision of incorporeal entities. The beatific vision cannot take place in bondage with the human body. That is why the soul flees the body at death, although it does not depart empty.

Aquinas says that the soul carries human habits into the afterlife. (*Summa Theologica*, 1, Q. 64, a 2). Thus, it predisposes us to meet God in a particular way, as from a lifetime experience of acting toward the good, or evil. But the question remains whether that is in fact a person meeting God. A person cannot act without a body, or as a separated soul. Aquinas is not unaware of the difficulty, although he does not raise the issue of personal identity as such. His resurrection theory remedies the deficiency of the incomplete person, while accomplishing the divine redemption promised in the metaphysics. It completes the divine telos. He says in (*Summa Theologica*, Q. 75, aa 1, 2): "that man may obtain the last end for which he was made; for this cannot be accomplished in this life nor in the life of the separated soul ... otherwise man would have been made in vain, if he were unable to obtain the end for which he was made."

Aquinas thereby supports a belief that is central to the teachings of the apostles. It is modeled on the death and resurrection of Christ. The Fourth Lateran Council expresses the belief that the dead shall rise again with their own bodies which they now bear about with them. Like Christ, they shall have a glorified body, including Christ-like characteristics of the luminous body, able to appear and disappear at will. The risen body shall possess agility, moving as quickly as the soul, and impassibility or have no response to pain. It shall be vested with immortality. However, the body shall also possess the characteristic of subtility, meaning it will be ruled by the soul. Thus it shall become a spiritual body. The risen body participates in the soul's more perfect and spiritual life to such an extent that it becomes itself like a spirit. Aquinas's eschatology recognizes that the disembodied soul enjoys an unnatural state without the body. Thus there will be rejoicing at the resurrection, since body and soul are made for each other. The resurrection of the body is God's gift to the faithful, allowing a fresh merger between the epistemology and metaphysics. This answers the *Euthyphro* dilemma: we are immortal because God wills it to be so.

Since the human body is incapable of seeing God on earth, does it see God in the afterlife because it assumes different characteristics? Indeed, Aquinas's view is that it becomes a spiritual body with spiritual characteristics. The belief in the existence of a spiritual body is a matter of faith, not reason. Although the belief is possibly true, it fails to settle the personal identity problem. Since I do not possess a spiritual body on earth, that might not be me in the afterlife. Aristotle points out that it is beyond the range of human power to attain that kind of vision. This is the main reason he argues for the reduction of soul to matter at death. But the belief in the spiritual body is part of the Apostles' Creed to which Aquinas is committed. The belief is difficult to support. For instance, what is the age of the risen body? Both Augustine (354-430) and Aquinas claim that it will be about 32, being the age of the risen Christ.

However, life expectancy does not reach 32 until the Middle Ages. That marks a preference for older, less agile, bodies. Life expectancy was much less in Ancient Greece, probably about 20 years. If we factor in infant mortality, the vast majority of humans throughout history have died about age five. Are most human beings aged before they are resurrected? In our day, we can expect to live for about 80 years. What becomes of the data stored in the brain between the ages of 32 and 80, or the missed experiences between five and 32? What about imbeciles whose brain never develops? Can we assume that individuals with mental disorders are restored to health at the resurrection? The traditional Catholic doctrine that the soul comes into being at the moment of conception also raises a question about the status of aborted fetuses? Medical science suggests that zygotes are routinely expelled from the mother's body as wastage in what she may experience simply as a late menstrual period. Is the fetus in heaven as a healthy 32-year old? Is heaven populated by unformed zygotes? Aquinas also interjects the cannibalism problem: If P eats the flesh of N who previously ate the flesh of Q, who awakens on judgment day? Following Aristotelian metaphysical biology, Aquinas says in the *Summa Theologica* that the principles of matter and form revert to the original body; "the flesh will rise in him to whose perfection it belonged more intimately ... as from the seed from which he was generated" (3, Q. 80, a 4). But surely the memory of cannibalism persists in the soul of the dead, although the risen body might not require food. Spiritual bodies might obey different laws. John Hick says in *Death and Eternal Life* (1976) that the laws of the afterlife world will not be those of physics. They will be the laws of psychology (p. 265). Such a world might be populated by spiritually embodied souls engaged in telepathic communication. It is a world filled with paranormal phenomena "producing visual and auditory images" that H.H. Price says in Edwards (1992) is like a dream world, fashioned by the power of our desires (p. 216). That world might be chaotic since the desires of one soul can be at odds with the desires of any other soul. Aquinas's world (GS), however, avoids chaos. It is a state in which (S), unaware of others, is fully absorbed in contemplation of the divine essence (G).

Why can't the spiritual body be the same as the original body? What if they are identical? John Hick details in chapter eight of *Faith and Knowledge* (1966) how a replica is the same as the original, if God creates it identical in every respect. His theory has been picked up by some contemporary thinkers, notably Paul and Linda Badham (1982), but Hick is the first to make the suggestion. Can a replica body be the same as the original body? What about the temporal difference between them? The replica comes into existence in the afterlife. Thus, it fails to satisfy a criterion of personal identity since it does not follow me in death. Furthermore, the genetic material of the first body is provided by the parents, whereas the second body is created by God. An illustration will help to emphasize the critical distinction between both bodies: Imagine that a ten-year-old child builds a model airplane. He sets it on the kitchen table and leaves for school. But the parent accidentally breaks it. The parent, not wishing to displease the child, purchases an identical copy of the model airplane. It looks exactly like the original model. Later that afternoon, a neighbor visits and asks who built the model? The simple answer is that it was built by a manufacturer. The complex answer is that it was built by the parent to deceive the child (to serve the end of not disappointing the child). The replica body generates a similar deception. A man dies but his body appears along with other resurrected replicas in another world. Do his friends recognize him? Or more to the point, is it the same person? Aquinas agrees it is not the same "bronze statue" if it is reconstituted. But the human is not a bronze statue. The metaphysics does not admit this view. He says in the *Summa Theologica* that the same soul remains after the body has perished. (3. Q. 79 a 2). Once again, we are reminded that the soul is thought to be the carrier of personal identity.

Presumably, the beatific vision occurs in timelessness. The person as a psycho-physical unit of body and soul is temporal, but manages to escape the body into timelessness at death. Does the risen body make its appearance in timelessness? Are we the same entities outside time? Even supposing that the same body could somehow be reconstituted from the atoms of a previous existence, which science doubts is possible, the time lapse between the last moment of death and the first moment of resurrected existence means I would not be aware of myself during the disembodied interval. The problem of personal identity requires bodily continuity between the two states. But if the soul is the essential thing about being a person, then, why does Aquinas say body and soul form a dynamic unit? If the body is not important to being a person, why are we embodied? This question leads to dualism. If we are human because of an immaterial substantial core that exists at the heart of personhood, (SB), then how do we remain the same person throughout life? The body is seen to change as we age. Yet, the soul also changes (hardens) through the development of moral habits. This is the person-making process. What, then, constitutes personal identity?

The existence of evil compounds the problem. If the person is drawn into eternal life by the will of God, or God's teleological plan (GSB), why do evil and suffering exist? In other words, once God enters into relationship with humans it becomes difficult to explain evil, unless God is evil. God creates the condition in which evil arises as a possibility. Thus, God must be indirectly responsible for evil. This problem offers a major challenge to (GSB) theorists. It is a main obstacle to the legitimacy of the metaphysical argument for immortality, although the problem is not insurmountable since moral evil is ascribed to the individual's free choices. John Hick has written a solid study of the issue in *Evil and the God of Love* (1977). The book develops an eschatology of "soul-making" processes in which good and evil struggle side by side in the life of the individual. Hick's central view is that we do not enter this world as fully developed individuals. The evidence does not suggest a fall from grace. Our moral life develops in response to the challenges of choosing between good and evil (p. 389). Although this view provides an interesting response to the existence of evil, it too is based on dualism. Hick's "soul" retains the seat of personal identity (soul-making). Our virtues, habits, ideas, and all immaterial characteristics of being human, do not individuate us as detached souls, but as persons. We develop neural tracts, for instance, from a lifetime of habits. The whole of the person enters into action. But how does a separated soul individuate anyone? It cannot be seen, measured, weighed, or even act without the body. We cannot distinguish between immaterial substances except by reference to the patterns or laws that characterize being human. Thus, the separated soul is nothing at all since it is said to be immaterial. Richard Swinburne's analysis (1986) of Hick's "soul-making" process suggests that souls must vary in composition or "soul-stuff" (p. 287). That being the case, we are asked to imagine the composition of a substance that is not made up of parts. How is that possible without reducing the theory to materialism?

Does the religious argument avoid dualism? The religious approach to immortality rests on the existence of God, and on the covenant to maintain the existence of the righteous in the afterlife. Religious justice prescribes a blessed future for the righteous and a contrasting punishment for the wicked. That view was expressed by the ancient Egyptians and is maintained in our day. The argument does not get off the ground without a belief in immortality. But the problem is that the existence of God does not necessarily imply immortality, it only makes it probable. The fact that God enters into relationships with us on earth provides a psychological promise of continued existence in the afterlife, but not a guarantee of it. Do we not frustrate the divine telos through our choice of evil? In the Christian religion, the salvific suffering and death of Christ redeems us from our sins. The belief in our continued existence in the afterlife as disembodied souls remains for the traditional Christian a matter of profound faith, however. This is not surprising, since it is difficult to provide a reasoned argument to justify the belief that a person is a soul.

The resurrection theory compounds the problem since it is not clear how mind and body can interact in the afterlife. Yet, the view is a fundamental Hebrew belief; "And when after my skin ... is destroyed, then without my flesh shall I see God."

(*Job* 19:26). It expresses an essential core of the Apostles' Creed. The two main versions of the Creed, Roman and Tertullian, were formulated about the first or second century after the death of Christ. According to the *Catholic Encyclopedia* (1907), the Roman Creed specifies the necessity of a belief in the resurrection of the dead and the life of the world to come. It carries great force for the faithful since it is given the authority of an *ex cathedra* utterance. Thomas Aquinas, the main philosopher on Catholic doctrine, insists that the Creed is only called into doubt under pain of heresy (*Summa Theologica*, 2-2, Q. 1, a 9). That being the case, Catholic thinkers are understandably reluctant to challenge the belief, or to comment on it. While both versions of the Creed refer to the "resurrection of the body," they remain silent on the status of the disembodied soul. The Tertullian version contains the reference to "life everlasting" without explanation. The life of the disembodied soul is highly attenuated. It dwells in "*Sheol*" a Hebrew place of waiting, or "*Barzakh,*" according to the Islamic Koran (the Arabic Ar-Rahman), the soul or "Beneficient" is unable even to praise God. The apostle Paul likens it to a state of sleep. According to Eastern commentators, the soul of the dead exist in the "*bardo*" state, a temporary condition. For the Catholic Christian, the text of Neuner and Dupuis (1983) contains the official doctrine of the Church as expressed by Pope Paul II: "the church affirms that a spiritual element survives and subsists after death, an element endowed with consciousness and will, so that the human self subsists, though deprived for the present of the complement of the body" (p. 691).

The temporary state of disembodied existence is also accepted by Islamic prophets. God gathers the living and the dead at the last judgment and re-embodies the dead. The grace of God is all that saves us from annihilation. The faithful of the Judaic, Christian, and Islamic tradition all profess a belief in the resurrection. While the belief does not involve contradiction, it is accepted without sufficient thought. The belief is underdescribed. If the connection between mind and body is necessary on earth, how does it become unnecessary, even for a time, in eternal life? How can the brain-dependent self that is currently thinking, sensing, willing, doubting, function without the body? If the disembodied soul exists, how can it act, enjoy or suffer the pleasures of being human without the human body? Can a replica, astral or even spiritual body feel my pain, my pleasure?

We need more information on what death is like to the dead. What do the dead do? Do they enter into relationships with other dead, can they act without the body? Does the evidence of parapsychology shed light on the nature of death as such? First of all is death a state, a condition in which the dead are active or passive? Paul and Linda Badham (1982) use the near-death experience (NDE) as proof of life after death. If it can be shown that consciousness or soul can function without the brain, then the soul can exist indefinitely without the body. The NDE suggests, especially to Paul Badham since he has continued to work in the area, that this is indeed the case. If we can establish that consciousness can exist without the body, even for an instant, we have found a window to survival, but not necessarily to the sustained activities of the soul. My inclination is to be skeptical about the success of parapsychology. The study of personal survival raises hotly debated issues in contemporary philosophy because no empirical evidence supports the claim that we do in fact survive the death of the body. What mediums report about the dead is generally underdescribed. Better explanations of "paranormal" experience exist or are more plausible. The problem facing mediums is that nothing of the person is actually observed to survive death. Yet, the major world religions are reduced to psycho-babble in the absence of life after death. Still, we can glean some insight into the nature of death in other ways, even if death should turn out to be inconceptualizable. The etymology of explanation suggests this possibility. We can look to being's unconcealment for an explanation of death, once we give full weighting to the sterility of the conceptual approach.

The evidence of faith provides an instance of a possible explanation of the fate of the dead. However, the primacy assigned to faith by both the Catholic and the Protestant or Reformed Church of England invites the possibility of conflict between reason and faith. Aquinas and Martin Luther (1483-1546) raise faith above reason. That option pours fresh fuel on the flame of dualism. Aquinas suggests that reason and faith are not opposed because they issue from God. Yet, whenever conflict arises between them, primacy is assigned to matters of faith. Luther goes further: in times of conflict, not only is reason mistaken, but faith moves us into a realm where reason is incompetent. This view is not attractive to non-believers.

The existence of undeserved suffering is inconsistent with the belief in God and the afterlife. How can an All Powerful, loving God allow the suffering of innocent people (and animals)? If God is not seen to care for us in this life, how can we expect God to love us in the afterlife? Why is it that everything God makes dies? Is death not evil? Does this implicate God in the existence of evil? Further, since death is real to us, might we not die in the afterlife? What sort of God is it that enters into relationship with us? The Swiss psychoanalyst Carl Gustav Jung (1875-1961) suggests in *Answer to Job*, first published in German in 1952, that the God-making process parallels our own (Hick's) soul-making development. In Jung's view, God and persons provide evidence of being evil as well as good. Of this, more later.

The aging and dying of the human body devalues the person's life. The body is seen to die and rot, while the soul is accorded special (immaterial and immortal) privileges. This is manifest in Hebrew, Christian and Islamic beliefs. To value something (from the Latin *valere*) is to view it as being strong, of worth. That description fits the soul, but not the body. The resurrection theory announced in the Creeds confers artificial dignity on the body. The body is a poor second cousin to the soul. But if the soul needs the body to operate on earth, how can it function before the resurrection?

What about our psychological desire for survival? Does it carry sufficient and necessary proof of immortality? The psychological argument arises out of the longing of the human heart for the ultimate good. Since the goods of the earth are fleeting, the craving for the ultimate good is fulfilled in the afterlife. The problem with this (T0homistic) view, however, is that it undervalues temporal goods. Many human experiences are fulfilling, including activities like gardening, listening to music, walking, sailing, or completing a project.

If the belief that God cares about us is true, then, it must include the fact that we are unique individuals with individuating characteristics such as genetic structure, blood type, dental identification, unique fingerprints, eyes, and the like. Anything less than the survival of those same individuating characteristics in the afterlife results in a depersonalized relationship and indistinguishable selves.

The resurrected body cannot be the same body that ages and dies. That cannot be me in the afterlife. What if I own the new body; does that make it mine, or satisfy the problem of personal identity? The view that it does is taught by the Church of England Doctrine Commission of 1938, and by the Catholic Bishops of Holland in their 1965 *Catechism*. While the sense of ownership is comforting, the problem is that the belief smacks of dualism. My body is not a possession. I do not own it the way I own books and a computer. I am my body. The resurrection doctrine needs rethinking. Virtually all contemporary thinkers have abandoned the old model. Even if God gives me a new body to restore the eschaton destroyed by sin, can the separated soul recognize a foreign body as its own? Will it not reject it in the way the body rejects a transplanted organ? The new body constitutes a radical change to personhood. Even if the new body is an improvement on the old body, it is not me. Stephen T. Davis (1989) makes the point: "the whole person, body and soul alike, is what is to be saved" (p. 120), although he fails to develop the implication:

> We human beings are born, live for a time as psycho-physical beings, and then die; after death we exist in an incomplete state as immaterial souls; and some time later in the eschaton God miraculously raises our bodies from the ground, transforms them into "glorified bodies," and reunites them with our souls, making us complete and whole again. (*Ibid.,* p. 121)

Is the case for embodiment overstated? If 60 percent of my body weight is water, then, as Badham suggests, much of my personhood passes through my intestines on a regular basis. Do we become less of a person for passing water? This line of inquiry is absurd. Yet, the person is diminished without body parts such as the corpus callosum. Are some parts of the body more critical to being a person? Most of the body can be replaced by artificial parts. Recent discoveries in biotechnology suggest the possibility of cloning duplicates of ourselves. How, then, is temporary disembodiment an affront to personal identity? While no serious objection is presented by the loss of a limb, the critical issue is not the quantitative determination of body parts, but the principle of embodiment.

What exactly is a principle of embodiment? The term is used to invoke the sum of patterns or laws of cosmic interactions that combine to individuate me. The scientific community agrees that the universe began as a Big Bang about eighteen thousand million years ago. It has taken that long for the process to produce conscious life. Our conscious, individuated existence is the result of a finely tuned process that did not come about by chance. The universe had to be precisely engineered to emerge out of two fundamental cosmic forces, expansion and gravitation. After the Big Bang, the universe would continue to disperse without the force of gravitation. Yet, with too much gravitational force, the universe could not expand. It would be caught up in a black hole of infinite gravitational force. Human life originates out of the finely tuned tension between these opposing forces.

Although Aquinas uses the evidence from design to argue for the existence of God, his view is not based on science, but on the exemplar cause or divine blueprint of creation. Today, science fine tunes his belief. We now have a better grasp of the exact conditions that must be in place to generate life. And we can go further to explain how cosmic relations, and their fortuitous variations, produce the unique genetic configuration of an individual human life. The human genome project, for instance, is an ambitious project to identify the 3,000 genetic abnormalities that individuate human illness. The Thomistic argument for personal immortality is even more challenging since it must explain how our atoms can be us in the afterlife. If we consider that the human brain contains billions of neurons, with connections numbering in the trillions, in an incalculable number of atomic and molecular reactions, the feat is no less than a miracle. Although if God wills this, we can imagine it to be the case, but science provides a better suggestion. When the argument is formulated from the perspective of the laws or patterns of relations that generate us, we can shift the focus to those relations. Thus, the argument is made simple by imagining the continued existence of those patterns after our death. What counts is pattern, not the particular realization of the pattern, but the pattern or law itself.

Aquinas backs himself into a corner. Has he been waiting 700 years for his body? When his body is resurrected, which is difficult to imagine since his atoms are scattered throughout the universe, interacting with other atoms and leading to the possibility of new life forms, will that be Aquinas in the afterlife? God cannot accomplish the impossible. When individual atoms are reduced to packets of energy, they cannot be individuated or reconstituted into a person's body. Saint Paul prefers to think of the risen body as being spiritual (1 *Corinthians*, ch. 15). Still, he has been waiting 2,000 years for his body. If Paul can endure that fate, perhaps putting up with disembodiment is a matter of discipline. It might begin "one day at a time," and with patience and training lapse into a week, then a year. Possibly, a chosen few can go on forever without a body. It is little wonder that the world religions continue to think of persons as being souls.

A basic antipathy to the body underscores the tradition from Plato to

Descartes. Does Davis sense this when he adds; "How one can simultaneously be both 'at home with the Lord' and in 'an incomplete state' is a tension that perhaps remains in the theory" (p. 122). Davis knows a lot more than he says: the disembodied soul cannot be the same individual. According to Fergus Kerr (1989) the tradition represents human beings "as angels fallen into flesh" (168). Why that focus? Well, being an angel has a certain pomp. Some of the world's best thinkers, Plato, Aquinas, Descartes, Locke, Kant, and Henri Bergson (1859-1941) celebrate the angel in us, as they over describe our immateriality. But the representation of persons as disembodied entities devalues not only the importance of human embodiment, but also the nature of our activities in the afterlife. What sorts of things can we do without the body? The body is not only the soul's means of action, it is also the means for the soul's most eloquent expression of action. For instance, how is conjugal love possible without the body? The body allows us to enter into communion with the other at the most sacred level of existence. The disembodied state is for ghostly contemplation without action. This cannot be the sense of the divine telos since it does not bring the person to final perfection. What if the body is spiritual?

How is the spiritual body my body? It possesses different characteristics from the physical body. While there appears to be benefit to walking through walls, the point is that it is not a human activity. We witness a pandora's box of formless souls, unable to act, express themselves, or interact with others. Souls are indistinguishable since they are everywhere the same. Heaven is boring. Following an unspecified period of time, (can time be specified in the absence of moving parts), the prodigal body rises out of scattered atoms, as astral body, replica, spiritual entity, or body double to rejoin the separated soul. Does the new body have physical parts, is it detachable? If it has physical parts, it can be reduced to atoms. It can die again. If it does not have physical parts, it is not human, or me. Is there a mind-body problem in the afterlife? Perhaps the reunion is tentative, as the soul prepares for a second departure from the body, a new death beyond death (reincarnation?). The separation of body and soul might breed disharmony in the afterlife. Can we trust a soul that leaves us?

To Descartes goes the dubious credit of raising our divinity to its most dizzying heights in dualism. Cartesianism is most at home in the epistemic (GS) configuration in which the "I" or disembodied thinking thing is divine-like in its characteristics. It does not have a body since the extended has no place in the immaterial world of pure thought. Descartes does not say at the time of his doubt that the man Descartes exists, but that he can conceive of himself not to include a body (*Principles of Philosophy,* 1, Principle LX). Although he can suppose that he has no body, he cannot say "I am not." A study of the thing that thinks, the essential Descartes, reveals, he says, the innate idea of God's existence. Together, the thinking thing and God strike a metaphysical agreement to secure the whole of knowledge on a mathematical foundation. The holy alliance is struck to accomplish salvific work; it provides a favored method, a metaphysics (*Meditations*, 1641) as existential foundation, and an epistemological vision. Descartes is on a divine mission. Like the "Holy Spirit," he is charged with the task of freeing us from the illusions of the past. His analysis of his dreams confirms that mission. Descartes's *Discourse on Method* leaves no doubt that he holds the church in high esteem. He knows what happened to Galileo, so he wants to avoid that kind of confrontation. He is an accomplished strategist:

> the revealed truths which lead to heaven are above our comprehension, I did not presume to subject them to the impotency of my reason; and I thought that in order completely to undertake their examination, there was need of some special help from heaven, and of being more than a man. (Part 1)

He is not insensitive to the politics of the day. So, his divine mission is disguised. His mathematical method consists of intuition, deduction, analysis and synthesis. The *Meditations* reads as a theorem in analytical geometry. The *cogito ergo sum* is not the result of a deduction, but of an intuition as required by a proper mathematical starting-point. The intuition is a signal that the thinking thing, not unlike Aquinas's speculative intellect, has an open connection to the divinity. Descartes's first deduction leads to the discovery of a criterion of truth. It embodies the methodology of analysis and synthesis: In "analysis" we suppose that the solution to a problem is at hand, while in "synthesis" we verify that the solution proposed by analysis is correct. Descartes's challenge is to open with a legitimate starting point. He finds it in his radical doubt. The "clear and distinct idea" serves notice that there exists at least one indubitable truth: the existence of the doubting thing. Synthesis makes use of that insight as a criterion of truth. But Descartes can go no further without explicit reference to God, or his own divine mind.

The existence of God is known intuitively, since it is an innate idea. Although in Descartes's opinion the belief does not require proof, he advances three arguments to convince the skeptic that God does in fact exists. The first two arguments are an unacknowledged commentary of St. Anselm's ontological argument. The third is the most cartesian since it pulls the existence of God from within the walls of reason. Does he succeed? As every critic already knows, once he lays claims to being a doubting thing he cannot hold clear and distinct ideas without simultaneously positing the thinking thing into non-existence. Fortunately, God guarantees the perdurability of the doubting thing in the absence of doubt. The whole of Descartes's physics collapses without God. God secures the foundation of the new science. Descartes invites God to validate the whole of the physics, especially at times when the thinking thing is busy with other matters. What a comforting partnership! The thinking thing is fully divine. The goal of rational mechanics is indeed to see the world the way God does. The ways of reason reduce the whole of reality to increasingly comprehensive identity propositions. Like God, we look at the atom and see the whole of the cosmos. The method teaches us, not only to overcome the illusions of the body, but how to be God. The irony is that cartesianism leads to the progressive elimination of God in some forms of contemporary thought. Once Descartes assigned functional tasks to God, the stage was set. We became God by taking on these same tasks. Analytical philosophy, for instance, is not inclined to assign any responsibility to God. Today, the God of Descartes is unemployed, or non-existent.

Does Descartes express any hesitancy about being divine? He has moments of doubt. The connection between mind and body is troublesome. In a letter to Princess Elizabeth of Bohemia on 21 May 1643, he reveals that our notion of the soul's power to move the body depends upon our having the notion of their union. But he has no idea how such a union is possible, if not by giving the unextended mind a seat in the pineal gland. One might have expected a lesser thinker to abandon claims to the divinity of the thinking thing. Kant saw the absurdity of seating the unextended in the extended, and offered the Transcendental Schemata as his own substitute connection. But once Descartes wrote the *Meditations,* the stage was set. Cartesians made what they could of it.

This brings the view of the human being as a divine, eternal essence to a full stop. Descartes writes a classic tragedy. If God dies, the whole of the physics collapses. But in our day, God is dead (Nietzsche). Descartes's desperate attempt to prove that a world beyond consciousness exists, or that he has a body, fails. He overlooks several necessary characteristics of being human, such as the role of the body. If my brain is removed, I am dead. Although pulmonary, vascular functions can be maintained on life support systems, in that event my life is that of a breathing corpse, which is not a human life. A second major flaw is that Descartes overestimates the powers of the speculative intellect. This is characteristic of rationalism in general. It sends an important signal to the existential community that the case for thinking is overstated by the tradition. Thinking and living a life are different. The final flaw is that the soul's aspiration to divine status fails to express the sanctity of a human life. It is an insult to both God and human beings. It overstates the cleverness of persons and undervalues the omniscience of a divine being.

Two

THE NO-PERSON VIEW

The philosophy of John Locke (1632-1704) is at the outset an attempt to settle the matter of Descartes's dualistic metaphysics. But he conducts the inquiry from the point of view of epistemology rather than metaphysics. Locke tells us in the Epistle of *An Essay Concerning Human Understanding* (1690) that he proposes to inquire into the nature, origin, and limits of human understanding "so as to know which subject the understanding is or is not fitted to deal with." The *Essay* leaves no doubt that the understanding is not made for abstraction. Suggesting that the origin of all ideas is empirical, Locke opens the work with a repudiation of Descartes's doctrine of innate ideas. Outside consciousness is a world of extended particles whose characteristics include size, number and motion. They interact with the external senses to produce sensations or secondary qualities in us. Although the world of extended particles is objective, our reaction to sensations is subjective. Locke says that secondary qualities: "are nothing in the objects themselves but powers to produce various sensations in us by their primary qualities" (*ibid.,* Book 2, ch. 8, sect. 10). In chapter 12 of the same book, he informs us that complex ideas arise out of combining simple ideas, setting them side by side, or separating them from all other ideas. Since all ideas derive from experience, the limits of understanding extend no further than the sensations that are their origin.

Unlike Descartes, Locke does not identify the person with immaterial substance. His discussion of personal identity appears as chapter 27 in the second edition of his *Essay Concerning Human Understanding* (1694). What constitutes personal identity for Locke? Since no self can exist without experiences, personal identity is not the identity of a substance. He finds it in the identity of consciousness; "For the same consciousness being preserved, whether in the same or different substances, the personal identity is preserved" (*ibid.,* 27, sect. 13). Self depends on consciousness, not on substance. Locke cannot bring himself to seat personal identity in the view of self as substance. As John Foster (1991) points out: "He thought that two momentary substance-stages qualified as stages of the same person only if they shared the same consciousness" (p. 241). Locke defines "self" as being "a conscious thinking thing, conscious of pleasure and pain, capable of happiness or misery, and so is concerned for itself" (*ibid.,* 27, sect. 17). Person is the name for this self, a thinking, intelligent being, one that has reason and reflection, and can consider itself as itself, the same thinking thing, in different times and places. Thus, being a person posits the consciousness of being the same thing in different times and places. Memory is the connecting link between successive states of consciousness. My personal identity is assured when I recall that I am the same self now as then. I know myself to be the same person I was yesterday because memory establishes a connection between both states of consciousness or self. Can I be held accountable when I do not remember committing a particular act of which

I am accused? The answer is no. Locke says that on the great day wherein all hearts shall be laid open, no one will be held accountable for what he knows nothing of.

But Locke's theory of personal identity is problematic. The memory of conscious states or stretches of consciousness is not a necessary and sufficient condition of personal identity. It erroneously prescribes the existence of a subject which memory records. Locke's argument is circular. He is seen to implicate the self as substance in the continuity that consciousness and memory prescribe. Might not consciousness reside in different bodily states over time? In the body transplant case, it would not be me then and now, although consciousness might suggest it is the same individual. If, however, a faulty memory fails to confirm the belief I have about being the same individual over time, then Locke says I can go no further. But as Joseph Butler points out in the first appendix to his *The Analogy of Religion* (1736), being a person constitutes a criticism of the memory theory. Butler says in Perry (1975): "And one should really think it self-evident, that consciousness of personal identity presupposes, and therefore cannot constitute, personal identity, any more than knowledge, in any other case, can constitute truth, which it presupposes" (p. 100).

If consciousness constitutes personal identity, as Locke claims, might I not be different persons over time? How, then, can I anticipate tomorrow or remember yesterday when these events are not occurring to the same person? This is contrary to the conviction we have about ourselves as being the same person over time, since consciousness sometimes fails to hold between two stages of the same substance. Butler's criticism of the memory theory points out that a person is either a substance or the property of some substance:

> If he, if person, be a substance, then consciousness that he is the same person, is consciousness that he is the same substance. If the person, or he, be the property of a substance, still consciousness that he is the same property, is as certain a proof that his substance remains the same, as consciousness that he remains the same would be; since the same property cannot be transferred from one substance to another. (*Ibid.,* p. 104)

Locke seems to anticipate the difficulty. Although he views memory as a criterion of personal identity, he recognizes that it is subordinate to the criterion of bodily continuity. In Book 11; chapter 27 of his *An Essay Concerning Human Understanding* (1690), Locke invents imaginary cases to support his belief: the rational parrot; the mayor of Queensborough who thinks he was Socrates in an earlier life; the prince and the cobber exchanging souls; and the case of two distinct states of consciousness present in the same individual, the one by night, the other by day ... .

Bodily identity, memory, and consciousness are criteria of personal identity. But they do not constitute it because a new person might be said to come into existence with each new stretch of consciousness. A well known rejoinder to Locke's identity theory is taken from the example provided by Thomas Reid's "gallant officer" analogy in Perry (1975): a boy was flogged for a misdeed, given a standard for bravery in adulthood (while remembering the flogging), and made a general in later life (not remembering the flogging). But if the general has no memory of the flogging, then he is not the same boy that was flogged or the same adult that remembers receiving the standard; S3 recalls experiences of S2, and S2 recalls S1, but S3 does not recall S1, therefore S3 is not S1.

Locke's difficulty is compounded when we attempt to establish a connection between our *pre-mortem* and *post-mortem* existence. In order to survive death, we need to establish the identity of the same person in the afterlife. But bodily continuity and the memory of having lived before are not proof the same person survives in the afterlife. Memory, as we saw, presupposes personal identity. It is necessary evidence of it, namely, of the existence of a subject that has bodily identity and remembered experiences, but not sufficient proof that it constitutes the same person. Even if we could establish that the same soul survives death, that is hardly enough to make it the same person.

Bishop George Berkeley agrees with Locke on the subjectivity of secondary qualities but takes the argument to the next logical step: since primary and secondary qualities cannot exist separately, it follows that the whole of reality is subjective. His *esse es percipi* affirms that reality cannot exist outside the realm of perceptions. God is used to maintain the existence of things in the absence of a finite perceiver. Berkeley says in *The Principles of Human Knowledge* (1710) that the existence of God is an obvious fact: "we may even assert that the existence of God is far more evidently perceived than the existence of men" (1. 147). While his belief has emotional appeal, it follows the path of least resistance. It is more expedient to invoke the existence of God as the guardian of identity than it is to elaborate an impossible theory on where things go in the absence of our perceptions, why they choose to return, or how they know to return as themselves. However, once Berkeley insists that spirits are more real than persons, he is in trouble. He develops a view of perception that makes more sense in the spirit world than it does in this one.

David Hume rejects the inconsistency of Locke's memory theory. Hume says in his *A Treatise of Human Nature* (1739) that it is incumbent on those who support the theory to explain how we can extend our identity beyond memory. Further, Berkeley's claim about the spirit world also fails to provide the solution he wants, as no evidence exists to support such a belief. Hume pushes the matter to its logical limit. In a section on personal identity (section 6, part 4), Hume muses on the origin of the "self":

For my part, when I enter most intimately into what I call *myself*, I always stumble on some particular perception or other, of heat or cold, light or shade, love or hatred, pain or pleasure. I never can catch *myself* at any time without a perception, and never can observe anything but the perception. (P. 252)

What we call the self is "nothing but a bundle or collection of different perceptions, which succeed each other with an inconceivable rapidity, and are in perpetual flux and movement" (*ibid.*). The "self" turns out to be the name we give to a bundle of associations. Hume is the original "string-theorist"; we are nothing but strings of impressions: "If any one, upon serious and unprejudiced reflection, thinks he has a different notion of *himself,* I must confess I can reason no longer with him ... I am certain there is no such principle in me" (*ibid.*).

So, there is no evidence to support the existence of a self, or of any kind of unitary structure. Thus, the belief in the existence of a necessary causal connection between substances (or selves) is equally false. The belief in the soul, God, including the religious hypothesis, for instance, is only a particular method of accounting for the visible phenomena of the universe.

Unfortunately, the first appearance of Hume's *Treatise* was not well received. So, he courageously sharpens the first part, giving it more force, and publishes it anew under the title *An Enquiry Concerning Human Understanding* (1748). He continues to think poorly of the "vain reasoners" that speculate about matters of God and religion: "Whence, do you think, can such philosophers derive their idea of the gods? From their own conceit and imagination surely. For if they derived it from the present phenomena, it would never point to anything farther, but must be exactly adjusted to them" (*ibid.,* p. 500).

The annihilation which some people suppose to follow upon death, and which entirely destroys this self, is nothing but the extinction of all our perceptions. He concludes the *Enquiry* with a devastating condemnation of metaphysics:

When we run over libraries, persuaded of these principles, what havoc must we make? If we take in our hand any volume; of divinity or school metaphysics, for instance; let us ask, *Does it contain any abstract reasoning concerning quantity or number?* No. *Does it contain any experimental reasoning concerning matter of fact and existence?* No. Commit it then to the flames: for it can contain nothing but sophistry and illusion. (*Ibid.,* p. 509)

Hume's analysis of causality devolves traditional truths into statements of preferences. According to Alasdair MacIntyre's *After Virtue* (1981), this is philosophical emotivism: "the doctrine that all evaluative judgments and more specifically all moral judgments are nothing but expressions of preference, expressions of attitudes or feelings, insofar as they are moral or evaluative in character" (p. 11). Emotivism attains full fruition in this century, as is evident from the success of G.E. Moore's "Intuitionist Principle." In emotivism, we express the forced choice of a "communicated passion of sympathy" toward each other. The passion grounds our moral judgments. It is a forced choice because the success of the social order depends on the will of individuals to naturally sympathize with others. Doing so is to our long-term advantage, although our shared affections and sympathy do not always tie us together.

Hume substitutes a relativistic rule of social order for what used to be an objective standard. His rule is relative because it reduces to passion the traditional view of virtue as an habituated character state. We pursue what appears to be in our best interest. Hume creates a society where individuals seek to secure what is useful or agreeable to them. But that emotive vision may preempt any conception of society as a community united in a shared vision of the greater good. The belief in the existence of objective moral standards is unfounded. MacIntyre says that what was once morality has disappeared: "moral judgments being expressions of attitudes or feelings, are neither true nor false, not secured by any rational method, for there are none" (*ibid.,* p. 11).

We have entered the age of moral decline. MacIntyre defines his own work as a confrontation with emotivism (*ibid.,* p. 21). In our day, the focus in (language) philosophy is to examine the meaning of sentences such as the ones used to make moral judgments. The study of meaning has become the new ontological reality. While analytical philosophy overtly rejects emotivism, the analytical study of moral terms used in everyday language is expressed through a relativism of context. The effort to discover the nature of the moral imperative translates roughly into "I approve of this." Is that so different from emotivism?

Derek Parfit's *Reasons and Persons* (1984) follows Hume in the development of a non-religious ethics. According to Edwards (1992), Parfit's book is "one of the most challenging and imaginative philosophical works of recent decades" (p. 324). Given Edwards's philosophical maturity and insight as Editor in Chief of *The Encyclopedia of Philosophy* (1967), we might expect a lot from that recommendation. But anyone searching the pages of the book for a solution to our moral dilemma will be disappointed. Parfit is a "string-theorist" in the Humean tradition. He claims that nothing about us corresponds to being a person. Why do we think of ourselves as being persons? He traces the habit to the uncritical use of language. We use the term as a matter of convenience to indicate complex associative patterns. In reality, the substantial self or subject of experiences, including the human soul, do not exist. It follows that the propositions of ethics are unfounded. Yet, Parfit expresses a strong desire to write ethics. He invites us to join him in the development of non-religious ethics.

The tradition's conception of human nature as an expression of Eternal Law is at an end. Natural law ethics is without foundation since the human nature on which it is based is deconstructed. So, we begin anew through the development of a different understanding of being human. Perhaps it can be shown that what Hume and Parfit reject is the traditional view of the person as universal essence, or separate soul. There seems to be ground for doing so since the tradition is rooted in dualism. Although Edwards thinks that dualism is the *sine qua non* condition of immortality, that view is a knee-jerk response to a dated conception of being human. His reaction is an attempt to reclaim the baby from the bath water. But he reclaims the wrong baby. Dualism arises out of a deficient metaphysics, one in which matter is viewed as being the extrinsic limitation of form. In that perspective, matter limits mind from the outside. But a more consistent metaphysical belief, one born out of systems theory, views matter as ultimately reducible to mind. In that event, the mind-body problem disappears. Matter arises where mind stops. Human death is the reduction of body to mind. Thus, the afterlife is not populated by disembodied souls. The reduction also shifts the focal role assigned to consciousness as it arises as the intrinsic limitation of personal identity. Consciousness does not define what I am, although it is one of my characteristics. This metaphysical view executes a double play, the one to avoid dualism, the other to maintain personal identity in the afterlife. For this to be the case, however, I must be a relationship of body and mind, and of consciousness and personal identity, rather than a substance or mere subject of experiences.

Both the mind and body are thought to be essential features of the self in relationships. For instance, the statement, "I hurt myself," means that I am hurt, not as a separate substance but as a being in relationships. The whole of the pain is transposed into my way of interacting with my world. Thus, the pain in the arm is ultimately reducible to my way of seeing the world. It is an intrinsic modifier of my relationships. For instance, the pain transfers into the way I carry the tool or meet the other. At the micro level of relationships, mind is evidently embodied. We have no experience of what it might be like to express pain as a disembodied mind. If that were the case, my pain could be expressed in your body, which is absurd.

Consciousness as such does not suggest embodiment. Consciousness is a gap or space that exists between a given set of antecedent conditions and behavioral effects. For instance, when I feel the pain in the arm I rub it. Consciousness exists between the pain and the response. It allows me to function as a negotiator between cause and effect. But I do not exist outside that causal sequence. When I feel a pain in my arm, I do not simply send a hand which happens to be attached to my body and to my brain and nervous system to do the job. My consciousness of the pain is an expression of all that I am. It presupposes my existence as a human in pain. This particular act of consciousness expresses an instance of the sort of being I am. Remembering Joseph Butler's admonition that consciousness does not constitute personal identity but presupposes it, we now see that any instance of consciousness is always reducible to personal identity as a narrowing or focusing in time. I need not be conscious to be who I am. First, I continue to be me even when I do not have a sore arm. But that would not be the case if personal identity were reducible to consciousness. I would also cease to be me when sleeping or unconscious, for instance. Second, we can affirm that consciousness is a property of who we are, which Locke could not do. The next rung of the epistemic ladder allows us to see that personal identity arises at the point where matter and mind fuse into a dynamic unit. Dualism vanishes because matter always specifies or limits the intellect. It does not constitute the intellect, although it provides an instance of intellection. My personal identity arises as my place in the relations that make me who I am. Consciousness is an intrinsic limitation of that place, while matter is the intrinsic limitation of mind. Of this, more later when the issue is raised to the wider realm of the person's relationships in being. This view of being human accords poorly with Edwards and Parfit. Edwards is skeptical about the possibility of personal survival because he is a dualist. Parfit says that no person exists in any instance of life or death. We have already examined some of the problems associated with dualism. We can now take a closer look at why Parfit rejects the idea of being a person.

Parfit bases his conclusion on the study of split-brain cases. These are cases in which a patient's left hand literally does not know what the right hand is doing. In a normal individual, the *corpus callosum* joins the two hemispheres of the brain into a single operating unit. However, when it is severed the patient functions, not as two persons but as no person. Parfit says that the split-brain case is what drew him to the study of philosophy. He claims that in split-brain cases the person's consciousness devolves into each of the separated hemispheres of the brain, or that two separate streams of consciousness exist. But they cease to be co-conscious as neither stream appears to be aware of the other. Parfit says in Edwards (1992):

> One of these people looks fixedly at the center of a wide screen, whose left half is red and right half is blue. On each half in a darker shade are the words, 'How many colors can you see'? With both hands the person writes, 'Only one'. The words are now changed to read, 'Which is the only color that you can see'? With one of his hands the person writes 'Red', with the other he writes 'Blue.' (P. 308)

Since each stream of consciousness is unaware of the existence of the other, Parfit concludes that no person is there, or single subject of experiences. These cases are unsettling because they challenge "some of our deepest assumptions about ourselves" (*ibid.*, p. 315).

Parfit goes on to explain his view on what it means to be a person. In the "Ego" theory, a person is a substance or subject of experience. Parfit uses Descartes's "thinking thing" to illustrate the model. He is undoubtedly right to reject the existence of person in that sense of the term. However, we can be persons in other ways. In Parfit's "bundle theory," the experiences of living a human life are explained as consisting of a series of states and events, tied together by various kinds of strings such as the relation between the experiences and later memories of them. Since no self exists in the absence of causal relations, as Hume points out, the simple view of persons is mistaken. Susan Blackmore (1993) also carries the no-person idea into her own work. She studies the near-death experience. One of her observations is worth citing in full since it mirrors Parfit's no-person view: "We are biological organisms, evolved in fascinating ways for no purpose at all and with no end in mind. We are simply here and this is how it is. I have no self and 'I' own nothing. There is no one to die. There is just this moment, and now this and now this" (p. 263).

At first blush, the split-brain case might lead us to wonder if two persons exist given the evidence of two unrelated streams of consciousness. Can we not suggest that each stream of consciousness marks a personal identity which, in turn, arises at the junction where matter meets mind? The evidence does not support that view. Furthermore, Occam's razor suggests a simpler route in which we treat the split-brain person as being sick. The split-brain case is not the norm. It provides an instance of a patient suffering from a neurophysiological disorder. Parfit thinks that the number of persons is none. That is because he mistakenly thinks that being a person can only mean being an immaterial substance, but it does not. A person is not a substance, or abstract essence. We are not subjects of experiences. Parfit addresses a mistaken issue. He is a devout Materialist with strong views against dualism. While materialism is an attractive alternative to dualism, it is not the best way to represent being human.

An interesting feature of materialism is that the parts of the human are seen to constitute the highest possible degree of unity. But the issue is boring since the parts, not unlike the soul, are everywhere the same. His materialist agenda is that there never was a person, not that the split-brain case reduces the number of persons to none. The problem with materialism is that it fails to provide a complete account of the life of a person. It is a limited, reductionist explanation of the whole by the part. The explanation of the part by the whole is more promising. The existence of two unrelated streams of consciousness in an individual does not suggest that no person is there, but it does suggest a shift in the relationship between the brain's two hemispheres. The patient's behavior is the consequence of a neurological impairment in which the brain fails to achieve the integrating function that is normally due to a healthy brain. The reports of truncated streams of consciousness is as it should be, given the damage to the corpus callosum. Thus the twin reports of the left and right hemispheres, the lack of integration between the information provided by the left hand and the right hand, confirm not the anomaly but the integrative role of a healthy brain. Imagine now that something wonderful happens to Parfit's patient: Neurosurgeons successfully reconnect the patient's severed hemispheres. Since the data of the split-brain experiences are stored in each hemisphere, the patient will merge these files into a fully operative brain. The two streams of consciousness will integrate and the patient will know just how sick he was.

But Parfit is right on several counts. He is right to reject dualism and the traditional representation of being a person. We are not disembodied souls. He is also right about the person as a being that enters into relationships, even if only between associative states of the person. But the problem is that he does not go far enough. He needs to widen the web of relationships to include associations at the level of the divinity in us, the other, and the environment. This is systemic thinking, a progression toward the part from the whole. The string-theory, however, is reductionist. To suggest that materialism alone specifies what it means to be a human being returns the subject to a new form of epistemic dualism between the whole and the part. The effort to reconstruct a non-religious ethics on a secular basis is well intentioned, but poorly conceived. It is analogous to Descartes's attempt to paint everything with a single brush stroke.

One additional point needs to be made about the no-person view. Parfit says that the view is not new, since it was held by the Buddha (*Gautama Siddhartha*). The mention of the Buddha holds a certain appeal for people. But the Buddha's view on "emptiness" (*sunyata*) has positive meaning. It does not refer to the absence of the subject, but to a state in which the purified personality does not crave the (illusory) pleasure of being a "self," or ego. Craving causes suffering (*dukkha*). Suffering means emptiness, imperfection, or lack of wholeness. Thus, the way of the Buddha teaches, not about egolessness, but about relationships. The being that suffers lacks enlightenment or wholeness.

Buddha's philosophy is expressed in "Four Noble Truths," and the "Noble Eightfold Path," the Path being a subset of the fourth Noble Truths. The first truth is to know that suffering exists. The second, is being aware of craving. The third truth is found in the awareness of the causes of suffering. The fourth truth follows the middle-way expressed in the eightfold path. It offers an escape from the round of "*samsara*" or the re-becoming that characterizes craving. Thus, the Buddha does not teach a no-person theory, but a process of becoming whole by moving out of the ego. Yet, his teachings are often misread.

Francis H. Cook's article on the nature of Buddhist theory in Davis (1989) appears to provide such an instance since it supports Parfit's view. Cook claims that the Buddha teaches the no-self view. The article provoked an interesting rejoinder (in the same book) by Badham and Hick that confirms my own view. In my view, the Buddha does not introduce the no-self theory, although moving into relationship with the All takes place through a process of moving out of self-interest. The focus is on being one with the All rather than on the part. The dispute indicates some of the confusion that exists between the self and the All. Once it becomes clear that the All is the true reality, as in systems theory, the moving out of self is seen as only a process.

Parfit's use of the teleporter analogy confirms his reductivist view of the I. The story invites us to imagine that a finite set of living neurons is moved to a distant planet. As expected, Parfit claims that the determination of who arrives at the other end depends on the number of neurons moved. If less than a majority of neurons is sent no one arrives. That may be explained in part by the fact that no one leaves. The teleporter case is based on bad science. Some humans appear to function normally with only half a brain. So, our personal identity can remain with less than a majority share of the original neurons. A hard blow to the head causes neural damage leading to accelerated memory loss and possibly to loss of consciousness. That loss tells us something about the rapidly disintegrating condition of the brain at the point of impact. In the teleporter analogy, no one arrives because the brain totally disintegrates and the traveler dies. But we can imagine the teleporter case from a different perspective. Say that my relationships are shifted from point n to p. Then, that will be me in p, if that is me in n.

Three

The Existentialists

Whereas British philosophers follow Hume's influence leading from Bertrand Russell and Alfred Ayer to Ludwig Wittgenstein (1889-1951) or Parfit, an alternative path is taken by some European thinkers in which the void left by the no-self theory is filled through human action. The parameters of action are contained in the works of three seminal thinkers, namely, Søren Kierkegaard's *Concluding Unscientific Postscript* (1846), Martin Heidegger's *Being and Time* (1927), and Jean-Paul Sartre's (1905-1980) *Being and Nothingness* (1943). Taken together these works combine an impressive focus on subjectivity and freedom with the being-there character of the human project. Their revolt against rationalism centers on three main themes. First, Kierkegaard dis-empowers philosophical reason to assign primacy to subjectivity as the mainspring for a religious leap into the arms of the godhead. The alternative demise of traditional values is expressed by Friedrich Nietzsche (1844-1900) in the human affirmation of a personal "Will to Power." Second, the movement is characterized by Heidegger's condemnation of the tradition and the rejection of eternal truths. In that event, we begin anew with the *Dasein* as a being toward relationships. *Dasein* is a term Heidegger uses to mean "human being." The rejection of dualism is central to his metaphysics. We find ourselves as already being in the world. Thirdly, the view of Sartre represents the individual as being totally alone in the world, although free to inaugurate the projects of a human life. Heidegger and Sartre use the phenomenological method to describe the condition of being human. In this brief chapter, I single out Sartre's work since he, better than anyone else, provides a solid descriptive account of metaphysical despair and the challenges that arise out of the demise of absolutes. The work of Heidegger and the character of our being "thrown" into the world shall also merit special study as we continue to expand the sphere of human relationships.

Once we rid ourselves of absolutes such as God, eternal essences, natural law, and the objective grounding of morals, what is left? Not much. Albert Camus (1913-1960), a close friend of Sartre, concludes that the whole business of seeking to act rationally is absurd. The individual that recognizes the sterility of rationalism can abandon the pretense of making sense of the world. Camus resigns himself to the benign indifference of things. The key to happiness lies in not attempting to make sense of our predicament. Once hope is removed, no disappointment is possible. But Sartre is more courageous than his friend; he is a humanist willing to run the risks of philosophizing in an age without values. His work opens with an awareness of freedom as responsibility. We can choose ourselves through our acts. So where do we start?

We have no unified vision of where to go. So, how can we start anywhere? The non-existence of God suggests the absence of absolute values to guide conduct. There is no human nature, no *a priori* code of ethics to help us distinguish between right and wrong. Everything is permitted because no moral standard guides conduct before action. Sartre begins the long reconstructive surgery in a key work, appropriately titled *Being and Nothingness* (1943). Consciousness–a secretor of negativity–distances itself from the world of the "*en-soi.*" The world is seen to be a massive, naked, frightful, meaningless pastiche of existence. Not much can be said about it since it does not become. The world of things is complete and hides nothing from us. It is simply "there," without sufficient reason. The realization of our sheer contingency is frightening, as he explains in *Nausea* (1938). We cannot kill ourselves because death is not a possibility. It closes the door on possibilities. But we can say "no" to things. We begin to do so in the first act of consciousness. The infant, which is nothing but freedom, commits the first act when it becomes aware of itself as being other than what it sees. It defines itself by knowing itself to be other than what it knows. Thus, consciousness forces us to gain distance from things. Unfortunately, the process of defining ourselves entails treating others as objects. Sartre's play *No Exit* (1946) makes the point that the process is hell. In the end, the other is my judge, defining me in a way I cannot define myself. The other's gaze is hell because it fixes me in a state where I am not. Yet, human existence is a process, not of being fixed, but of separation from things. The gap widens in the life of a human being as consciousness continues to secrete negativity. Sartre uses the argument as one of his proofs for the non-existence of God: The belief that infinite consciousness can simultaneously exist as infinitely distant from being and as fullness of being at the same time, is contradictory. Death is what finally marks the end of my human project. It defines me. Has it been worth it? No, the Sartrean individual remains alone, without exit, living life in the insane asylum of human existence. So why bother?

We have a self-inflicted responsibility to join together in order to overcome common problems such as the scarcity of food. Sartre is a humanist. He sets out to redress a world where injustice and the denial of freedom prevail. His *Critique of Dialectical Reason* (1960) is a call to common action to overcome our most urgent problems. His work merits a Nobel Prize and international acclaim. If an epitaph marked his work, it could read: He bravely faced the despair that arises out of the loss of absolutes and from being alone. So where do we go from here? We can go to the second face of existentialism where the sacred is reintroduced in secular life. The work of Gabriel Marcel (1889-1973), for instance, focuses on the view of the other as being a loving extension of the self. The social self now replaces the bankrupt metaphysical self.

In Christian existentialism, the "resurrection" also focuses on new life in this world. As a consequence of the "risen Jesus," and baptism, we are no longer "dead to sin," or alone in the world. Some early Christians talk as if the resurrection has already taken place, although St. Paul rejects this interpretation. He seats it in the afterlife. Still, this is original existentialism.

Summary and Conclusion

I have criticized the traditional view of being a person because it did not provide a cogent argument for being human, and for being immortal. My criticism extended to contemporary philosophy where the argument for immortality is a non-starter without dualism. But in my view, dualism generates the problem of personal identity in our *pre-mortem* and *post-mortem* existence.

The conception of the disembodied soul is simply too angelic to be human. It does not support a belief in personal survival. Aquinas can be forgiven since he was a mystic, but we lesser mortals cannot abscond from the relationships of ordinary life. So where do we go from here? The first stop is to examine the relationships that make us who we are. The second step is to cast our relationships on being's unconcealment as focal point. Being's unconcealment is the gateway from thanatology to eschatology.

The Existentialists make a solid contribution to human life as choice, responsibility, and adventure. The central thing about us is not our eternal nature, but the fact that we become persons through what we do in relationships. We live in a finite world in the presence of good and evil, life and death. We regard beliefs as tentative and experimental, and life as rooted in the everydayness of successes and failures, pleasures and pain. We are as often in error, sin, loneliness, despair, and anxiety, as we are in truth, love, grace, compassion, tolerance, and hope of becoming better persons. The natural law does not exist in human nature as fixed, but in our processes of becoming through relationships, good and bad, in history. The task of detailing some of our adventures lies ahead.

The character of our "being-there," to borrow Heidegger's expression, reveals our generic indebtedness to being's unconcealment. We stand in the presence of truth before entering into relationships. Being's unconcealment, specifically the nothing surrounding it, is a focal point in the reduction of consciousness to personal identity, matter to mind, embodied mind to being, being to the nothing, or creator, and the creator to God.

The person I become knows itself as a being toward the good and evil tendencies of the human psyche. I also begin in my relationships toward other human beings. And I begin in my relationships toward nature. My fundamental associations characterize me as a person. I am nothing in the absence of my relationships. Hume and Parfit are right about this aspect of being human. But they are wrong to reduce the range of relationships to emotivism, or to focus on the part. The evidence supports the claim that the person is in process toward the whole. We are not only beings toward death, but also beings toward immortality in divine timelessness.

For this to be the case, however, my relationships must be shown to survive in the afterlife. Being's unconcealment is called upon to play a critical role in that regard, while quantum physics is enlisted to support religious beliefs. Why this route? The secularism of the age expects and deserves as much.

Why the existence of God is important.

Some people, even persons who believe in God, think that the existence of God is an abstruse subject, far removed from the real business of life. In their view, life should be pretty much the same whether God exists or not. Given the definition of God as an all-powerfull, all-good being, however, the idea that God's existence doesn't matter is implausible. (可以当信当为)

If God exists, then all our actions are seen and judged. If there is no God, then many of our actions go unseen and unjudged. If God exists, every event in our lives, every even in everyone's life, has a meaning because it is part of God's plan, even if that plan is unknown to us. If God does not exist, the existence of the human race is meaningless, in the sense that its existence is not part of anyone's plan or purpose.

Even more significantly, If God exists, good will ultimately triumph over evil. All decent (主流的) people are frustrated by the worldly success of mean and unscrupulous (不地为) individuals. Nevertheless, the theist is consoled (安慰) by the thought that, since God exists, the success of the wicked is only temporary. The atheist (无神论), contemplating 思考 of the success of the wicked, must live with the though that the wicked may forever get way with their crimes. Theists live in a word of divine justice and divine (神的) meaning. Atheists live in a world of irregular justic, in which the meaning of events is supplied only by themselves and their fellow human beings. The theist and the atheist live in different mental and emotional universes.

Four

PERSONS EXIST IN RELATIONSHIPS

1. Meaning of Terms

One of the first concerns that arises in the language of being a person is the use of "metaphysically suspect" terms such as "God," "spirituality," and "the religious experience." Hence we begin with a clarification of those terms.

The term "God" is paradoxical. The meaning of "God" is relative to culture, an expression rooted in the natural order, but the God of major world religions is also transcultural, objective, and universal. That paradox feeds the propositions of morality. The reality of God is characterized in several ways depending on which arm of the paradox is visited. For instance, 12-Step literature imagines God as being a power "greater than self." But in Hebrew thought, God is an "Abba," possibly a loving father. Still, the God of science and philosophy is functional and impersonal. In mysticism, the God of Meister Eckhart (1260-1327) exists beyond description, since naming God limits God. God is rational, but loving. God is impersonal, but deeply embedded in human affairs. God is a spiritual substance. Yet, the existence of God is manifest in concrete relationships. God is immaterial, but nothing material is outside of God. God is also viewed as being an all powerful, necessary, self-caused, loving creator. Yet, God must be indirectly responsible for the existence of evil in the world. The followers of world religions claim to enter into relationships with a loving God, but God did not respond to the cry of the faithful at Auschwitz, or to the undeserved suffering of millions in our own day. Human suffering can lead to the denial of God. The reality of God, including the denial of God, reflects a person's experiences. Why is that? The simple view is that the existence of God is not self-evident. Some philosophers, such as Hume, suggest that we cannot logically venture beyond the natural order.

This belief provides a clue to the paradox. It seems necessary to distinguish between God as creator and the reality of God beyond creation. The intellect fixes on God as creator, situating the ultimate cause of the natural order in God. This view implicates God in the imperfections of the world. It leads some philosophers into agnosticism or the denial of God. But the God of religion also exists beyond the creator, or the imperfections of the world. This view moves us beyond the limits of reason. However, the evidence must be found to legitimate a leap of faith. The evidence exists in the unconscious realm of the psyche. We can know the effect of the divinity in us, although the reality of a transcendent God remains unknowable in itself. The ways of the human heart, other human beings, and being's unconcealment suggest that God exists.

So, we move on two fronts to explain the paradoxical character of God: First, to the creator as uncaused cause of the natural order. Second, to the God that exists beyond the creator. The evidence that the psyche moves us toward the universal order is contained in our own search for absolute truths. The human being exists, not as substance, but as the output of God's loving processes, beginning with the creator in us.

The effect of God in us is manifest in our own creative processes. We become human through our relationships. The denial of God limits the pursuit of the good to the terrestrial order, whereas the affirmation of God raises our relationship to the good beyond the natural order. Both views enact processes at work within us. Theists contend that atheists know a great deal more than they pretend to know, but atheists claim that theists over describe emotional experiences. They both struggle with the existence of good and evil in psyche.

The human strives toward universal good as Aristotle says. Evil is the frustration of that tendency or divine telos within us as Aquinas says. How evil can be a tendency of the psyche and frustrate the divine telos in us is a tension in (my) theory that remains to be explained. Evil is not the absence of good. The mind hungers for universal truths, however. For instance, Euclid opens his geometry by first formulating his postulates in universal language. He says that the straight line can be extended indefinitely. How does he know this, if not as a tendency of reason? This view provides a model of scientific inquiry that persists in our own day. The shift into non-Euclidian geometry does not suggest that the mind has modified its structure. The psychological principles that accompany past and present scientific inductions suggest that the search for an absolute, universal truth, such as the existence of God, is characteristic of the mechanism at work whenever we think. The conceptual shift from the homogeneous space of Euclid to the heterogeneous space of Einstein is not surprising, since reason and reality converge in dynamic propositions. An element that was taught to obtain from reason is now shown to provide from experience. But the essential character of the dialogue remains unchanged. Our tendency toward good and evil is also made concrete in the particulars of experience, unfolding God's telos in history. So, morality is an evolving business. The lesson learned from Auschwitz and the undeserved suffering of innocent victims in our own day is that we often as not follow the evil tendency within us. The tendency of the psyche toward good is not always manifest in history.

God is the object of religion. The term religion is from the Latin root *religare,* meaning "to bind," and the Sanskrit *Yoga,* or "union." The "God connection" is made between consciousness and the unconscious or hidden aspects of psyche. God exists in our unconscious mind, but is made manifest, or conscious, through the use of informed, culturally sensitive symbols. We develop symbols, or metaphors, in response to God calling. These symbols, rich in historical tradition, arise through the phenomenological description of the effects of God in us. For instance, Christians view the cross as a profound symbol. Saint Irenaeus says in *Epideixis* that it symbolizes the central event of the Christian belief. The "meditating Buddha" plays an equally central role in the religions of Indian origin. The religious community meets in such metaphors.

Sceptics commonly assert, "God is just an idea in people's minds." But this cannot be true. If God exists, exists everywhere, not just in people's minds. What exists in people's minds is just the concept of God.

Spirituality is the existential experience of using metaphors to make religious connections. The religious experience, when authentic, generates the healing powers of the divinity in us, extending to the range of feelings and thoughts we have about the world. The spiritual experience is existential because it promotes changes in us leading to social action, or sacramental changes in the environment. A spiritual experience is necessarily transformative, raising consciousness to new heights. It results in a deeper relationship with the sacred, the other, and the environment. However, a spiritual experience is not always religion based.

Religious studies are the phenomenological study of spiritual enframing. The phenomenological method is used extensively to describe the two main forces of the psyche; our being toward good, and our being toward evil. The individual acting toward evil seeks (consciously or unconsciously) to frustrate the divine telos.

2. Relationships

It is not human nature that allows us to forge relationships, but the relations that trace the locus of being human. What sorts of relations define us, or make us human? The evidence suggests that a human being is the outcome of psychological, ethical, and metaphysical relationships. Since I possess reason and can act morally, my relationships of origin must be intelligent and ethical. The (metaphysical) laws, or patterns, that individuate me suggest that an intelligent, loving, creator enters into relationship with me. In the beginning God and the creator enter into relationship to beget us. The creator begets the cosmos while God begets the likeness of God in us. Further, the non-dualistic view of the universe points toward the possibility that the creator is God. God's creative act sends us on an errand to become God-like. We do so by sharing in the responsibility of co-creating ourselves, other human beings, and the environment. In this event, the distinction between God and creator is epistemic rather than ontological. However, this view implicates God (and creator) in the existence of evil. The natural world delimits the possibility of becoming supernatural. We realize the divine telos through our free acts in the natural environment. The temporal and the eternal reside side by side in the same particle of human existence. We begin with a study of good and evil within our own psyche. Our psyche is an instrument for moral action. We move toward others, as well as the environment, because of a tendency within psyche to (morally) empower or dis-empower everything we touch.

To love or empower other human beings is to form a mutual personal identity with them, defining ourselves through them. This view of the loving person is represented by the character Aristophanes in Plato's *Symposium*. Aristophanes has in mind to praise the God Love:

the original human nature was not like the present, but different. The sexes were not two as they are now, but originally three in numbers; there was man, woman, and the union of the two, having a name corresponding to this double nature, which had once a real existence, but is now lost, and the word 'Androgynous' is only preserved as a term of reproach. (P. 189)

Human nature was originally one, and we were whole, but Zeus saw our wickedness and cut us in two. Aristophanes exhorts us to piety, that we might avoid evil, so that the God Love can return us to our natural state of being whole. The philosopher Gottfried Wilhelm Leibniz (1646-1716) objects that a complex presupposes the identity of the simples which compose it, however. Phenomenology, for instance, describes the contents of self, or subjective correlate of experiences, to provide insight into the nature of things in themselves. The view is based on dualism. The belief that a person is a center of activity, or subject of experiences, does not express a primary datum since it is abstracted out of our relationships. Although relationships individuate us, the whole gives meaning to the part, not the part to the whole. We do not enter into relationships because of what we are, but become what we are through our loving relationships. They take place in three main movements toward reality, namely, the psychological, the ethical, and the metaphysical aspects of being human, or becoming persons.

Our psychological movement toward God is an expression of the human heart. It is not primarily a rational process, although the tendency is not unreasonable. It appears to arise out of a pre-discursive drive, or instinct toward wholeness. John Hick (1976) says "God has so made us that there is an inherent gravitation of our being toward God" (p. 250). He is absolutely right. Most of us are aware of our God connection, but the strongest evidence that this is the case exists in dim-witted individuals. Some brain damaged individuals, for instance, express strong religious needs without having the slightest insight into the existence of the God connection. I am not referring to the "blindness" of faith, but to the religious practices of some idiots. However, healthy, rational individuals can also be unaware of that tendency in psyche since reasoning can obfuscate the obvious.

But what explains my describing myself in terms of some relationships rather than others? My fundamental premise is that love governs what we become. The ancients viewed this as moving toward the divine telos. The legitimacy of that view is argued here. The first evidence of this characteristic exists in the human psyche where we move toward God as a common focal point. The God experience places us in the presence of a birthing process in which we become ourselves by being divine-like. The tendency to move toward God, or away from God in the case of evil, is manifest in psyche. If God is the All, nothing is outside God. God is in all things, and *all things are in God.* This is the view of panentheism (not pantheism). Thus, God must in some sense be responsible for evil as well as good. God weaves an infinite number of relationships, only some of which are known to us, such as our psychological tendency toward good and evil. This tendency is the fundamental stuff of being human. Choosing evil, however, is a tendency to break away from the divine telos.

Loving relationships provide the objective ground of ethics, securing the person-making process in universalist soil. We exist in a system of relationships taking place at many different levels. Our relationships are psychological, spiritual, interpersonal, and material. For instance, the culture of the table and fireplace contain a rich expression of who we are, as we gather to break bread and tell stories about our person-making experiences. The error of string-theorists lies in the attempt to reduce our relationships to materialism, or to the psychological associations between stimulus and response (behaviorism). They are self-centered, or individual like, standing as epitaphs to remind us of lost battles in the struggle toward wholeness. The rich variety of stories we tell around the fireplace moves us beyond the realm of separate substance, or causality. They reveal our nature as family. Our religious stories, for instance, are stories about belonging to cosmos. Parfit's interpretation of the split-brain case reduces being human to a physiological thread, opting out of the wider spectrum of relationships through which we become persons. Contemporary science, in contrast, affirms the relations view of being human. We exist in the world, a place in which we weave relationships toward good, evil, the face of others, and the face of the world. We are not anything separate from our associations with things, or the intricate web of relationships we weave in systemic thinking, or the view that the whole has greater reality than the part. The view of ourselves as being a separate substance is an illusion of the past, one that promotes not only dualism, but a false sense of our place in nature.

Heidegger's pioneering work *Being and Time* situates persons in the stream of lived experiences from the first moment of birth. To be a person is to "be there" in the world. His term for persons is "*Dasein*." This section lays the foundation for three central characteristics, or modes of being-there, namely, psychological, ethical and metaphysical: (1) Our psychological tendency unfolds a self toward good and evil. Evil is not the absence of good, but a distinct and separate order of being. (2) The ethical perspective of the person arises at the intersubjective level where we freely choose to empower, or to dis-empower, other human beings. This is the social self. It has metaphysical primacy over the individual, or epistemic self. Being moral arises as the projection of our own inclinations toward others, as extrapolations of the psyche. Evil is the deliberate abuse, control, exploitation or forcing of natural relationships into unnatural states. Moral judgments include conscious and unconscious processes alike, drawing on reason, logic, feelings, emotions, and the divine light within us. (3) We enter into the metaphysical mode of being a person in our inclination toward the unconcealment of being. In brief, we become who we are as a consequence of relationships taking place in the web of psyche, other human beings, and being's unconcealment.

The tradition seats natural law in the human essence, or human nature. That view belies a fundamental dualism which generates the problem of personal identity. The present study avoids dualism, although we do not enter with equal vigor into each aspect of our relationships. It is a matter of temperament, or place in the relationship cycle (culture), that certain individuals tend to focus on chosen forms of relationships. For instance, meditation feeds on the presence of the divinity within psyche, whereas the social self comes to life primarily in the presence of other persons. Some persons draw strength from belonging to a church, others "belong" to nature. We are different, although we share a common characteristic of belonging in loving relationships, animated by a common core of person-making possibilities.

A revised natural law theory invites a process of discovering God in history rather than in the eternal truths of human nature. This view is expressed by all major world religions. It exists in the religions of Judaic, Christian, and Islamic origin. It is consistent with Buddhism and Confucianism. Religionists view us as being transcultural, person-making entities. According to Xinzhong Yao (1996), Confucianism details a process of the individual becoming human through relationships. In Judaic thought, family and community–today especially, global– are primary objects of love. In Christian thought, the person is invited to enter into loving relationships with the divinity within psyche, and to love the other with the same intensity as the divinity in self. We are also charged with the responsibility of civilization and the construction of a better world (social action). Thus, to be human is to enact this vision in history.

What becomes of human nature? The "I," "self," "subject," or "ego" is an artificial construct, the result of a deduction, or of extrapolated abstraction. Stopping the moment of phenomenal experience, we discover it as an outcome, or subjective correlate of relationships. The distinction between subject and object is artificial since no pure "I" exists outside relationships. Thus, natural law cannot be expressed in the individual as essence. The life of a person is not rooted in the subjective correlate of the relationship, or the objective correlate taken separately, but in a mode of existence superimposed upon the two in such a way as to make relationships primary and possible. While the phenomenological method provides some insight into the nature of these correlates, being a person is dialogical process. The error of dualism lies precisely in the attempt to view the whole from the perspective of the parts: mind, body. It reduces us to one aspect of the correlate. The tendency to view the part through the whole is more promising.

An equally vivid sense defines us as beings toward evil, however. Resentment, for instance, is an instance of psychic discomfort with an aspect of self, the other, or nature. The evidence unequivocally suggests we are beings toward evil. Devil worship, wars, weapons, Auschwitz, nuclear bombs, for instance, reveal a psychological tendency within us toward the celebration of evil. The evidence of cruelty, slavery, oppression, tyranny, mutilation, and torture of other human beings arises out of our tendency toward evil. Furthermore, the deliberate pollution and degradation of the environment also reveals the evil aspect of being a person. What do we make of evil? The *Proverbs* of Solomon, son of David, King of Israel, warn against it: "The sage speaks: avoid bad company" (1:8-19). The map to wisdom is announced in the same *Book of Proverbs*: "do not forget my teachings, let your heart keep my principles, for these will give you lengthier days, longer years of life, and greater happiness" (3:1-2).

The presence of the divinity within us also introduces the existence of Satan (and evil) as a member of God's inner court. This is an unexpected turn of events. C.G. Jung includes the existence of evil in the effects of the divinity on the human psyche. But Kierkegaard focuses on the purity of heart (*den enkelte*) that moves the authentic religious commitment. It exists in subjective truth. Gabriel Marcel views other human beings as an extension of the divinity within self. This means we can choose to empower or dis-empower others. Martin Heidegger expresses a profound reverence for being's unconcealment. The spiritual experience of meeting God (or Satan) is celebrated, not only in the evil we do, but also in our struggles against evil. Our world is filled with suffering.

Social action enlists a hegemony of the person as a being toward good. The existential connection between us is often richest at the level of suffering where resonance and empathy overcome the artificial distance of language and culture. We know ourselves as transcultural beings in need of healing.

The self-help movement arises as subjectivity in action. It is driven by a transcultural, transpolitical, source of spiritual empowerment, providing evidence of the primacy and power of the social self. The exploited are persons united in a single spiritual voice against suffering (evil). The Canadian Council on Social Development identifies the following types of self-help groups: groups for addictions, mental and physical health, family-related problems, friends or relatives of people with illnesses, aboriginal peoples, stigmatized groups, social advocacy, third world self-help, and economic self-help. The self-help movement draws heavily on the realm of feelings and emotions, as well as on reason and logic. It softens the coldness of high technology. Technology needs to become more like self-help. Liberation Theology, for instance, is a movement in which people are encouraged to take charge of their own well being through the development of publicly owned agencies such as the cooperative movement, and issues like low income housing. Christianity offers a model of self-help, or Liberation Theology, like Jesus, is seen to restore power to the people by inciting them to follow the authority that lies in their own heart.

Five

PERSONS AS CORRELATES OF GOOD AND EVIL

1. Persons as Correlates of Good

The opening pages of Alasdair MacIntyre's intellectually sound book *After Virtue* (1981) invite us to imagine that the natural sciences had somehow suffered the effects of a catastrophe:

> A series of environmental disasters are blamed by the general public on the scientists. Widespread riots occur, laboratories are burnt down .... and people begin anew using remnants, bits and pieces of scientific language here and there. Chaos prevails. The language of morality is in the same state of grave disorder as the language of the natural sciences in the imaginary world I have just described.

Three years later, Derek Parfit's *Reasons and Persons* invites us to join him in the development of a non-religious ethics. He imagines that both human history and the history of ethics are just beginning (p. 454). But can non-religious ethics be an ethics without absolutes? Non-religious and religious ethics appear to value the same sorts of social goods: peace, justice, freedom, and fundamental rights. But what is the standard of these values if not the objective language of ethics? What supports the base of non-religious ethics? Can it be developed in the absence of an absolute, human nature, natural law, person, God. Non-religious ethics provides no grounding for our moral life, no objective reason for being moral. If eternal truths do not exist, why do we enter into associations with others? Unless there exists a divine telos or ultimate end toward which we strive, one that transcends the conception of truth as relative to context, there can be no global community of purpose. The person without a vista of the absolute is plunged into a subversive relativism. According to Hans Küng (1991) we need an objective mission statement to develop as persons: "there is one thing that those who have no religion cannot do, even if, in fact they want to accept unconditional norms for themselves: they cannot give a reason for the absoluteness and universality of ethical obligation" (p. 51).

Perhaps we can use the metaphor of a dying patient's hospital career to represent the gradual demise of eternal truths. What happens when we die? The process begins in somatic death, a condition which is not necessarily irreversible, although it is incompatible with the continued existence of life. If the patient's condition is not reversed, it progresses into cellular death beginning with the death of the neo-cortex or higher thought processes and continues into the death of the mid-brain and brain stem. The legal (and philosophical) definition of death is the death of the whole brain. The metaphor opens:

Somatic death: Nietzsche announces in *The Gay Science* that God is dead. The year is 1892, although public knowledge of the death of God does not occur until about 1905. God had been unwell since the first appearance of Hume's *Enquiry Concerning Human Understanding* and Ludwig Feuerbach's (1804-1872) *The Essence of Christianity* (1841). The advent of two World Wars, the Holocaust, and the Bomb do little to reverse the patient's condition. The patient's condition worsens as Heidegger denounces the errors of traditional metaphysics as well as the death of Descartes's absolute. This completes the patient's somatic death cycle. Henceforth we would come to know ourselves as beings toward death rather than as beings toward the resurrection. Sartre and Camus begin the long process of reconstructive surgery to rebuild God to our likeness. The one proceeding from nothingness to a vision of consciousness as secretor of negativity, the other resigning himself to the benign indifference of the nothing. We stand between two nothings. But they are not sacred horizons. We come from nothing and move toward nothing. We live in the age of despair. Philosophers divide into two main streams of thought, the one following Heidegger, the other Wittgenstein.

Cellular death: The patient moves quickly into the stages of cellular death or irreversible coma. The year is 1953 because of a discovery that the DNA or genetic structure of any living thing is interchangeable with any other living thing. Human beings are not special. The belief in human nature dies. The death of natural law theory follows in the wake of that death. As the patient's burial is anticipated, some environmentalists such as Lynn White deliver the eulogy, citing natural law theory as responsible for the dying state of the environment. In the 1970s, the patient's condition deteriorates even further by advancing into mid-brain death when a scientific report by D. H. & D. L. Meadows, J. Randers, and W. W. Behrens III, known simply as the "Meadows Report"or *The Limits to Growth* (1972), is ignored. The patient finally moves into brain-stem death in 1984 with the appearance of Derek Parfit's *Reasons and Persons.* On the eighth anniversary of the death of persons, Paul Edwards reflects that all is well. The patient is buried. We can now take the first steps toward the development of a non-religious ethics. A few years later, authors begin to reflect on the problems caused by religion. John Dourley publishes a Jungian critique of Christianity, *The Illness That We Are* (1984), citing the politics of religion for too frequent Holy Wars, while Merold Westphal's *God, Guilt, and Death* (1984) argues in eloquent voice that the main argument for the existence of religious beliefs centers on the fear of death.

But an important sequence cannot be left out of the metaphor. In the definition of death, the patient's condition is verified after the lapse of a 24-hour period, ensuring that the death was not pronounced prematurely. For instance, hypothermia and barbiturate poisoning interfere with the measurement of death. Recent developments suggest that the death of absolutes was pronounced prematurely. Our barbiturate poison, inducing our false sense of values, is materialism. Yet, materialism awakened us out of our dogmatic slumber. The patient is shaken by the onslaught, we begin anew. In 1979, Virginia Black launches *Vera Lex* as the international forum of the natural law society–a search for absolutes, or universals. About the same time, new developments in quantum physics suggest the reconciliation of science and religion. The patient is restored to life. The natural law is suspected of being alive and well and living in many places, beginning with the human heart, but continuing into interpersonal relationships, and into our dialogue in being. Yet, God's presence in our psyche remains largely unconscious. We are agnostic in some measure.

Why do some persons enter into public relationships with God whereas other equally sensitive individuals fail to acknowledge doing so? Was St. Paul's vision on the road to Damascus merely a discharge of the occipital lobe, or did he really see something supernatural? Pragmatism judges a belief by the way it works. If God is dead, persons must be dead. Paul did see something because the experience transformed his life. Atheists insist he did not see anything supernatural. What else does psychology say about the religious experience?

Spiritual psychiatry, such as the type introduced by Jung, suggests that the secular ambition to develop a non-religious ethics corresponds to an unconscious psychic desire to enter into relationship with God. Why else, for instance, would Parfit feel the need to develop ethics? Presumably to rid it of falsehoods, that is, the search for truth in parsimonious language. But once we reject the existence of absolutes, nothing is left to explain his interest in "other absolutes." However, his ambition makes sense as a manifestation of the unconscious need of the psyche to be one with God. For instance, the work of Descartes suggests a desire for a God connection. The mystical interest which John Caputo (1978) discovers in Heidegger's thought points in the same direction. The existence of a psychological need to interact with God, or at least a creator, is also evident in the work of some cartesian philosophers such as Baruch (Benedict) Spinoza (1632-1677), Nicholas Malebranche (1638-1715), and Leibniz. God is also assigned functional responsibility in Newtonian science. We are psychologically predisposed to act toward God.

What does Descartes see when he turns within the *cogito?* He sees God, since God is explicit and philosophically necessary to his philosophy. But, at first, he acts as if that was not the case. The problem is that he cannot complete his doubt without positing consciousness into non-being. What the philosopher sees is his own being in relationship with God. This is evident from his insistence that the idea of God is innate, if only potentially so. Descartes's doubt awakens the sleeping divinity to salvific activity. Every serious student of Descartes recognizes that the whole of his system collapses without God. How can we imagine, for instance, that the statement "I exist as a doubting thing" is not contradicted by the crucial principle of his method, the clear and distinct idea as a criterion of truth? Once Descartes lays claim to having clear and distinct ideas, he is no longer a doubting thing. He ceases to exist, since he only exists in virtue of doubt. Although one can doubt something in clear and distinct terms, one cannot simultaneously lay claim to absolute doubt. Supposing we grant the validity of the "I think, therefore I am" and the subsequent validity of the criterion of truth, Descartes can go no further. How to imagine the continued existence of the doubting thing in the evidence of clear and distinct ideas?

Descartes never intended to work alone. The God within psyche maintains the existence of the thinking machine in the absence of doubt, or in the presence of clear and distinct ideas. The idea of God and religion is never far from his mind. The *Meditations* (1641), a work dedicated to the Paris theology faculty, bore the subtitle "in which are demonstrated the existence of God and the immortality of the soul." It begins the turn to the self and to the discovery of belief in God. That belief in God is seen to be entirely reasonable and rational. Descartes takes reasonable precaution in the *Discourse on Method* (1637) to express understanding for matters of theology. He is "politically correct," as we have seen. Furthermore, Rule Twelve of his *Rules for the Direction of the Mind* (1701) distinguishes between the study of corporeal substances and the investigation of incorporeal substances. We need to insure, he says, that the understanding is divested of all references to the corporeal in order to accord the incorporeal world the serious consideration it merits. The study of his personal life also leaves no doubt that the existence of God, the soul and immortality play a major role in his belief system. Perhaps this spills over into the *cogito* since it is animated by a profound God consciousness.

However, Descartes's God consciousness is mistakenly put to work at the service of analytical geometry and physics. Ethics continues to suffer from this functional displacement since an important aspect of human relationships cannot be expressed mathematically. God is used as the solution to problems. For instance, God guarantees the permanence of matter when the *cogito* is busy elsewhere. The functional character of God extends to science. God not only conserves personal relationships, but also mass, energy, and inertia. It is argued by the survivalists Paul and Linda Badham (1982) that God will wish to preserve the relationships begun in this life into the afterlife (p. 122).

The connection between being spiritual and being religious suggests we can be spiritual without being religious. But religion as process of reconnecting is necessarily spiritual if it is authentic. Religion contains the invitation to enter into relationship with the sacred. Spirituality is a positive response to that invitation. Thus, Descartes's *Meditations* is spiritual, but not religious. It is spiritual as metaphysics, or in the attempt to provide an existential grounding for the physics. Our being toward good is a spiritual tendency of psyche. Derek Parfit's work does not appear to be authentically religious, although the preoccupation with ethics belies a similar spiritual foundation.

The teachings of Jesus as of all great thinkers are primarily spiritual. He does not come to introduce religion, but to announce the existence of God within the human heart, first declared by Isaiah in Hebrew Scripture. However, his teachings promote the religious view, since they bridge the gap between the conscious and the unconscious. It seems possible to recognize that a religious experience can also arise in the person's encounter with art, music, poetry, dance, a child's laughter, or even a tree when the experience connects with the heart. The work of Descartes, and of Parfit, is an effort of the heart seeking to do good. It awakens the restorative, creative energies of the unconscious. Reconnecting allows us to discover the presence of the eternal in the temporal, the sacred in the secular. For instance, the teachings of great spiritual leaders can move us to conversion and social action. The experience is transformative, often creating the need to develop a fresh language to express the newly discovered realities within psyche. Religion is vital to the spiritual life since it feeds and sustains us on our temporal journey, although it is not always authentic. Most persons do not have major spiritual experiences or conversions like St. Paul.

Still, the religious experience can contribute sufficient spiritual awakening to move us beyond the pleasure principle. People like Gandhi, Mother Teresa, and Martin Luther King, Jr., give evidence of a broad spiritual vision. Liberation Theology, for instance, is a grass roots movement where church is seen to reinvent church. It generates a spiritual movement that connects with the experiences of the poor, the alienated, and the oppressed. The Scriptures announce the presence of the sacred, or God, in the heart of all persons. This objective presence is articulated differently in diverse global cultures. Cultural diversity is to be celebrated since it adds to the varieties of interpretation of the sacred way. We share a common ancestry, although our values, attitudes, and beliefs differ. The purpose of prayer, meditation and contemplation is not only to enhance the awareness of our own divinity, but also to celebrate the diversity that exists among us. The existence of major religions is a manifestation of our rich diversity. Aquinas in Book 3, chapter 53 of the *Summa Contra Gentiles* describes knowing God as a process of knowing ourselves, as a subject within us. We use that insight as the gateway to knowledge of others, and of the environment.

Our fundamental existential restlessness introduces more evidence that God is present in the human heart. We are in constant movement toward the ultimate good promised within. We are simultaneously drawn toward things of the earth while needing to move on. Why is that? Although my explanation of events is speculative, it seems a plausible, reasonable belief to suggest that the fleeting nature of earthly goods frustrates us. We need to reconnect with an absolute source of values. Thus, we exist in a perpetual state of privation and yearning, as though in a state of psychic grief. We experience a psychological craving to be whole, an addiction that consumes us with a desire to be one with God. It seems possible to term this experience a "spiritual or generic grief" since it exists at the deepest levels of the psyche. The God experience is not known in itself, but only through its effects on the psyche. It manifests itself in our restlessness toward conversion. Although we do not know the ultimate good or God directly, we seem to remember our roots in God. We are called into transcendence. The memory of our divinity creates a longing, an unconscious yearning for reconnecting with God as the source of ultimate good. We miss the fullness of God as we might miss a loved one. We yearn to consummate the relationship with the God within us. Thus, each act of the person is simultaneously a source of joy and a source of disappointment. We exhibit a fundamental recognition of God within us, and an existential impatience with the life of sense. We continue to experience a psychological craving for transcendence. Our addiction to the greater good is executed as promised in the psyche. To grow in wisdom is to become increasingly aware of the gaps in our lives that separate us from God. The "God craving" seems to be what animates Descartes's mathematical ambition to reduce the whole of reality to clear and distinct truths. I believe that it also underwrites Parfit's desire to pursue ethics.

The existence of the divinity in psyche manifests itself in our relationships. They arise spontaneously, providing the spiritual foundation of metaphysics while animating epistemology. The existence of the divinity in psyche secures the ethical character of the person as a being in relationships with others and the environment. Although the development of epistemology is beyond the scope of the present inquiry, we can suggest that the spiritual light of psyche illuminates the contents of the brain, or raises beliefs into the realm of knowledge. The epistemic process is termed mind in the order of being and brain in the order of specification. The expressions of knowledge are irreducible to the data contained in the brain, but cannot arise in their absence. The intuited light of psyche also allows us to empower the other in human relationships by meeting them in their own divinity. The propositions of ethics are the result of that encounter. The presence of the divinity within also animates a technology that respects the being of things, or views things from a sacred perspective. The person's psychic desire to do good and avoid evil in human relationships is driven by reason or logic and subjective truth.

The life and thought of Kierkegaard provides a shining example of subjective reality, or the individual's psychic addiction to God. He needs to find an authentic, spiritual response to the presence of the divinity in psyche. It is authentic because it consumes him; he is willing to live or die by it. Being spiritual is no easy matter since it exacts a commitment from the individual to rise above the security of reason and logic. The path is through subjective reality, or truth.

Kierkegaard is struggling to express subjectivity in action in a world characterized by the excesses of reason and logic. His polemic contains a quality of spiritual impatience seldom encountered in the annals of philosophy. But his search is temporarily blinded by the fact that the God commitment exists beyond reason. He strives to make sense of traditional ethics, but fails to do so. It lacks the authentic commitment that is required of spirituality, the willingness to risk everything for love of God. The sterile reasoning of traditional ethics does not force the existential commitment prescribed by the psyche's encounter with God. But he finds evidence of an authentic spirituality, purity of heart, or *"den enkelte"* commitment in Abraham's willingness to sacrifice his only son Isaac for love of God. To an outsider, Abraham appears to be breaking the ethical law which commands us not to kill a human being. How to imagine being religious without also being ethical? Abraham's action, although not irrational, responds to a command that exists beyond the law. He experiences trust, a truth of the heart. The full measure of Kierkegaard's spirituality is unpacked in his second last work, *Concluding Unscientific Postscript*. Subjective reality is the spiritual foundation of the religious commitment. His earlier work *The Concept of Dread* details the preparatory anxiety of such a commitment. The religious response is made in fear and trepidation since it is not based on reason. The individual becomes willing to risk everything in answer to God's calling. Such is the courage of Abraham, the "shining hero of faith."

Subjective reality, unlike objective truth, doubles back on itself, moving dialectically on the arms of reason and faith toward God. The religious lesson Kierkegaard teaches us is that we do not enter into a relationship with the God within because we understand that it is beneficial to do so. We are driven to do so out of generic grief over our loss of God. We do not know that God fills us once the leap is taken. We fear letting go of reason. But like the trusting child leaping into the arms of the parent, God is there for us. In the leap we risk everything: But in that same act we also gain everything, eternal life. The religious leap, when authentic, is a self-sacrificial response to the presence of spirituality (and mystery) in the human heart.

The teachings of the major world religions are based on the subjective reality of the human heart, although the pluraculture has many different voices. Like Abraham, spiritual prophets are prepared to die for authentic truth. For instance, when Moses, Jesus, Gandhi, or Mohammed (570-632) denounce oppression, they risk everything. They appeal to the spirituality of the heart. The message "that the cripple might walk" is an invitation to the cripple that exists in every heart to denounce injustice. We are "crippled" because we fail to see beyond the world of sense. The insight of prophets is liberating since it frees us to pursue the higher good promised within. In our day, authentic science and religion are nourished by the same spiritual base.

Since the spiritual experience of death and resurrection in our lives exists at the meta-rational level of insight, it is best told in narrative form. Telling stories about our own conversions or enlightenment allows us to include a wealth of detail that cannot be expressed in analytical form. We tell relationship stories about ourselves. The experience of the heart is the narrative of the lived life, not as contemplative or discursive, but as existential encounter with the saving truth within psyche. It allows us to resonate and identify with the spiritual experiences of people who are different from ourselves. Telling stories enables us to set aside individuating differences and join as a people united in a common search for the ultimate good of persons. The narrative is told in a human language that we all understand, usually a story of suffering, social injustice, oppression, cruelty, unemployment, and hunger. But we also share stories of triumph, love, charity, risk-taking for others. The highest expressions of human triumph, or failure, meet in the transcultural, worldwide expressions of art, music, and poetry.

The work of Christ, as well as the work of the Buddha or Gandhi, is directed toward liberating people by awakening them to the power that exists within the human heart. This voice is the power of God within us. For instance, the Jesus story illustrates the model: Jesus does not tell people what to do. He speaks in parables. His first line is: Who does not know that? The hearers reply; yes, we all know that, it is common sense. But then Jesus says if we all know this how come we do not act accordingly? We all know the truth since it is inscribed in our hearts. He is extending an invitation to follow the ways of the heart. Jesus was punished for being subversive. The laws of the heart can conflict with the laws of the land. But that can only happen when the law of the land is not compatible with the ethical law within psyche. The Buddha and Christ both make it clear that the person is a being toward the God that exists within each of us. The desire to develop non-religious ethics is animated by the same spiritual need to overcome the artificial distance that prevents us from acting toward our common truth of psyche. The work of Parfit, and Hume before him, offers evidence, not of the denial of God, but of our deep-seated need to become God-like. It issues an invitation to the doubter in each of us to look beyond secularism by becoming aware of a deeper need to seek the ultimate good that is promised within.

2. Persons as Correlates of Evil

Equal evidence attests that we are beings toward evil. At first blush, the existence of evil in the human heart seems to disprove the existence of God. As John Hick (1977) says, the issue is posed as the fundamental dilemma of theodicy: "If God is perfectly good, He must want to abolish all evil; if He is unlimitedly powerful, He must be able to abolish all evil: but evil exists; therefore either God is not perfectly good or He is not unlimitedly powerful" (p. 5).

The dilemma was first formulated by Epicurus (341-270 B.C.E.). The tradition following Saint Augustine to Thomas Aquinas views creation as a good, and evil as the absence of good. The existence of evil is a serious problem in theodicy. Augustine appears to have been greatly preoccupied by the problem throughout his life. He distinguishes between two perspectives on evil; philosophical and theological nature. Theologically, God cannot be responsible for moral evil, although God as creator seems to be implicated in it from the metaphysical point of view.

Thomistic metaphysics views reality as being good, of which evil is a privation. Evil is an absence of being or a non-being; it is more like a malfunction of something that is good in itself. While Aquinas echoes Augustine's teachings on evil, he adds the specification that evil is an absence of good that is normally due to a subject. We are generally not accountable for physical evil. For instance, I am not morally responsible for the fact that my eyes have grown weaker with advancing age, although my vision is no doubt deprived of a perfection that is usually given to a well functioning eye. However, I might be said to be morally responsible for that state if the defect is the result of deliberately pouring acid into my eyes. At the same time, a normal person would not normally choose to do such a thing. Culpability is decreased by lack of insight. Why does evil exist? Aquinas says (*Summa Theologica*, 1. Q. 25 a 6) that God could not have created the universe better than He did. But how is a world without evil not a better place? God must have wanted evil. We are back to the original dilemma: How can we understand a perfectly good God as responsible for evil? Perhaps the existence of evil arises as the result of the Fall? The Augustinian tradition holds that the human species is created finitely perfect, but given a free-will. Human evil and suffering are rooted in the misuse of that freedom. We are deliberately cruel toward others. The decision to pursue our own self-interest by using others as *means* toward the attainment of selfish ends, conflicts with the good of others. Pursuits of self-interest naturally do not conflict with others' well being. We expect self-interest so as not to create dependencies which do conflict with others' well being. In that event, we treat others as ends in themselves. The human decision to pursue evil results in the alienation of other human beings. In that theodicy, a dichotomy results between heaven and hell. God calls us toward the ultimate good promised in heaven. Evil, suffering and death arise as the consequence of our decision to frustrate the end God intends for us. Persons are fallen beings. We have existed ever since under the righteous condemnation of God. God's grace is all that saves us from extinction. But the Augustinian tradition falls short of affixing responsibility for moral evil on the creative action of God.

Yet, it seems that God is indirectly responsible for the existence of evil since the possibility of committing evil must exist in the person. That is, the person must be inherently capable of evil. There must have been a predisposition in the person toward evil before the Fall, otherwise there would not have been a Fall. Following this line of thought, Irenaeus (130-202) suggests that evil is not merely the absence of good, but a reality in its own right. This view casts the Fall in different light. Technically we do not fall from grace since we do not come into existence as wholly good. We come into existence as a mix of good and evil. John Hick (1977) follows the Irenaean path to develop an eschatology of the person as soul-making process: "Man exists at a distance from God's goal for him, however. Not because he has fallen from that goal but because he has yet to arrive at it" (p. 283). A few pages later he adds that the person "did not fall into this from a prior state of holiness but was brought into being in this way as a creature capable of eventually attaining holiness" (p. 287).

This is a significant departure from the view of evil as privation of good. We exist as imperfect, immature creatures that undergo moral development to reach the perfection God intended for us. God said, "Let us make man in our own image, in the likeness of ourselves" (*Genesis,* 1:26). The two words "image" and "likeness" are not synonyms. Image suggests an exact reproduction, whereas likeness denotes a resemblance. So, we are a copy of God, but not an exact reproduction. We are finite, since we depend on a creator to exist. What does it mean to be made in God's likeness, if not as a being in relationships? Perhaps God and the creator are also in relationship? In that event, our likeness to God is best expressed as a likeness to the creator. This view fixes our soul-making processes in a finite world where good and evil choices are possible. It also implicates the creator in the existence of physical evil. To insist that we are made in the image of God ultimately leads to the unexplained presence of evil, or the denial of God, as Feuerbach already knows. However, the existence of evil in us is consonant with being made in the likeness of God. To be made in God's likeness, then, does not mean that we are infinite like God, or that God is finite like us. We cannot be infinite like God since we come into being and pass out of being. God is not finite like us since God exists outside the natural order. It is contradictory to assert that God is contingent. But God as creator exists in the natural order. To exist in the likeness of God, however, suggests that although we are part of the natural order, we attain some measure of perfection by following the divine plan within psyche, or God beyond creator.

Hick's soul-making point is well taken, although I prefer the term "person-making" to designate the process of moving toward the divine telos since it does not carry the dualistic connotation of "soul-making." Thus, evil exists as an independent entity. The moral life arises out of our free choices between good and evil, as they exist in psyche. That view accords with our temporality, since metaphysically, creation is finite. To be finite is to be limited, or not perfect. We are not in privation of perfection, although we are other than perfect as beings toward good and evil.

Our metaphysical dependence on the creator lays the foundation for the possibility of moral choices as we struggle toward the good in the face of evil. We could not engage the person-making process without the possibility of freely making choices between those opposites. Although God as Absolute Good is necessarily beyond finitude, the creator's causal activity places humans in the realm of finite or limited beings. In the Christian tradition, the clue to our evil lies in the text of *Genesis* and the serpent's words, "your eyes will be opened and you will be like gods, knowing good and evil" (3:5), and in God's words, "See, the man has become like one of us, with his knowledge of good and evil" (3:22). We draw two main conclusions from this: The first is that the gods are implicated in the existence of good and evil. The second is that standing in the presence of good and evil generates the possibility of ethics and morality, or the objective and the relative. In our day, the lack of a global ethics reflects our own will to control morality as an expression of cultural relativism.

But can we progress without good and evil? For instance, one of the cautions ethicists raise about the genome project is that the elimination of 3,000 genetic diseases can narrow the range of human relationships. Suffering is necessary for person-making. What about the second-order consequences of the genome? When we celebrated splitting the atom, for instance, we did not anticipate Hiroshima and Nagasaki.

Carl G. Jung's (1992) *Answer to Job* contains an interesting psychological study of evil. He sets the existence of evil within the human psyche as a parallel to the good and evil within God. The attitude we take toward others is a projection of our own psychic reality. It readily explains how we come to empower or dis-empower the other as a response to the good and evil that exist within our own heart. The relational character of good and evil is not as evident in the Thomistic perspective of the human as eternal essence. The view that we are created wholly good before the Fall does not explain how we come to choose evil. But the vision of psyche as being originally good and evil readily explains the free decision to follow (or refuse) the divine telos.

How do we explain the Fall, and the person-making process, if not through a vision of the person as a being toward both good and evil? A wholly good person would not fall. A created entity cannot be wholly good since it lacks the perfection of being self-caused. A metaphysical difference or distance from God arises in us from being finite. We emerge out of the God relation as contingent entities. The gap prepares the way for the possibility of morality. The conception of evil as privation does not afford that flexibility. The term privation only makes sense as the absence of what must have been an anterior presence. Thus it makes no sense to say that a container is empty unless I understand beforehand that containers are meant to contain. In Thomistic ethics, evil as privation always stands in some measure of good. It is ultimately reducible to the good. John Hick (1977) says it does not stand up to scrutiny. "To describe, for example, the dynamic malevolence behind the Nazi attempt to exterminate the European Jews as merely the absence of some good, is utterly insufficient" (p. 56). It suggests that Satan is not a totally evil entity, but is a good in lesser degree than most. It also suggests that some things are more evil than others simply for possessing less perfection. Is a bat more evil than a person because it possesses less perfection than we do? Evil must be other than mere deficiency. It must exist as a real force. Evil is to morality as the concept is to (Thomistic) epistemology. But does evil come from God? This is a baffling problem. If God is infinitely good, no room exists for evil. But evil exists. One of the most perplexing encounters with evil takes place in the Biblical *Book of Job*.

3. The Biblical Book of Job

The Biblical story of Job is one of the most intriguing books of the Hebrew Bible. Job is seen to be "the good man," as goodness was understood in times when the Hebrew Testament was composed. He is just in his dealings, pious toward God. He is kind to his children, just to his servants. In those days, it was thought that God rewarded the "good" by blessing them with wealth and power. The sacred drama unfolds as God accepts Satan's wager that Job will abandon and curse Him once He removes His blessing. Satan is seen to be a member in good standing in God's household. Having struck the wager, Satan departs to torment Job who becomes the victim of a chain of misfortunes as his wealth, power and family are taken from him. But he refuses to curse God. He falls to his knees in prayer. "Naked I came from my mother's womb, naked I shall return. Yahweh gave, Yahweh has taken back. Blessed be the name of Yahweh!" (*Job*, 1). One might expect this to be the end of the story, but it has only begun.

Once again God behaves in unusual fashion since He grants Satan a second opportunity to test Job. The controversial wager has sparked much debate among Biblical scholars, for how can a loving God let Satan torment an innocent human being? Job, poor worm that he is, living in a land where he was once sovereign, is now inflicted with boils all over his body and is forced to seek refuge in a "dungheap." He is in excruciating pain. His wife petitions him to curse God. She knows that Job will be cast into the shadows of inexistence for doing so, but still thinks that this course of action is in his best interest. Job is suffering beyond the level of human endurance. Again he refuses to curse God.

Job is visited by three of his friends, Eliphaz, Bildad, and Zophar. They sit and mourn with him for seven days, crying but not saying anything. The dialogue finally opens in three series of speeches (*Job*, 3-14, 15-21, 22-27), where Job and his friends oppose their different conceptions of divine justice. His friends defend the doctrine of divine retribution. They are anxious to establish their faith in divine justice, but they are perplexed. They never actually tell Job that he must have sinned to deserve such suffering, but they think as much. They hold the simplistic view that the good are necessarily happy or rewarded (a view which is false and unbiblical). Job protests his innocence but his friends grow more obstinate. Job encounters the universal problem of injustice. He protests his innocence but is repeatedly brought up against God's injustice. How can this be? He sobs, God must have made a mistake. He laments his fate; why was I born, does the universe make sense? It is the familiar story of how a just God can punish the innocent. It raises the profound question of whether we should behave ethically out of devotion to God or because we are ethical beings. In Plato's *Euthyphro,* Socrates poses the dilemma in the following way: "Is the holy loved by the gods because it is holy, or is it holy because it is loved by the gods?" Does some criterion of goodness stand independently of the gods, or do the gods decide what is good and what is evil? Job's plight suggests that he is at the mercy of a fickle God. He is a good man who is being punished because of God's changing whim rather than for anything he did.

A new character, Elihu, now appears and attempts to vindicate God's ways. Job finally decides he has suffered enough and calls upon God to give an account of his action. He boldly asks for proof that he has committed wrong and demands an apology. In Biblical times, this is an unthinkable act of defiance: no human can put in the dock a God whose wisdom and power are infinite. The *Book of Job* marks the first word spoken between God and "Man" in the Hebrew Bible. Satan plays a key role. He is seen to be a trusted member of God's inner court, enjoying free access to it. Satan appears to travel the earth and report to God on the attitude and behavior of humans. Satan knows that Job is innocent but he appears to be intent on proving his guilt. Satan is evil. The fact that God agrees to Satan's wager makes Him evil by complicity. Jung remarks in his *Answer to Job*, "Did God forget to check his Omniscience."

But God remains in charge: God's voice thunders forth from the whirlwinds; He is about to deliver Job's final crushing blow by showing him the vastness of creation. Where were you, says God, when I laid the foundations of the earth? Declare it if you have any understanding! The passage that follows is one of the richest, most eloquent texts of the Bible. It was written by an unknown author, a "Biblical Shakespeare" of sorts. God does not answer Job's question but humbles him even further: Where is the dwelling place of light ... and where is the place of darkness. Do you remember when you were born. Do you know if you will live many days ...? Job is awestruck by the presence of the Almighty (38:1–42:6). He has been privileged to see a side of God that no human being can fathom. Job experiences a profound spiritual awakening and cannot speak "I knew you then only by report, but now I see you with my own eyes" (41:1–6). He keeps silent and repents in dust and ashes. Surprisingly, God offers to punish his friends for their lack of trust. But Job chooses to forgive them.

Satan lost the wager. In a sense, Job's wife also loses her plea since she sought to separate Job from God by inviting him to curse God. Had he done so, he would have been banished from the sight of God. The Bible has nothing more to say about Satan. In a seeming anticlimax Job is then rewarded with more wealth and power than he ever had. He lives another 140 years and dies old and content. The story comes to a happy ending.

But how can a story which raises such profound concern end so simply? It does not tell us why Satan is evil or why suffering exists in the world, although God seems to be responsible. If that is the case, is God evil? The "evil act" is repeated countless times throughout history: Can a loving God allow the martyrdom of millions during the Inquisition, the suffering of millions of innocent victims at Auschwitz, the atomic bomb, the countless millions that die from hunger and disease in our own day? The injustice of the world is one of the reasons why so many individuals question the existence of a loving God.

The authenticity of certain passages of the *Book of Job* has been questioned. It is not known, for instance, who the writer of God's speech is. Authorship is attributed to "the Shakespeare of the Bible," but that tells us nothing. Further, the ending and Job's reward do not appear to fit the text. The authenticity of Elihu's speech is also questioned. Also no hard evidence suggests that Job actually lived. Yet, the facts appear to be historically correct. For instance, Job's wealth is measured in the number of slaves and cattle he owned, as is typical of Genesis stories. It was written about the fifth or fourth century B.C.E. and might have been composed by several authors. Setting these concerns aside, the story raises the important question of evil and suffering in the world.

Throughout history every major religion has wrestled with the problem of the suffering of innocent people. Why does God allow this? The answers vary. Christians focus on the salvific nature of suffering, uniting our suffering to the suffering of Christ. Buddhism views it as an illusion that is caused by seeking to "cling to things." We overcome suffering by following Buddha's path, or way of letting go of things. God does not create a world free from suffering. In Islamic religion, suffering is seen as a divine test to measure the worthiness of humans. In Hebrew religion, the Book's message is that faith must remain, even when the understanding fails. In Confucianism, the existence of suffering leads to an inner quest for harmony.

4. Carl G. Jung's Answer to Job

John Hick's soul-making theory falls short of assigning culpability for evil to God. But who, then, is responsible for evil? Carl G. Jung struggled with the problem of evil for most of his life. He suggests that the human psyche gives evidence of an intimate interplay between good and evil as manifestations of God's two Sons, Christ and Satan. His *Answer to Job* details how this comes to be. His psychological evidence implicates God in the existence of evil. The work continues a psychological inquiry begun earlier in *Aion* (1959). The numerous questions raised by his patients about God's role in the existence of evil lead him beyond that work. He bravely stakes the claim that God is responsible for evil. This marks a significant departure from the Augustinian belief that nothing evil can come from God. How can evil come from a loving God? The role of the divinity is explained in dialectical fashion as encompassing the antagonism of a Christ-Antichrist relationship.

Jung seems to be right about God existing in relationships. He further claims that Job's experience is an important chapter in the evolution of God. It enables God to become aware of Himself, or the "dark" side of God. The fact that God casually accepts Satan's wager suggests that God must have been unaware of evil, until Job made it clear. However, Job (humankind) now stands in judgment of the divinity, possessing insight that God did not have of Himself. The experience leads God to a fuller awareness of the challenges facing humans, as they too struggle against the dark side of psyche. God sends His Son Jesus to atone for divine guilt.

We also stand in guilt before God as authors of our own evil choices. However, once we become aware of the evil that lurks within the human psyche, we too can begin to take charge of events. While evil is not completely erased from the human scene, it loosens the control it has over us, as we become aware of its existence. Yet, God is ultimately responsible for placing us in this environment.

Jung views the good and evil within the human psyche as a reflection of the good and bad Son in God. Christ and Satan are brothers since they were begotten in the same way from God. Good and bad are somewhat like the right and left hand of psyche. Jung views psychic realities in terms of syzygies, or pairs of opposites. God can be notoriously unjust, but He also shows love for His people. Good and evil provide evidence of a yin-yang relationship in God and humans. Thus, everyone, including the deity, is in recovery.

In the beginning, God was misled by His shadow, Satan. However, once God becomes aware of His dark side through Job's suffering, Satan is cast out of God's inner court. But we are not completely rid of Satan. He reigns as the prince of darkness–the dark side of finitude–or evil.

Jung's *Answer to Job* presents a solution to the existence of evil as separate entity. The good Son corresponds to the psyche's movements toward ultimate good. The bad Son is our being toward evil. But can God be evil? Jung's analysis of evil provides an interesting challenge to Christian theodicy since Satan is assigned divinity. If God is evil, then, the Redemption might enlist God's redemption against Himself. In that event, Christ died to save God as well as humans. Jung cites a tradition in which God prays to Himself: "May it be my will that my mercy may suppress my anger, and that my compassion may prevail over my other attributes" (p. 60).

What do we make of this? Perhaps we can distinguish between God and our representation of God as creator. The God that "prays to Himself" is the creator. The creative act adds a specification to God, limiting pure act to the natural order. Thus, a creator generates finitude, or contingency. Although creation is good, it is not unreservedly good. It is metaphysically finite giving way to a forum where evil, suffering, death, and injustice arise as possibilities. The process of person-making takes place in that environment. Does Job awaken this reality in God's psyche? Jung's *Answer to Job* suggests this is the case. But perhaps the line suggests more than this as the awareness of finitude enlists us as co-creators of cosmos. Job becomes divine through the experience of suffering. Job is prepared to forgive his friends, but God seems unsure. God becomes aware of the creator in God after the fact of creation, as we become aware of the good and evil in us after the fact of our own person-making experience. The reality that lies beyond the creator is not responsible for evil, although God as creator introduces a condition wherein both God and persons become aware of finitude. We choose evil whenever we frustrate the divine telos, or act as other than divine. Thus, humans are responsible for moral evil, although the creator sets the stage. Satan rules over the existence of evil.

Job's victory over Satan suggests that humans are not helpless in confronting the power of evil. The Christian redemption rids God of creator to relegate Satan to the realm of darkness. Although no longer welcome in God's inner court, Satan exerts a real influence on God's telos, striving to frustrate it. However, humans remain indelibly stamped with Satan's presence within psyche. We are beings toward evil as well as beings toward good. In Christianity, the redemption opens the possibility of not being controlled by evil, as God overcomes the creator's metaphysical dark side. In the person-making process we become God-like or Satan-like. In Jungian psychology, we become less evil by being aware of its existence within psyche.

The struggle between good and evil promises more spiritual power for the human psyche. The existence of evil is turned to advantage in spiritual growth. Job saw this possibility as he glanced into the divine future. "I know that my Redeemer liveth" (ch. 19: 25). Job was overwhelmed by the knowledge of God's plan and fell to his knees. Job is fully aware of being a worm (finite or from the nothing), but he also knows himself to be a special worm.

5. Good and Evil as Ways of Framing Reality

It is unwise to underestimate the power of evil. Satan was once in God's inner court and displayed sufficient power to dupe the creator. The ensuing struggle in the divine court is reflected in our being toward good and evil.

Jung's account of the origin of evil stands in sharp contrast to the Augustinian version of the Fall. Did we fall from grace or do we enter the world as good and evil? The fact of our metaphysical dependency on creator (and possibly on the Reality beyond creator) suggests that we are thrown into a relationship of good and evil from the moment of birth. Persons are not consulted about being part of the process, as they find themselves in it. Once in existence, we echo the story of the Heavenly struggle. Our freedom operates within the parameters of the divine specification, or design. We, then, freely pursue good or evil in psyche. However, the responsibility for moral evil lies with us (and Satan) as we decide to follow or frustrate the divine telos.

While the world and all things contained in it are created finite, the limitation of existence by potentiality means that things are not perfectly good. The limitation of potentiality, however, is not the absence of the good. Our experience of finitude suggests that to limit is to stand as an opposite. The electron does not limit a proton by being less of a proton, but by standing in opposition to it. The unity of opposites, or syzygies, characterizes our experience of the natural order. Good and evil exist in a dialectical synthesis of opposites or struggle toward the realization of the divine telos. The process of person-making unfolds in that finite realm. We pursue good and evil on the installment plan and become good or evil in the measure of our choices. To choose good is to move toward God. To choose evil is to be attracted by the surface appearance of the created world. Satan, however, was cast out of God's inner chamber. We too can refuse the divine telos. We are predisposed to act toward good and evil from the first moment of our existence. Each act of the person is a payment of rent toward our final condition of moral perfection. The final state is attained in the afterlife, a place where the human heart hardens.

The propositions of morality arise out of a dialogical process between the good and evil tendencies of the psyche and the concrete practices of a locale. Thus, morality is the expression of a dynamic person-making process in which our condition of being good and evil, as fine tuned by past decisions, meets the particulars of each new day. While the tendency to behave morally is objective, being the expression of the divine light in us, our moral decisions are subjective since they arise out of the particulars of experience. Further, moral judgments are mediated through a finite human brain, susceptible to the ravages of injury, false education (ignorance), and mindlessness. We stand as often in evil as in good. Materialism claims that the whole of our religious experiences are reducible to brain states. In this view, statements of morality are relative to the neural activities of a person's brain. The criminal act, for instance, is explained chemically. But this is only one of the threads in our moral story. What about the criminal's ignorance? Are we not charged with the responsibility for making informed choices, even in the face of materialism? The criminal choice deliberately overrides the psyche's tendency toward the good and the consequences of harming self, the other, and the environment. And chemistry does not excuse the criminal's irreason, or mindlessness. If it does, morality reduces to relativism or luck.

The subjective character of moral decisions is born out of our moral choices. Subjectivity arises because of the tolerance or freedom of the ethical life. While a physiological condition, for instance, can decrease moral culpability, it cannot explain the original characteristic of good and evil in psyche. For as long as the individual is rational and free, the possibility of accepting or rejecting the divine telos exists. The evil act arises out of a deliberate refusal of the divine telos. Thus, although concrete moral choices are relative to culture, the ethical foundation of morality is objective. Our spiritual experiences intersect the string of psychological associations where matter meets mind. They arise because the ethical tendency generates the possibility of behaving morally. The strong appeal of materialism in society suggests we are easily misled by the surface appearance of things.

Heidegger provides evidence of moving beyond the surface appearance of reality. His way of framing *Dasein*'s psyche (being-there-in-the-world) reveals a tendency of psyche to empower (or dis-empower) events of life. For instance, Heidegger's view of death in *Being and Time* (pp. 279-304) empowers us toward death. He sees death as a possibility rather than an impossibility. We suspect he wants to raise the issue to the religious level, although he does not do so. He begins with the view of death as process, although his vision remains rooted in finitude. The fact that he transforms the negativity of death into something positive, however, suggests he sees more in psyche than he is willing to admit.

What does he see? According to Heidegger, death is not the end of *Dasein*'s existence, but an opportunity to transform finitude into something positive: An opportunity to make the best of the (brief) time allotted us. Death ranks highly in the scale of person-making processes. It is "the *utmost* possibility of impossibility," not to be outstripped by any other possibility. Heidegger, not unlike Leo Tolstoy's (1828-1910) *The Death of Ivan Ilyich,* motivates us to move beyond the view of death as event, or the simple end of life. Although Heidegger's work deals with the secular, it contains an invitation to move beyond secularism. If an event like death can be transformed into a person-making process, perhaps there is more. Is Heidegger more religious than he claims to be?

The interpretation Jung gives to Job's suffering is rooted in a similar awareness of finitude as source of inspiration. Being finite is inconsistent with being God, although it is not inconsistent with being creator. The existence of God does not suggest the existence of creator, although the awareness of creator suggests the possibility of God. Job's awareness of his own finitude sends him to his knees, as God too struggles with the dark side of God the creator. But seeing a preview of the divine plan (of God beyond creator) transforms Job's suffering into a source of inspiration. He rids himself of the view of God as creator.

A serious difficulty arises with Jung's *Answer to Job,* however. Do we have evidence that the human psyche parallels the divine psyche? The sense of evil as a separate category of existence breaks down, if we are made in the image of God. But it holds fast, if we are made in the likeness of God. We are not replicas of God since we are finite. But we do some of the things God does since the person-making process invites us to co-create the world.

God's unfolding of eternal truths takes place in history. Our process of becoming persons also takes place in history. Thus, we are like God rather than images of God (analogical). We are like God as persons in the making, but unlike God as finite beings. Does this absolve God from responsibility for the existence of suffering? It does not. God's free decision to create rather than not to create gives God a role in the existence of physical evil and suffering. Paul Helm (1988) recognizes this when he says, "God must be responsible for (physical) evil in some sense" (p. 164).

Irenaeus, Augustine, Aquinas, and Hick (1977) trace metaphysical evil to finitude: "Created beings must, in the nature of the case, be less perfect than their Creator; they must, then, in varying degrees be imperfect" (p. 148). Although God brings about the condition of finitude which makes physical evil real, our way of framing reality is a response to the awareness of our finitude. We can empower or dis-empower the finite by choosing to move beyond it, or to remain at the level of surface appearance. The existence of finitude does not make the idea of a loving God implausible. We need to consider why the world is finite and how character building can only arise in such an environment. The world is created for our sake. The divine intelligence must have understood that created beings would carry the imperfection of being created, but how else can we make moral progress?

The imperfections of our world are necessary. The possibility of moral judgments and the development of virtue, rests on freedom and finitude. God intends our use of the imperfect world as a necessary condition of human development. We get to choose between good and evil. The person-making process could not take place in the presence of a perfect world. We are not on earth to maximize our personal pleasures, or to dominate others, but to engage in the arduous person-making process. We limit our own growth whenever we substitute evil for good. We do not know why God chose to create or why God continues to create, but we can be like God in the creation process. Our struggle is expressed in the Biblical statement attributed to God, "I make weal and create woe" (*Isaiah*, 45:7). The reality that is God is beyond the person-making process, but God as creator shares in the struggle to conquer the evil within finitude. This is announced by all the major world religions. Christians such as Augustine, for instance, assign a key role to the redemption from sin, although he also over describes the process of contrition.

The existence of physical evil, earthquakes, floods, hurricanes and such causes pain and suffering. But no person-making progress occurs without struggle. Hick makes the point: The development of human character and virtues cannot take place in the absence of a struggle. How can someone be thought to be heroic, for instance, without a real risk to life? Imagine if bullets bounced off people, or if stolen money was mysteriously replaced by some divine power as soon as it was taken. In a world where there was no suffering, there could be no person-making activity. But why is suffering excessive? David Hume's *Dialogues Concerning Natural Religion* (1779) uses the evidence of suffering to deliver a resounding critique of theism: The first circumstance that introduces the argument is the profound suffering of animals. While Hume recognizes that pleasure and pain incite animals to action, he wonders why the pain of animals is so intense? Could not the creator have achieved the same objective by introducing the animal to a diminution of pleasure rather than severe pain? He goes on to add that the possibility of pain would not in itself amount to anything without a second inconsistency of nature: "might not the Deity exterminate all ill, wherever it were to be found; and produce all good, without any preparation or long progress of cause and effects?" To further the great frugality of nature compounds the problem of pain. Every endowment required to survive is distributed with such frugality, that any diminution of those powers "must entirely destroy the creature." Finally, the fourth circumstance under which pain and suffering arise is poor workmanship in "all the springs and principles of the great machine of nature." For instance, the winds unnecessarily rising to hurricane force, rain and heat are equally permitted to ravage the planet when they are excessive. These four circumstances, then, are reasons why Hume says God does not exist (pp. 254-257).

What are we to make of Hume's critique? His point on the excessive and apparently unnecessary suffering of animals is well taken. Hick (1977) says that the existence of excessive suffering is undeserved because animals are innocent. However, some suffering is necessary. The redemption of Christ, for example, would be pointless in a perfect world. While it is not possible to show that every single instance of suffering serves the divine purpose, Hick says there could be no "soul-making" process in a world that was designed as a permanent paradise. Our world is not created as a place where pleasure can be maximized, but rather as a place in which we can become more God like. In a painless world, we would not have to earn a living by "the sweat of our brow," or by the ingenuity of our brain. In banishing pain, we banish hunger, thirst, the need for heat. Then hunting, farming, and house-building would become unnecessary activities, as would the demand for skill and inventiveness. Without the person-building process there would be no need for exertion or for any kind of activity (pp. 318-336).

Humans are largely responsible for their own psychological suffering. It arises in response to finitude or to the way in which we frame the world. We originate moral evil, excessive cruelty, violence, and inhumanity toward others. The sinner cannot shed guilt upon God because our person-making decisions are free. But this leaves the problem of explaining why animals suffer beyond what is required for their own survival, since their choices cannot be free. Nor is there an answer to the undeserved suffering of people born with crippling disease. Hick (1977) says: "Our 'solution', then, to this baffling problem of excessive and undeserved suffering is a frank appeal to the positive value of mystery" (p. 335). However, the "value of mystery" argument only applies to cases where Hick's "soul-making" process succeeds: "And yet, so far as we can see, the soul-making process does in fact fail in our own world at least as often as it succeeds" (p. 336). His solution to this problem is to suggest that the process of "soul-making" must continue in the afterlife since the divine telos cannot be frustrated by the existence of evil but only by our choice to do evil (*ibid.,* ch. 16).

The existence of good and evil arises as our way of framing being. Our moral choices are guided by the tendency of the psyche. Moral evil arises out of the deliberate attempt to frustrate the divine telos, but we act toward moral good whenever we seek to conform to the ways of the divinity. Moral habits arise out of our sustained choices toward good and evil. The development of virtue (or vice) ceases at death. Does the struggle between good and evil continue in the afterlife? Hick suggests that possibility, since no human can frustrate the divine telos. But his view introduces the problem of personal identity. He seems to think that the divine telos prescribes our becoming absolutely good. Although the realization of the divine telos suggests a final victory of good over evil, we cannot completely overcome evil since it is integral to finitude and our way of framing being. The possibility of choosing between good and evil characterizes us. Once we can no longer choose between them we cease being persons, or finite beings. Thus, while it is not illogical to suppose the culmination of the person-making process, and the annihilation of evil, the victorious do not emerge as themselves and absolutely good. Our decision to choose evil must remain as a characteristic of finitude.

Death, however, is an opportunity for a final decision. A finite entity cannot of itself continue forever. While we can logically believe that God will maintain us in existence beyond death, we cannot rise above finitude without risking personal identity. One of the attractions of reincarnation theory is that enlightenment does not make us infinite. We cannot suppose that a contingent existent attains enlightenment, (if enlightenment is a possibility for humans), as other than a finite being, even if the number of reincarnations is infinite. What, then, is the point of Hick's soul-making process continuing in the afterlife? He does not aim for enlightenment but for a radical change in the nature of persons. Why would God wish to maintain relationships in which we continually strive to become other than ourselves? At some point, we might become fully aware of the evil within us, and not be controlled by it. In that event, we remain ourselves. What becomes of evil? It is annihilated since it irrevocably loses the hold it has on us. Yet, it must also be seen to lurk somewhere in the dark recesses of the void, as the final choice of evil-seekers, however. It might exist in the non-being, as fertilizer for a fresh round of human existence.

Argument for Atheism: The problem of evil

1. God is perfectly good.
2. A perfectly good being should want to destroy all evil.
3. God is all-powerful.
4. An all-powerful being can destroy any evil; therefore.
5. If God exists, there will be no evil; but
6. Evil exists; So.
7. God does not exist.

Human beings have reason and freedom of choice, and when they make choices they create their own lives. To worship is to lose self-respect; to worship is to deny the importance of one's own freedom. To do so is to cease to be human. So human beings should never do it.

1. something is God only if it is worthy of worship.
2. nothing is worthy of worship; So
3. nothing can be God; So
4. God does not exist.

Six

PERSONS AS CORRELATES OF OTHERS

The belief in the existence of a social self views the atomistic existence of the individual as being an abstraction. The problems that arise out of grounding ethical systems in the ego disappear as we shift focus toward the psychological interconnections that exist between human beings. Our first ethical indubitable is not "I think, therefore, I am," but "We exist, therefore, I exist." The evidence to test the legitimacy of this belief is found in several quarters, beginning with the cultural programming of contemporary science. In science, the perception of a connection between wholes and their parts is undergoing radical change, mirroring a similar shift in global politics, moving us toward a unified social teleology.

One of the characteristics of being human is that our psychological tendency toward good and evil moves out to empower or dis-empower other human beings. This view is developed in Gabriel Marcel's philosophy of participation. We only stand as separate entities when the love binding humans fails to prevail. But love, or "mystery," allows us to become one with others, creating a relationship that endures beyond the grave. Marcel moves us out of the realm of the isolated ego as "problem" to a place in the mystery of love where the celebration of life necessarily includes other human beings. His insistence on the "social self" leads him to the discovery of God as personal absolute. We reach God through other human beings. The connection between humans is not deductive, but spontaneous. The attitude we express toward others is spontaneous (metaphysical) since the other is an extension of the self. No self exists without others. But if the social self is given primacy over the isolated self, how do we measure individual worth, or avoid discrimination? The reply is that the individual as social being at large is rational, capable of learning values. In our day, the spirit of social communion and learning is valued in several corners, including an unlikely area such as war. Robert Humphrey's assessment of his wartime experiences leaves no doubt that the spirit of Marcel's philosophy is alive and well. The group dynamics of 12-Step recovery–enjoyed by millions worldwide–provides further evidence to support the success of the social self model:

> Rarely have we seen a person fail who has thoroughly followed our path. Those who do not recover are people who cannot or will not completely give themselves to this simple program, usually men and women who are constitutionally incapable of being honest with themselves. There are such unfortunates. They are not at fault; they seem to have been born that way. They are naturally incapable of grasping and developing a manner of living which demands rigorous honesty. Their chances are less than average. There are those, too, who suffer from grave emotional and mental disorders, but many of them do recover if they have the capacity to be honest. (*Alcoholics Anonymous*, p. 58)

The movement away from the isolated cartesian self toward the social self mirrors developments in contemporary science where the part only acquires meaning in relation to the whole. The classical view of science where the world is composed of independently structured atoms or elementary particles breaks down at the level of the very small. In quantum physics, the characteristics of matter include the environment in which matter is observed. So, the same matter appears as wave or particle depending on that environment. But if the laws of matter no longer hold in sub-atomic physics, the explanation is that the whole individuates the characteristics of the part. The interdependence of matter and observation suggests that matter is a living system, irreducible to the aggregate of point-like characteristics. In analogous fashion, persons are not isolated atoms, but instances of a social phenomenon in which the dynamics of social interactions give reality to the individual. The following will help to clarify this view.

Whereas the drama of the person as a being toward good and evil is born out at the psychological level, our ethical associations with other human beings arise as a projection of the attitude we have toward them. Morality is a statement of cherished values in human relationships. The base of moral judgments is rooted in the presence of God within psyche. This presence provides an objective, absolute grounding for morality. But the base is always expressed in the soils of circumstances. Thus, the ethical base is objective and universal while morality is subjective and relative. The natural law is not expressed in the subject as such since no subject exists outside relationships. The natural law is expressed in human relationships rather than in human nature. We enter into relationships with others from the moment of birth. In the process of becoming persons, the other emerges as an extension of the being toward good and evil that exists within psyche. The existence of physical evil plays an important role in the moral life since our decisions could not be moral without the possibility of choosing evil. My free decision to harm my neighbor, for instance, arises out of the evil that exists within my own psyche. But that decision is tempered by the good within me. No human act is purely good or purely evil since it always arises at the term of a dialectical interplay between good and evil within psyche. The moral life arises out of that person-making process. The decision to empower the other is a reflection of the stage of love I find within, while the decision to dis-empower or harm the other is the result of the stage of evil I find within me.

The process of person-making is one in which we make choices about empowering or dis-empowering other human beings. The love I have for others is purest when it arises as a response to the divinity that exists in the other. Two hearts meet in spiritual resonance and identification to celebrate the love of divine communion with other human beings. At that point, the divinity in the other meets the divinity in self. The "I" and the "thou" act as one in God. That process leads to the discovery of a personal absolute. It empowers individuals to function as a social unit. The failure to see the divine in the other is a consequence of our movement toward evil. The process of person-making allows us to become more God-like. Fritjof Capra (1992) expresses the dynamics of human love in his own work: "We are born as individuals, but our task is to become persons, by deeper and more intricate, more highly developed relationships. There is no limit to becoming more truly personal" (p. 95).

We enter into relationships with others in two fundamental ways: We can treat others either as means or as ends in themselves. In the first case, a tendency to use or exploit the other treats the other as object. Kant's deontological ethics recommends we always treat persons as ends, never as means to further selfish aims. But Kantian ethics promotes individualism. His three postulates of practical reason de-emphasize the role of community in social action. For instance, the relationships the Kantian agent establishes with God transpire at the level of the individual. This is incomplete since I can treat the other as an end, but never see him or her as being an extension of myself. The only requirement for "holiness" in Kantian ethics is that my will conform to a principle of universal legislation as exacted by the categorical imperative. In that view, the only act that has any moral value is not one done out of love of people, but from reverence and respect for the moral law. The categorical imperative invites us to set personal interests aside, though "the heavens should fall in the process." It does not merely recommend, but commands strictly.

In my opinion, Kant's ethics is based on a false sense of what it means to be human. Kant's God does not play a role in being a person, but appears in the afterlife as an "external examiner" to measure the individual's degree of holiness and to dole out happiness as it coincides with an individual's moral goodness.

The French philosopher Gabriel Marcel also treats the other as an end, but seems to possess a genuine concern and love for other human beings. His philosophy contains an unsystematic exposition of persons as beings toward other persons. It is unsystematic because it takes place at the level of mystery rather than problem. It is based on the empowerment of others from the divinity that exists within. The difference between both philosophers is most striking in their view of the divinity. For Kant, the absolute is an impersonal, omniscient administrator, while for Marcel, God is a personal absolute. We meet God in human relationships, not in private. God is involved in the joys and sorrows of other human beings. To fully appreciate the point, we need to remind ourselves that Marcel's philosophy opens as a revolt against certain forms of dualism, including the technocratic mentality, or the practice of treating others as means. In the cartesian machinery, the person is a duality of thinking and extension. Other minds in the system must be like our own mind. This mirrors Newtonian physics and the mechanistic view of the universe as composed of individual atoms. In the social arena, it leads to a philosophy of exploitation, reducing the other to functional roles.

Marcel rejects the identification of being a person with the functional representation. The "problem" mentality is characterized by the impersonalism of mathematical relationships: unavailability, denial, and betrayal. The typical illness in our day is a feeling of not belonging. We lack affect and appear to ourselves as detached, unrelated to others and the world. We become so accustomed to the artificial atomism of the age that we lose sight of our own psychic tendencies. Marcel's solution, however, focuses on the subject's *being* dimension. Human relationships are characterized as taking place in the realm of mystery, or the irreducible divinity within psyche. That presence is love. The process of becoming aware of its existence invites the ascent into the "mystery" of human existence. Mystery is not degradable to the level of problem. It is enacted in Kierkegaard's subjective thinker rather than in Descartes's thinking thing. Mystery and subjectivity intimately involve us. To stand with the other in the presence of mystery is to recognize that together we form a holy subjective alliance. The other is an extension of the self through an intentionality of divinity. No dualism occupies human relationships because the self cannot exist without the other.

Marcel does not affirm I am, but we are. The reality of God is all-inclusive. Further, nothing lies outside us since God is within us. The sentiment of love we express toward others is the consequence of God within psyche. It transforms human relationships from the level of problem to the level of mystery. To stand in the presence of mystery with the other is to look upon the other the way God does, not to judge or condemn but to empower. We never attain perfect communion with the other in this life, although each loving human act is a payment of rent toward that goal. Love bridges the distance between us. It moves the outside to the inside so that what was before me is now part of me. For brevity's sake, Marcel's essential thought can be sketched as follows:

Others as Means	Vs. Others as Ends	Incarnation
Having Dimension	Being Dimension	I am my Body
Primary Reflection	Secondary Reflection	Intersubjectivity
Others as Problem	Others as Mystery	Others as Body-Subjects
Exploiting Others	Available to Others	Personal Absolute
Denial	Fidelity	Hope
Loss of Self	Reclaim Others	Person-Making

Love, then, is what moves us into not merely treating others as means, but of seeing them as an extension of ourselves. The social self is more real than the individual self, although participation begins with my own embodiment or incarnation. To be incarnated is to be invested with flesh. But I am not invested with flesh as a "computer with meat" since I am my body. The human body is not a possession. Embodiment takes place in the realm of mystery. Thus, Marcel strongly objects to the reductivism of empiricism.

The relationship I have with others is analogous to my own mode of being as incarnate mystery. To dwell in the realm of mystery with the other is to affirm the sacredness of the other. It is to empower them, as an extension of my own divinity. Authentic love is divine. This view is in sharp contrast to seeing others as an extension of my own evil. Evil puts an end to loving relationships, reducing them to the level of object. Carl G. Jung, for instance, views projection as a process of inscribing my own fears and insecurities on others. The other becomes what I dislike about myself. However, we are largely unaware of this mechanism, and go to war under the control of evil within psyche. Evil is characterized by denial, unavailability, infidelity, and exploitation of the other. It leads to the death of self. But we thrive on the personal, caring, loving relationships struck with the other. The tendency toward good is characterized by availability, fidelity, and the joy of standing in the presence of a loving absolute. The divinity fills our lives with hope.

Our being in the world through others at the level of mystery anchors the success of the self-help movement worldwide. The other is available, not to judge or use the other, but to admit the other into a source of healing within psyche. Communion with the other takes place at the level of intersubjectivity through the medium of resonance and identification. To resonate with others is to share with them a non-conceptual world of common experiences. It is to draw strength from similar experiences of alienation. The self-help experience is profoundly spiritual. It is rooted in the intuitive vision of the sacred in the suffering of another human being. Loving the other means being available to the other for the sake of the other. The phenomenology of love suggests a ''letting be'' of the other so as not to control, judge, or dominate the other. The experience is termed "intuitive" because it is not mediated through reason. It arises beyond the pale of speculative reason, at a place where two hearts meet to celebrate the divinity within psyche. For instance, the action that moves a parent to love a child is not animated by reason, certainly not by the tendency to dominate and control the infant. Love is meta-rational. The discourse between mother and child is one in which the mother empowers the child by teaching the child to draw on an inner source of divinity within the human heart. The mother is not a teacher as much as she is a liberator, pointing to the law within.

Marcel's philosophy of death can now be stated in its most powerful dimension: the death of a loved one does not bring the relationship to an end. We continue to exist in the other, and the other in us, through God as a common focal point. To be available to the other at the level of mystery is to affirm that death raises the relationship to a higher level. Communication with the dead takes place at the level of mystery, although it ceases at the level of problem. The skeptic denounces the possibility of such communication. But let the skeptic dwell on the nature of the bond that exists between lovers. If it be such that it cannot be reduced to the level of problem, then how can death put our end to it? How can the physical separation of lovers put their love to an end, if the relationship is based on mystery? It cannot. The love becomes more intense, purer.

When a loved one dies, according to Marcel, we do more than reproduce memories of the likeness of the deceased within ourselves, as a skeptic might have it, since we are actually seen to gain fresh insight into the nature of the afterlife. Communication with the dead takes place at the level of love, at a place beyond reason where belief does not have to make logical sense to be true. The spontaneous consonance between the living and the dead is played out at the level of the divinity within psyche. The connection with the dead stretches out beyond the present moment to encompass the dead from time immemorial. The vestiges of love move outwardly to encompass the world. How is that possible? The imagery of communion between the living and the dead tests the limits of the language possibility. The insight is often better expressed in the language of poetry, music, and visual art. The heart has its own logic, a logic which reason does not understand, but that enjoys its own standard. But the insight is not for poets alone since recent developments in quantum mechanics make it clear that standing in the metaphysics of love provides science with similar insights.

David Cockburn (1990) builds his own "social philosophy" on the fundamental principle that our first inclination toward other human beings is expressed in the spontaneous attitude we have toward them. We do not react to people on the basis of knowing who they are or because we possess a metaphysical insight into their being, but we react to them spontaneously: "metaphysics does not ground the attitude but is an expression of it" (p. ii). Fergus Kerr (1989) follows in a similar Wittgensteinian tradition as Cockburn when he says: "We found our mental and spiritual activities on our primitive reactions to one another in our common world" (p. 129).

We do not catch reality "in a net" since it is part of the bustle of everyday life. Language is the expression of that reality. No abstract reality exists beyond language. The dualistic view of the person as substance or subject of experiences reverses this ordering by suggesting we need to know who a person is before we can react to them. But if that were the case we would never interact. It takes a long time to know who we are, and even longer to know others. In fact we do not succeed in knowing ourselves completely. Wittgenstein is right to put an end to the solitary picture of the "I" or subject as disembodied consciousness. He thereby avoids the ambiguities created by unnecessary abstractions. His emphasis is on what we do in our life as the best model of the mind. Contrary to Plato's belief, the human body also tells the story of that life. The attitude we have toward others requires an identification of the person with the extended, tangible human being. No dualism here.

Whether we deduce the metaphysics out of the epistemology, or the epistemology from the metaphysics is a matter of profound significance. Aquinas's conception of natural law deduces the epistemology out of the metaphysics. But this generates an abstraction in which relationships are not spontaneous. I had an opportunity to discuss this point with Cockburn when I was in Wales, and we agree that the traditional understanding of metaphysics as the study of essences or what things are introduces dualism at the level of our attitude toward other human beings. For instance, Cockburn cites recent efforts in the philosophy of mind as being studies of the "mind" rather than persons. But a second sense of metaphysics might avoid this problem. Thomistic metaphysics introduces an important distinction between the concept and the idea, meaning that in meeting others we spontaneously become the other before the awareness of doing so arises. The "concept" is a means to insight, not the term of an insight. It was introduced by Aquinas to avoid the "critical problem" of having to think about what something is before knowing that it exists. Given this more normal use of the term, we can give sense to the idea that ethics is grounded in that brand of metaphysics rather than epistemology. But the situation is problematic if metaphysics is seen to be a search for categories before the epistemology. In that event the ethics will be dualistic. In ordinary language philosophy, Cockburn (1990) says, I discover myself not in some "pre-linguistic inner space of self-presence, but in the network of multifarious social and historical relationships in which I am willy-nilly involved" (p. 69).

What, then, does the spontaneous attitude toward others reveal about persons? Quite simply, it confirms the view that the person's relationships with the other is the result of being a person, not the result of wanting to be a person. Our attitude toward others is spontaneous because it characterizes being human. The relationships of love I have with others empowers them because they arise out of a spontaneous consonance between the divinity that exists within two psyches. Furthermore, given that the reaction to others is spontaneous, personal identity emerges not out of some metaphysical depths of an isolated subject of experiences, but as the reaction of a being in relationships. What we first observe about the other is not a thinking thing, since consciousness is ultimately reducible to personal identity, which in turn arises at the intersection where matter meets mind, but the manifestation of a being in multi-level relationships. The attitude itself does not have a ground because no person exists without relationships. The conception of the person as an abstract category always leads to an epistemological paradox of sorts.

The conception of the person as a being toward others illustrates the nature of natural law philosophy as a species-sustaining value system. In any dynamic system the part always acts primarily for the good of the whole, and only secondarily for itself. Thus, the individual self-perfects through a process in which the good of the group or society is placed above the good of the individual. The belief that action should be directed toward the welfare of the other is based on a belief in a fundamental equality of all human beings. In a recent article (1994) Robert L. Humphrey explains how such action also depends on the promotion of self-development values in the individual. He draws his examples from his considerable overseas army experiences in multiple countries. As a former Director of project Target (*Thai American Relations Guidance Education Training*), he has a rich stock of experiences from which to draw. He opens his lectures with a personal story, taken from his wartime experiences. In one such story he narrates an experience from Iwo Jima:

> I took command of the only six (teenage) American Marines who were still left in the front-line rifle platoon. Four of the six were understandably stressed-out. They were keeping their heads down far too low in their fox-holes at night (not watching for infiltrators). One night, two Japanese soldiers crawled between the fox-holes of two of those boys who were not properly peeking out. The next morning, I warned them that the Japanese would crawl in on them and kill them. It happened again. I raged at them. It still did not work. One of the two remaining, healthy, young fighters (Johnson, an experienced hunter from Texas) told me quietly, You are telling them the wrong thing, Lieutenant. Tell them the Japanese will crawl past them *and kill us others*: That Worked. (P. 8)

This is an amazing story. It confirms the systems approach to human relationships, namely, we act primarily for the good of the other. It goes further by recognizing the need for fundamental principles of action. Some moral principles, such as the protection of life, are worth dying for. Humphrey says: "The best men voluntarily do the dying, if necessary, to save the group whose members are less morally fit" (p. 9). The measurement of compliance with this natural law, he says, is the individual's mental well-being. The higher the development of the spiritual, mental well-being of the individual, the greater the ease with which the individual is willing to sacrifice his or her own life for the welfare of the group: "The men hated, and apologized for, showing fear that endangered others. ... But when others' lives were not in danger, we felt no embarrassment about showing fear" (p. 11).

Humphrey's discovery is rooted in a basic principle that was articulated earlier by Marcel, namely, that the connection between wholes and their parts is spiritual, as a spontaneous union with others through God. He is willing to place spiritual principles ahead of selfish interests, thereby grounding the social self in a community of caring persons. However, the social self evaporates in the absence of values (such as honesty). Values are learned "through emotional impact from either an actual experience or a well-presented account" (p. 13). Humphrey's view articulates an insight shared by individuals in 12-Step recovery programs. In *Alcoholics Anonymous* (1980), for instance, Tradition Twelve says, "Anonymity is the spiritual foundation of all our traditions, ever reminding us to place *principles before personalities*" (emphasis mine). This translates roughly into a belief in the fundamental equality of people. Thus, the individual is invited to move out of an emotivist-egoist self in order to care for others in need of help. The psychological mechanisms of resonance and identification bridge the gap between the social and personal self. Once the good of the social order is seen to prevail over self-interest, God, or a "Higher Power," is invited to do for us what we could not do for ourselves. The *Anonymous* book states the belief as Step Six. "We're entirely ready to have God remove all these defects of character" (p. 59). Given the presence of God in psyche, the individual is empowered to develop moral virtues. A psychological "change of heart" transforms an illness into a small victory for the good. This also seems to be not only Humphrey's view but the main argument in systems theory: Since the reality of the part depends on the primacy of the whole, the movement toward the whole is a stage in the self-development of individual values.

The just and righteous community is based on this foundation. The paradox of moving out of self to regain self suggests that love is presence and absence. My phenomenological description of love (1995) reveals that the loving attitude or letting-be of the other takes place as a process in which I lose myself in the will of the other (pp. 163-172). But love as absence redirects my energies toward the personal "clinging-self," or independent subject of experiences. No human being truly exists in the absence of love. The social self invites us into a loving communion with the other, serving as a powerful reminder of the insufficiencies of the personal self. We stand together in a loving community sharing personal strengths and weaknesses so that together we can step out of the alienating characteristics of being-alone-in-the-world. The stepping out of self enlists a dialectical process of affirmation and negation in which the personal self is simultaneously possibility and impossibility of forming community. Ari Hirvonen (1995) in a commentary on Augustine's view of community suggests that "the possibility of there being a just community implies the self-renunciation of the fixed identity and the transparent presence of community" (p. 268). Hirvonen echoes my own ethical beliefs when he says that justice and righteousness are not determined by immutable norms, "but by a style of action in a relation of fellowship between partners; hence it always comes back to the question of responsibility toward the other ..." (*ibid.*). The letting-be of the other (love) is the foundation of becoming more truly human.

The insufficiency of the personal self is also apparent in regard to our relations with the environment. The proof that we do not stand outside our environment, but find ourselves already inserted in that environment, exists at unexpected places, namely, in the field of chemical dependency. Research in addiction medicine suggests that the sudden loss of tolerance experienced by some heroin addicts is partially conditioned by the environment where the drug is normally administered. One of the risks of heroin addiction is death from an overdose, but the risk of dying is greater when the substance is ingested in an unfamiliar environment. A study by Shepard Siegel of McMaster University and his associates Rily Hinson, Marvin Krank, and Jane McCully (1982) supports this view:

Siegel reasoned that the tolerance to heroin was partly conditioned to the environment where the drug was normally administered. If the drug is consumed in a new setting, much of the conditioned tolerance will disappear, and the addict will be more likely to overdose. (P. 45)

While more study is required to establish the exact neurology of the environmental connection, the fact that such a connection exists is not surprising to philosophy. The next chapter examines that environmental intimacy.

Seven

PERSONS AS CORRELATES OF BEING'S UNCONCEALMENT

1. Overview

Sailors already know the majesty of nature. The wind, the heat or cold, the sun, the moon, the changing color of the sea, each of these holds us captive. Survival depends on the sorts of relationship we develop with the elements. Too much complacency results in the death of the relationship, as does too much timidity. Being is in charge, it beckons forth and invites us to dwell in its truth. The awareness of that primacy feeds poets and scientists alike. Although we are one in existence, being's unconcealment is both master and slave of the relationship, as every sailor knows.

The reducibility of matter to mind, mind to being's unconcealment, being's unconcealment to creator, and creator to God ... is based on the principle that essence is the intrinsic limitation of existence. The ultimate reducibility of the former to the latter suggests that the one arises where the other ends. This view is not only consistent with Thomistic metaphysics (Carlo, 1966), but systemic philosophy avoids dualism by viewing the part from the perspective of the whole. So, the place where God, or the divine activity, ends characterizes creator; where creator ends marks being's unconcealment, and so on. This is to say that our view of the natural order, or the creator's work, is made possible through being's unconcealment. We can go no further with our disclosure of being than creator allows. We can go no further with our disclosure of God than creator allows. We can go no further with our disclosure of matter than mind allows. The underlying assumption that runs through the argument is that dualism being a non-starter, we need to look at the natural order from the perspective of the reducibility of essence to existence (as an instance of act and potency) to safeguard our personal identity in the afterlife. A consistent application of the primacy of *esse* argument demands as much. So, matter (B) must be ultimately reducible to God (G). The investigation into the afterlife can be conducted within the bounds of reason since B implies (is ultimately reducible to) G.

The conception of the person as a being toward God is played out at the level of being's unconcealment. The view is carried in three stages. The first is in the reducibility of matter to mind. The second is in the reducibility of embodied mind to being's unconcealment. The third arises as the reducibility of unconcealment to creator and God. Being's unconcealment provides evidence for the existence of the creator as immanent within the natural order. The root of that possibility is seated in God's transcendence.

2. The Reducibility of Matter to Mind

In 1996, I read a paper on the mind-body problem at a philosophy department seminar, University of Wales, Lampeter, UK, that opened with the tongue-in-cheek reference to the title page "Fragmented Notes on Dualism." What made me think there would be an interest in a paper that promises disunity on the title page? The title was used to make the point that dualism also opens with a fragmented, if not incomplete view of reality. Thus, dualism is unattractive. Yet, we have no shortage of papers on immortality that begin with dualism as premise. But they end in failure since they cannot account for personal identity. Epiphenomenalism as an alternative theory is also inadequate since it involves circular reasoning: while we can point to the causal influence of brain on mind by isolating the corresponding activity of the brain, we cannot argue the causal influence of mind on brain without invoking those same neural patterns. It seems to me that the mind-body problem is expressed in better language when it is approached not in reductivist either-or terms, but from the inclusive both-and perspective. Descartes's attempt to explain the interaction through the pineal gland is indefensible. If it is true that our ability to recognize falsehood is all that is required to spot a fallacy, then the problems dualism raises with respect to personal identity suffice to debunk the theory. According to Kai Nielsen in Davis (1989): "work at the cutting edge of the philosophy of mind by such philosophers as H. Putnam, D. Dennett, Paul Churchland, T. Nagel, and Derek Parfit, to mention a few, takes dualism to be an utter non starter" (p. 54).

Materialism provides an attractive alternative to dualism, since the theory possesses great unity, and unity is a sign of perfection, but it need not be our first choice. The problem with materialism is that the parts are homogeneous. They cannot account for the diversity of persons. Although mind and body appear separate at the superficial level, my own view is that matter is ultimately reducible to mind at the deeper, sacred order of existence.

In the language of Aristotle, the coming into being and passing out of being of things is explained through the agency of fundamental principles of change. He says that potency limits act, as we saw earlier. His realism corrects Plato's idealism. Aristotle is unequivocal about the intimate connection that exists between matter and form; the engagement of these principles constitutes a dynamic unit of substance. Our familiar world is not filled with sightings of form existing separately from matter, (contrary to popular ghost stories), since form cannot exist without matter. The phenomenon of human death is explained as a change in the locus of co-principles. Form reverts back to the potentiality of matter. Although that change enhances the privation of matter, form does not separate from the substance. Aquinas goes on to frame death within his Christian perspective where form or soul separates from substance. For as long as the person lives, the body limits the immateriality of soul, but the process ends at death.

We can now take a closer look at the relationship between a limiting principle and the perfection it limits. The limiting agent functions in one of two ways, namely, as intrinsic or extrinsic limitation. The distinction can be situated in context of the Plotinian world of eternal forms. In order to distinguish God from "creatures," the human essence must be really distinct from the divine existence. The human is not eternal. The discussion of the metaphysics of creation is found in the famous controversy of Giles of Rome and Henry of Ghent at the end of the thirteenth century. According to Giles of Rome, potentiality functions as the extrinsic limitation of form. However, Henry of Ghent argues against this belief since it suggests that the limiting principle pre-exists the creative act, rendering the doctrine of a *creatio ex nihilo* incomprehensible. The solution to the dilemma is contained in Aquinas's belief that matter is the intrinsic limitation of form. William Carlo (1921-1971) expresses the view (1966) that essence is ultimately reducible to existence. If he is right, it means that the body is the intrinsic limitation of mind. The distinction between the extrinsic and the intrinsic limitation of mind by the body is important from the point of view of personal identity. While Aquinas stresses the ultimate reducibility of essence to existence in the metaphysics, it collapses in his eschatology where the soul's departure from the body causes death. The doctrine of the ultimate reducibility, however, also suggests that at human death the soul carries the body in its wake. According to this belief, mind encapsulates body. They form a unit in both this world and the afterlife. This simple solution avoids dualism while solving the problem of personal identity. But how does the reduction of body to mind avoid materialism or animism?

We can imagine that the conception of body as the intrinsic limitation of mind places the body where the mind ceases or ends. The operations of human understanding never take place without matter, although these operations are not reducible to matter. Aquinas's belief that essence functions as the intrinsic limitation of existence, marking the place where existence ends, so to speak, marks the place of mind and matter. Matter limits mind as potency limits act. To say that the outer fringes of mind, the delineation of mind, specifies the place of matter is not to suggest that all material things have mind. Only some material things are living things. Fewer yet possess a capacity for reasoning. For those who may wonder how we can imagine the intrinsic limitation of mind by matter, the answer is that it is no more difficult to imagine this than the extrinsic limitation of matter. Dualism is based on that fundamental belief. The Thomistic suggestion stands dualism on its head and in the process dissolves the distance between body and mind. In ordinary experience, if we connect two bodies of water, one at five degrees Celsius, and one at fifty degrees Celsius, do we not expect water at higher temperature to limit water at lower temperature? How imagine the water at fifty warming itself at the expense of the water at five degrees Celsius? The explanations of mind-body interactions from the perspective of intrinsic limitation confirms that view. It avoids all the difficulties of dualism without loss of benefit. Since matter is ultimately reducible to mind, to think is to think as an embodied being. D. R. Griffin confirms this observation when he says in Davis (1989): "Since the cells composing the brain are sentient, they are not ontologically different in kind from the experiencing mind" (p. 93). But this is not to identify the brain with the mind, as numerically identical. They remain distinct.

That view retains much of the Thomistic connection between mind and body while avoiding the problems posed by his conception of the resurrection of the body. The mind is both dependent and independent of the brain. The brain literally limits the mind since the mind cannot function without it. Yet, what the mind produces is irreducible to the content of brain. To put the matter as simply as possible, if someone strikes me on the head with a hammer it will affect my thinking. However, it will not explain what I am thinking as my brain is being crushed. The inseparable unity of mind and matter is essential to a proper grounding of epistemology. The existence of the brain accounts for the observable, measurable character of learning, while the existence of mind explains the immaterial character of learning. Both are required to explain human understanding: the immaterial character of learning cannot be explained materially since it violates laws which physical things cannot violate, such as the irreversibility of space and time. Furthermore, our beliefs depend on contents which cannot be expressed in physical terms, such as what is the color of virtue, the weight of honesty, the KSP of love. In addition, learning includes a content that cannot be exhausted by any number of material drawings.

Although Paul Edwards's philosophical position (1992) is somewhere between dualism and behaviorism, he too is intent on refuting materialism. He uses the following arguments to make his own case on the immaterial nature of thought: Firstly, the privacy argument; we can't tell what someone is thinking by examining what goes on in the brain. Secondly, the fact that certain features of our experience such as the smell of a flower cannot be explained through behaviorism. Thirdly, the property of intentionality; an atom in the brain can't represent anything. Yet, mental states are directed toward a target. Fourthly, immateriality; mental states do not have mass, weight, bulk. They cannot be explained by matter alone (pp. 25-30). Edwards's view supports the thesis that mind is both dependent and independent of the brain. The real distinction between them raises the insoluble problems of dualism, while the ultimate reducibility of brain to mind avoids dualism and safeguards personal identity. Aquinas's error was to open his metaphysical argument with mysticism rather than end with it. His body never had a chance.

Let me be the first to formulate some objections to my belief. If mind is immaterial, an unextended substance as Descartes says or a spiritual substance as Aquinas says, then it is not composed of parts. It does not occupy places in space. How, then, is it possible to imagine the perimeter of that which has no parts as coming to an end? How can body arise where mind ends? We reply in two ways. The first is that we are finite beings. We do not exist necessarily, but only contingently. This means that we could just as easily not exist as exist. But for the grace of God we would not exist in this life or in the hereafter. The conception of matter arising where mind ends is an expression of our finitude. The second reply is that the paradox that seems to arise out of the reduction of the material to the immaterial reflects what transpires in our own psyche. We appear to ourselves as a mix of the eternal and the temporal, as beings that know themselves to be immortal while knowing themselves to be mortal. Thus, the reducibility of the material to the immaterial evokes a vision of the temporal as the intrinsic limitation of the eternal. We are not eternal as such, but in rare moments of spiritual ecstasy, some mystics (such as Aquinas) claim to grasp the presence of the eternal in the temporal. Human death is oxymoronic: the phenomenon of death is simultaneously meaningful and meaningless. It is meaningful because, as Heidegger says, it is the utmost possibility of impossibility. We can chose to be powerful before death. But death is meaningless because it is not an experience. No one lives through his or her own death. Death is timely and untimely. The individual that dies runs out of life, but death is not the absence of life. Death is a source of inspiration, but it can arrive by chance. No one knows the appointed time of death. As Sartre says, I can die of a heart attack on my way to the gallows. The possibility of my death can fill me with despair, but it can also fill me with hope. Death is a process that defines me, although the nature of death as such is unknowable. The proposition "all humans are mortal" is analytic (contains nothing new) because no person has proof of his or her own death, or data on the nature of death as such. We can choose to be powerful in the face of death, but it precludes the future. Human death is a process rather than an event of the living.

A further objection to the reducibility of the material to the immaterial is that nothing of the physical body is actually seen to accompany the dead into the afterlife. Death seems to be the utter end of human life, while the body is buried or cremated. How, then, do we justify our claim of embodied immortality? It is met in two steps. The first movement arises out of the character of the person as an entity toward being's unconcealment. The second is from quantum mechanics and the relativity of observation. Science announces that matter can appear as either a particle or a wave motion depending on the environment. It seems possible to suggest that the human body can also appear as wave or particle (embodied or disembodied) to a divine observer, exhibiting physical characteristics in the natural order, and immaterial characteristics in a different realm. Nothing is illogical about that belief.

An important distinction between understanding and explaining a phenomenon moves us in this direction. To understand an event is to grasp the necessary reason of the event; to conclude that given the nature of the event, it could not have been different. Thus, we understand that persons can only act as persons. But being human is not a clear and distinct concept. For instance, we cannot understand the afterlife or provide the causes of continued existence other than through an appeal to divine grace. The process of explanation holds more promise, however.

Explanation is a process of discovering the sufficient reason of a consequent from within the folds of an antecedent sufficient condition. Reason explains the event because it recognizes the identification between the antecedent and the consequent. We know, for instance, that when the conditions affecting the properties of water are set at 100 degrees Celsius, and 76 centimeter mercury pressure, the properties of the substance will be seen to boil. The distinction between explaining and understanding suggests that while we cannot understand the nature of death as such, the process can be explained. What, then, is the sufficient reason of death? The conception of the ultimate reducibility allows us to discover the sufficient reason of death in being's unconcealment. The nature of the afterlife is explained by tracing, not only the material to the immaterial, or matter to mind, but embodied consciousness to being's unconcealment. Being's unconcealment, in turn, reduces itself to the creator, and possibly to God, as the psychology of thought suggests.

This explanation is not an appeal to the evidence of parapsychology, an area about which I remain skeptical. Even if we could establish communication with the dead, we would not understand it. That is, the data are interpreted from the point of view of the living, not the dead. Yet, reputable research is conducted in this area. For instance, the near death experience (NDE) has been receiving a great deal of attention since the seventies, as has the phenomenon of telepathic communication.

The possibility of reducing the material to the immaterial suggests that the immaterial or soul carries something of the body into the afterlife. If the issue of personal survival is to make sense, we must suppose that the habits, knowledge, beliefs, volitions, and virtues acquired in this life accompany us into the afterlife, mapping out our own disposition in eternity. But since our person-making habits are developed as embodied consciousness in relationships, an aspect of these follows the soul into eternity. Gabriel Marcel, as we saw, makes the point that the loving relationships we establish on earth are taken with us into the afterlife.

Perhaps a simple example will illustrate the reducibility of matter to mind: Imagine that we are walking along a path and hear the sounds of a waterfall. We might wish to walk toward it in anticipation of the splendid view. Then as we arrive to witness the water tumbling into the river bed, a strange and wonderful thing happens. A sudden unexpected drop in water temperature brings about an abrupt change. The temperature plunges below the freezing point of water. And the waterfall begins to freeze. There at a place where the frozen waterfall ends is the form of the water, marking it, giving it an identity as this waterfall rather than another. So it is with the individual. There in matter, at a place bordered by nothingness, at a place where mind ends is the form of the mind, giving the person a personal identity.

3. The Reducibility of Embodied Mind to Being

Not only is brain reducible to mind, but embodied mind is also reducible to being. It functions as the intrinsic limitation of being. The person's way of framing the environment, for instance, provides an indication of the ways in which we limit nature. The environment can be viewed in two ways: One is at the superficial, functional level of exploitation; the other way arises at the sacramental level of respect for nature. Good technology is sacramental. The sense of *techne* suggests an art for "letting be"; it does not seek to "stockpile nature," but respects the natural restorative processes of nature. Good agricultural technology, for instance, allows the natural energies of the soil to restore themselves. Similarly, good medicine does not go against the nature of the human body, but allows it to heal itself.

We enter into spiritual communion with being. We shape being and being shapes us. Together we form a unit. Being is not maintained in existence by the activities of consciousness, but is a condition of consciousness. Heidegger's *Dasein* as "being-there" suggests that consciousness does not deduce the existence of things. We begin life as inserted in a world that is already there, disclosed as the horizon of *Dasein*'s possibilities. *Dasein*'s metaphysical fingerprint is already on being from the first moment of *Dasein*'s existence, before the epistemic life of consciousness begins. Our fingerprint is on the whole of cosmos. Our movements and sounds, for instance, carry into space forever. They accompany us into the afterlife, along with the whole of our moral and physical habits and person-making relationships. We form an inseparable unit with nature. This is the sense of the reducibility of embodied mind to being's unconcealment. This view is confirmed by science. Fritjof Capra (1983) says:

> Quantum theory ... reveals a basic oneness of the universe. It shows that we cannot decompose the world into independently existing smallest units. As we penetrate into matter, nature does not show us any isolated building blocks, but rather appears as a complicated web of relations between the various parts of the whole. These relations always include the observer in an essential way. The human observer constitutes the final link in the chain of observational processes, and the properties of any atomic object can only be understood in terms of the object's interaction with the observer. This means that the classical ideal of an objective description of nature is no longer valid. The cartesian position between "I" and the world, between the observer and the observed, cannot be made when dealing with atomic matter. In atomic physics, we can never speak about nature without, at the same time, speaking about ourselves. (P. 78f)

What an interesting turn physics is taking! If I could somehow examine my own brain, subject it to microscopic analysis, I would find at the subatomic level, at a place where matter fuses into mind, that I could not distinguish between the observer and the observed. I would see myself looking at myself. In this mirror vision of my action on the environment, brain, mind, and being become indistinguishable. I would not recognize where one ends and the other begins. This is hardly surprising since the artificiality of dualism has long been disclosed. In that world of physics, I can see myself in the act of thinking, immersed in the fire of knowing. I am that being seeking to see itself knowing, that sees itself looking. Thus while the fusion of embodied mind and being is disconcerting to cartesians, it returns us to friendly territory once again to a time before the industrial revolution and the excesses of arrogant reason. It reveals the artificiality of the cartesian machinery as the device of an impatient mathematician seeking to play God by reducing the sacred to the theorems of analytical geometry. In that moment of insight where embodied mind is seen to merge with being's unconcealment, I discover my own metaphysical "inner child" and remember my roots in the All of creation. I remember that I am my body; I am being; I am the All. Nature is not something I possess or control. Marcel's exclamation, "I am my body," means that the distinction between the outside and the inside blurs. I don't have a brain, I am my brain. I don't have a garden, I am my garden. The death of the environment is the death of the whole person. The embodied I that is currently thinking is a being in motion along with other particles in motion. We connect as a network of interlocking systems in the foci of interstellar space.

4. Why Something Rather than Nothing?

To Blaise Pascal (1623-1662) goes the credit for expressing in eloquent voice the fragility and greatness of the person. Our fragility is that we are but small, thinking reeds. Our greatness comes from knowing our profound insignificance. That insignificance is expressed in the most profound discoveries of art, science, and religion. It leads us to raise the question why there is something rather than nothing. The preoccupation with this question, the basic question of philosophy, reverberates fully in the work of Heidegger. What, indeed, is the root of the possibility of being in a situation in which I can give voice to my finitude? Heidegger cannot answer the question he raises. It points beyond the question to the root of the possibility of raising questions. The possibility of raising questions is questioned. Perhaps the answer to the question is at a place in poetry, dance, art, music; a place where the word cannot travel. We are now standing in the presence of an awesome absolute, undoubtedly the evidence of a creator, and possibly God. When Sartre faces this possibility, he quivers like a wretched worm unable to shake the epistemological dust of cartesianism from his brow. He is unwilling to accept being-there as gift. He rejects all absolutes. Heidegger, however, also stands in awe before that gift, battling against it, but accepting it in his more mystical moments. This seems to be the case in his series of lectures on technicity, especially his fourth lecture, "*The Turning*," where he details how "Being" comes-to-presence in the atomic age. We appear to desecrate being.

What is the benefit of standing in the presence of being as sacred? It depends on how it is framed. We can be awestruck by the gift of being's unconcealment. We can note that it is freely given to us. It is the power that animates good science and religion. Without the gift of standing in awe before being's unconcealment, Albert Einstein (1879-1955) thinks that science is as good as dead. Nothing is left to feed it. But the gift can also dumbfound us. Being's unconcealment is the power that elevates Aquinas's philosophy into silence. But it plunges Kierkegaard and William James (1842-1910) into the depths of depression. Kierkegaard arises from the metaphysical ashes to root subjective truth at a place that exists beyond the sterile arguments of Rationalist ethics. James, being of a more practical temperament, opts for Charles de Renouvier's (1815-1903) belief in the efficacy of the will. Believe that life is worth living, he says, and that belief will help create the fact. But two other visionaries, Sartre and Camus are not so fortunate. They cannot restock the coffers of reason once it is placed in receivership. Kant also partakes of the philosophic vision. He acquiesces to the fundamental unknowability of things. But his representation of reality as noumenal presents reason with a sacred alternative route to metaphysics: a *Critique of Practical Reason* to house metaphysics at a place in human insight where reason could not impose its rotting carcass. These insights startle us into thought. Why is there something rather than nothing? That "why?", as Aristotle pointed out long ago, is the seed of our epistemic life.

5. The Concept and the Idea

One of the clearest expressions of the gift of being's unconcealment is contained in a critical distinction Aquinas establishes between our concept of the world and our idea of the world. The Latin root of existence is "*ex*" and "*sistere*" meaning to "step forth, emerge." The concept is the means for the stepping forth of being into unconcealment. The tradition from Plato to Aristotle focuses on the emergence of "whatness or substance" as the essential character of the stepping out of being. Why is that? Greek philosophy expresses the belief that the world is eternal. The fundamental concern is in explaining the diversity of things. But Aquinas already knows why things exist and he shifts the focus toward this given truth. He is fascinated by God's creative activity. If we follow the turn from Aristotle and Aquinas, we note the role of being in decoding the nature of stepping out. The process takes place through a questioner. But the questioner is already fed by being's unconcealment to raise the question about being. The questioner does not stand outside being raising questions about being, but is that same questioning being that finds itself thrown into raising questions. Aquinas's theory of the concept intends to preserve the primacy of that indubitable given. He calls it the effect of

God's creative activity. At the epistemic level, we acquiesce to that metaphysical primacy in a theory of direct perception. This focus, or way of framing being, is maintained through the high middle ages to Descartes. But it falls into a period of forgetfulness during the cartesian era to continue dormant in some forms of philosophy today. So it is appropriate to raise it anew.

Why does Aquinas need a distinction between concept and idea? The distinction serves an invaluable function in my explanation of the journey toward the afterlife. The role of the concept is process like. It is a mechanism designed to safeguard the objectivity of knowledge. Aquinas saw the need to ensure that the knower, in the primary operation of knowledge, fuses with the being of things rather than with a mentalistic representation of the being of things. He anticipates the phenomenological critique of cartesianism. Let me clarify:

The first operation of knowledge, according to Aquinas, lies in our conceptual union with the being of things. It takes place before the mind begins the activity of composing and dividing. Thus, if what I know is the rose (as the rose knows itself), then, the mind cannot actually be knowing the rose in the primary operation of understanding, since that is to know the mentalistic representation of a rose. I must become the rose before I can know myself having become the rose. The concept, then, is the means or road toward that ideal, or the objectivity of knowledge. The idea is the term or end point of the epistemological journey. It arises in the second operation of understanding. The idea arises through the production of an entity to the likeness of the conceptual union, forming something to its likeness so that it can function as the exemplar of knowledge. The idea is the concept having been examined. Both operations occur simultaneously. The specification of the agent intellect by the conceptual becoming of the other spontaneously triggers the order of operation and the production of the idea. The concept feeds reason, but the idea is the digestive tract at work in the life of reason.

The intuition of the speculative intellect is the means for a pre-discursive, pre-thematic consonance with the being of the thing. The artist can paint the rose by first becoming the rose, fusing with it as an entity belonging to the rose before taking distance to capture the experience on canvas. The artist already lives the experience of being a rose before the imitation begins on canvas. It is a lived experience, filtered through the lenses of attitudes, beliefs and values of the artist. The work of art corresponds to a way of framing reality. Since it takes place in a cultural setting, the expression of art is historical. It tells the tale of our person-making process. Art forms express the varied perspectives, or beliefs, of the artist. Art evolves, being the expression of cultural relativity. But the possibility of standing in dialogue with the rose is a given. We stand in the presence of an absolute, although the interpretation of standing in the presence is relative to context. Standing before the rose gives evidence of our standing in the presence of mystery. The experience is offered equally to every artist. But not every person is an artist, moved by the gift of our being-there. Standing in wonder opens the possibility of authentic science and religion. What else is a religious experience, if not a springing forth from the truth of being? We need not wait on being. Asceticism, for instance, consists of various practices such as meditation, fasting, to purify us. It prepares us for an appreciation of the gift of being-there.

We develop rituals and symbols to reenact the experience of making such connections. The artist, the woodcutter, the religionist, the baker and candlestick maker each uses ritual to prepare their way of encountering being's stepping out into unconcealment. They begin at the place of intuition. And provide us with stories about the experience.

Aquinas tells the story of the "transcendental properties" of being to reflect the beauty of being's stepping out. His transcendentals allow us to savor the different textures of the gift of existence. The vision of being in the characteristic of unity, truth, and goodness provides a gateway to the "stepping forth" of existence. Framing being as unity, for instance, allows us to view the rose as being-along-with-us, clinging to itself, resisting destruction, in an age of divisiveness. The whole of nature resists destruction. That ecological awareness sensitizes us to the delicate balance of nature, the fragility of our own being. To hail flowers as truth is to stand in being as unconcealment, filled by the insight of being-there. To see being as good is to engage the possibility of filling the appetite for existence we share with cosmos, in cosmos. To see being as beauty is to resonate the intuited truths of unity, truth, and goodness. The transcendental vision is no less than a profound spiritual awakening. In our day, the insight animates the environmental movement and the turning toward biocentric ethics.

The "critical problem" arises from mistaking the idea for the concept. When Descartes and the cartesians begin philosophy with the idea rather than the concept they unwittingly substitute mental constructs for the being of things. They do not wait on the stepping out of being, but forcibly dislodge secrets from being. He pays an epistemic penalty for that behavior: In *Meditations* five and six, Descartes extrapolates the stepping out in one of two ways; either the existence of things is an extension of spatial reasoning, or we cannot know things. His dilemma is unavoidable. Once the intellect rejects the gift of being's unconcealment, paradoxes are destined to appear. The gift of being's stepping out is clearest in the realm of human death, at the place where being refuses to be for us.

But before we examine that aspect of being's unconcealment, one additional point needs to be made about its primacy. Aquinas's metaphysics unloads being's primacy into a conception of human nature as substance, as we saw. But once we make the shift to a view of the person as a being in relationships, we can avoid some of the epistemic problems encountered in the tradition. So, the concept points to the primacy of relationships, whereas the idea is the relationship as known. When we procreate, for instance, the child is born out of a relationship. Although the human being is fully individuated at birth, it arises as the outcome of existing patterns, or laws. The pattern comes first, the characteristic of being human only later. The (systemic) concept celebrates that primacy without betraying the epistemology. The representative role of the concept is as critical to the success of the epistemic life, as our tendency toward good and evil is to the possibility of the moral life.

6. Being and Human Death

The majority of articles and books on death view it from the perspective of life. But the question what is death like to the dead subsequently resolves itself into an absurdity. This is not surprising. If death is thought to be the absence of life or activity, it is absurd to wonder what sort of life remains when life is absent and stranger yet to raise the issue about the sorts of things the dead do when not doing anything. My distinction (1995) between nothing there and nothing-there avoids that absurdity through an appeal to a reversal in the ground of the possibility of absence. So the dead are nothing-there because the possibility of life no longer exists at death. The realization that we cannot understand the nature of death as such, also follows this line of thought. But if the nature of death as such is inconceptualizable, we can explain why this is the case. In seeking to explain death, however, the focal point shifts toward systemic theory, as we move beyond consciousness to the laws and patterns governing consciousness. What better way to explain death than through the appeal to a shift in the laws and patterns of being's unconcealment?

What is death like to the dead? What would the dead tell us about themselves, if they could speak? We must look to being's unconcealment for an answer. Death is not something we do since it is not an experience. In that sense, no connection exists between dying and death. The expression "you look half-dead" really means that you look to be well on with dying. We are never more or less dead. Death is the removal of the possibility of having experiences. We can distinguish between dying and death in the following way: whereas dying entails a gradual loss of consciousness, death is the removal of the possibility of being conscious. Death is not something we do or fail to do. On the occasion of human death, being refuses to be for consciousness. Death is simply a "recall" of being's unconcealment. Thus, the possibility of framing being no longer exists at human death.

The distinction between understanding and explaining something can now find full expression. We cannot understand the nature of death as such since nothing of human life is present at death; no living person is there to interview. In fact, once we recognize that death is not an experience we know why the nature of death as such is inconceptualizable. We can now begin the search for an alternate route. That alternate is the explanation of death. The person always exists in relationships with being. No person exists without such relationships. If we split the moment of phenomenal experience, we observe the presence of a subjective correlate of consciousness fusing with an objective correlate or being as stepping out. But the subjective correlate does not exist without the objective correlate, and vice versa. They form a dynamic unit. This is precisely the point of Wittgenstein's critique of idealism and empiricism. But we have artificially split the atom of human experience as a cardiologist might stop the pulse of the human heart to take a closer look at the mechanism. We shall not tardy. The inconceptualizability of death means that we cannot grasp the nature of death as such through a study of the human subject. However, we can explain death as such through the human object, namely, being's unconcealment. At that artificial place in epistemic surgery, the explanation of death moves us to an antecedent condition of life, to a place that contains the sufficient reason of embodied consciousness. Consciousness always exists in relationship to the stepping out of being. Thus, since death as such is not the absence of consciousness, we look to being's unconcealment to extricate the sufficient reason of death. For as long as we live, or die, an ongoing dialogue takes place between consciousness and being. Being is given directly to consciousness in a free gift of unconcealment. Being is intelligible. It lets itself be known. This is not something we do, as is clear from the error of Descartes. Being's unconcealment ceases at human death. Being no longer steps out; it refuses "to be" for us. Death is an abrupt cessation in the unconcealment of being; a mysterious reclaim in being where unconcealment becomes concealment. Death is the ontological reclaim of the possibility of raising the question why is there something rather than nothing. At that point we no longer stand in awe, not because the situation isn't the utmost possibility of standing in awe, but because the possibility of standing in awe is removed.

This view of death does not add undue emphasis on the gift of existence. We come from the nothing and move back into the nothing. It is no more difficult to imagine our non-being before birth than it is to imagine our no-longer being after death. One difference is apparent. We come into existence as beings in relationships with God in our psyche, others, and the environment as sacred. Possibly God will want to maintain the relationships struck with us in this life. In fact, short of God's annihilation of the entire cosmos, having been brought out into finitude, we are destined to remain an eternal dimension of that order of being, even if only as a memory in divine timelessness. God cannot rid God of the creator. We are sustained in existence by God's omniscience and by the fact that nothing lies outside of God. So the reversal in being's unconcealment must carry us along. Thus, the no-longer being of death is the removal of the possibility of the temporal, opening up several new prospects such as the possibility of existence in duration beyond time.

The silence that arises at the place of being's no longer stepping out at human death is accompanied by a reversal or mirror image of being's stepping out. At that point, the person stands in the presence of God. This is explained through the ultimate reducibility of being's unconcealment to the creator and then to God.

Eight

PERSONS AS CORRELATES OF GOD

1. The Reducibility of Being's Unconcealment to the Creator

So we belong to a network of person-making relationships at the psychological and interpersonal levels of existence. We also belong to the environment. The psychological level of relationships enables us to become God-conscious, providing an ethical base for our relationships with others and being. The concern we express toward being also raises a moral issue because the attitude or way of framing being expressed by persons is either secular or sacramental. In the secular mentality, we operate at the superficial level of existence. For instance, I define myself by a particular street in a town where I live. On that street is a house where I sleep. Behind the house is a yard. And in the yard a tree. It is a familiar tree, yard, house, street, city, that allows me to make sense of my life. I belong to it. But my relationship in that world is raised to the sacramental level when I move beyond the surface appearance of things to recognize the interdependence of all things along with the existence of patterns, or laws. My relationship is sacramental when it fixes on patterns.

Carl Sagan says that the universe is about 15,000 million years old. The appearance of human beings is a recent phenomenon. Paul and Linda Badham (1982) note the even more recent appearance of Christ in history. If we compress the history of the universe into a single year:

> The big bang happened on January 1; our galaxy came into being on 1 May; our earth was formed 14 September; primitive life began on 16 December; man emerged on 31 December at about 10:30 PM; and at 11:59.56, four-hundredths of a second before midnight, Christ was born. How can Christ be the center of the universe? (P. 53)

The Buddha's birth is equally recent since it occurs at 11:59.48, or eight-tenths of a second before Christ. But a deeper lesson is learned from this, the lesson of creation. It provides us with an insight into the relativity of the temporal horizon and the cosmic nature of both Buddha and Christ. The focus on the reduction of being to the creator is an awakening to the existence of cosmic unity. It moves beyond the four million years or so of human existence to the vista of the eternal God. God exists in timelessness beyond the creator and temporality. The creator is without sufficient reason without God. Possibly, the creator is God. In that event, our temporality is but one string in the infinite number of possible relations toward God.

2. The Nature of God in Heidegger's Philosophy

It seems possible to forgive Descartes's reductivism because he was a pioneer. He could not know that the success of his mathematics would engender disastrous epistemological and ethical consequences. The subsequent attempts of the cartesians to deduce the existence of a world outside the *cogito* is an embarrassment to philosophy for it leads to skepticism, or solipsism. Skeptics undoubtedly know a great deal more than they pretend to, but they find serious difficulty with the claims we can legitimately make about the world. The view is expressed as the ancient "*diallelus*" problem of circular reasoning. We cannot know if things really are as they seem to be unless we first know which appearances are true and which are false. In a footnote to the preface of the second edition of his *Critique of Pure Reason* (1787), Kant remarks:

> It still remains a scandal to philosophy and to human reason in general that the existence of things outside of us ... must be accepted merely on faith, and that, if anyone thinks it good to doubt their existence, we are unable to counter his doubts by any satisfactory proofs.

One of the characteristic traits of rationalism is that everything outside mind is either rejected or accepted on the basis of faith. Contemporary philosophy finds value in Heidegger's exclamation that we have no need of such proof since we are already in the world. He says in *Sein und Zeit* (1927) that the scandal of philosophy is not the absence of satisfactory proofs for the existence of reality, but the belief that such proofs are required: "If *Dasein* is understood correctly, it defies such proof, because, in its Being, it already is what the subsequent proofs deem necessary to demonstrate for it" (p. 205).

His point is that the *Dasein* as an entity refers to a way of being rather than to a way of knowing, as we have seen. This is a focal point in his rejection of Christian theology. In fact he rejects all absolutes, including God. But he appears to give assent to the existence of what might be termed "the God of being's unconcealment." Fergus Kerr's article, "Getting the Subject back into the World: Heidegger's Version," in David Cockburn (1991), contains a refreshing account of Heidegger's argument. According to this view, Heidegger rejects the traditional representation of human nature because of the problems it creates. He traces the origin of human nature to two main sources, one Greek, the other Biblical. In Greek philosophy, the human being is defined as a living thing that has reason. This creates the impression that the human is an interior "I" looking out at the world. The Moderns imagined that a proof of that world was necessary. The second element that distorts the meaning of being human is the Biblical allusion to our divinity. The belief that we are made in the image of God (*Genesis,* 1:26) generates a transcendent view of ourselves. Heidegger's critique is that we mistakenly think we can function beyond ourselves. In the tradition, the interior "I" and the divinity connect to discuss common problems. The first item of business is the existence of the world and the assurance that it continues to exist in the absence of the "I." But Heidegger does not provide much evidence on why this business is carried out. He briefly cites two authors belonging to the Reformation. Yet, he goes on to reject Christian theology on the basis of this investigation. It is not surprising that Kerr should wonder about Heidegger's philosophical competence (pp. 173-190).

Heidegger offers us two examples of theological residues in philosophy; the first is the belief in eternal truths; the second is the existence of the "idealized subject," in Edmund Husserl's (1859-1938) sense of the term. Heidegger's rejection of the first belief is based on his claim that no truth is possible without the *Dasein.* *Dasein* is the entity that discloses or understands truth. This is not to say that Newton's laws, for instance, were untrue before Newton, but simply that they did not exist. On the second point, Kerr takes it that by our preoccupation with the "idealized subject of experiences," Heidegger is rejecting a tradition that moves from Descartes, J.G. Fichte (1762-1814), Kant, to Husserl. Husserl's attempt to reveal the existence of a transcendental subject as absolute datum of experience ignores the familiar fact of *Dasein*'s immersion or being-there in everyday life. Thus, no pure "I" or subject of experience as imagined by the Rationalists exists.

Heidegger's polemic against eternal truths and the disembodied self also appears to imply a rejection of God since a deity is the only entity that can exist outside time. Our claim to transcendence is that the "I" connects with that deity. According to Heidegger, the elimination of the desire to transcend ourselves is a precondition of a true account of the being of *Dasein.* However, Kerr is suspicious of what Heidegger intends by "God." He might not be referring to God as understood by Jews and Christians. Further, Kerr is critical of Heidegger's attempt to implicate the proof for the existence of the external world and whether it can be known, with the problem of the knowledge of God and the possibility of proving God's existence. He says that Heidegger "leaves the details tantalizingly sketchy." I am not a Heidegger scholar, but I too find it difficult to sort out the nature of God in Heidegger's philosophy. Heidegger represents God as a functional deity, possibly a creator, but he also appears fond of Meister Eckhart's non-functional God beyond creator.

3. The Existence of the "Nothing" as Creator

Heidegger's *"Zu den Sachen Selbst,"* and Kant's *"ding an sich"* are vastly different. What Heidegger signifies by "the thing in itself" is not, as we might expect, a thing standing outside consciousness, but a mode of being that encompasses the *Dasein* as truth-disclosing entity. Since the *Dasein* replaces eternal truths, and traditional philosophy is at an end, he begins anew. The plan to do so is announced in *Sein und*

Zeit. The task is to work out the being of the *Dasein*. The *Dasein* is the entity that enters the inquiry into the being of entities. What is the ultimate root of the possibility of *Dasein* analysis? It is a given possibility, and the inquiry cannot be completed. Yet, the raising of the question points beyond itself.

John Caputo (1978) claims that Heidegger's mysticism is influenced by Eckhart (p. 9). He suggests there might be a mystical element in his thought, although Heidegger is not necessarily a mystic. So, the psyche reveals the existence of a psychological tendency toward God, although Heidegger might not be aware of it. The existence of God is more evident in loving relationships with other human beings. *Dasein*'s focus, however, is directed toward being's unconcealment. Does Caputo's evidence suggest that Heidegger sees the existence of God at that level?

Eckhart's influence on Heidegger is clearest here, although Heidegger does not represent God in the traditional way. Caputo suggests he replaces God by Being and soul by *Dasein*. The *Dasein*, first of all, invites Being into a *Zu den Sachen Selbst* communion. The moment of fusion with being's unconcealment points to God's role in illuminating the possibility of being-there. In other words, God's light shines on being to create the possibility of *Dasein*'s entry into communion with being's unconcealment. His view of death as "utmost possibility of impossibility," or source of inspiration, also suggests this openness, as we saw.

That view is manifest in our experiences of the world. The desk at which I sit, for instance, is extended in the space of my office. But it does not occupy the whole of this space. It comes to an end. The desk would not be a desk if it did not have a boundary. Heidegger identifies the ending of the desk as the nothing that surrounds it. However, the nothing appears to be something, since it marks off the desk from other objects in the room. What, then, is the something of the nothing? Heidegger's inaugural lecture at the University of Freiburg in 1929 sheds light on this question. He opens the lecture by situating the question, "What is Metaphysics?". He says that the sciences wish to know about beings, their relationships, their causes, their effects, and otherwise nothing. But what is the being of the nothing? The nothing is not a being. It is cut off from being. It is neither this nor that. Yet it is encountered. Like the Buddhist idea of *"shunyata,"* the nothing is experienced. It is in the fact that the nothing is there that the experience of the something arises. The nothing raises being into the light of truth. For instance, the rhythmic silence that separates musical notes, the dramatic pause of speech ... add content. So, if Heidegger's nothing of being experience extends to the nothing that surrounds the Big Bang origin of the cosmos, we can catch a glimpse of the creator at work. The evidence that someone is at work here is suggested by the patterns or laws that govern the expansion and contraction of the universe. Of this, more later.

Caputo claims that Eckhart uses this same experience to move beyond being. To Eckhart, the nothing is God, "He who is." To experience the nothing is to recognize that we could just as easily not exist as exist. It is a reminder of our human finitude and fundamental powerlessness before God. But that view suggests that the nothing is itself surrounded by something, a "second nothing," or divine horizon. So, being's unconcealment points to a creator of the nothing, and to the possibility of a God beyond creator. In that event, the creator is a specification or instance of God at work. So, the argument moves on two levels. First, the nothing surrounding being points toward a creator. Second, the nothing surrounding the creator, arising at a place where the created nothing ends, points toward God, or an Uncaused Cause beyond the creator. We move beyond the natural order to encounter God.

This view is familiar to us since it is housed in the psyche's religious connections. When the sentiment is authentic, the religious connection generates a spiritual awakening. Job, for instance, gives evidence of that awakening as he experiences direct communication with God, or the horizon of the nothing. He becomes aware of his own psychological relationship with God. His experience is profoundly spiritual, yet humbling. He knows himself to be standing in the presence of the Almighty. He has ventured beyond the range of human comprehension. In that moment of spiritual insight he sees his profound insignificance and falls to his knees like a worm before God.

The first trace of God, God as transcendent, exists in us, but moves outwardly to connect with the horizon of the nothing that surrounds being. Heidegger experiences the nothing, and his psyche senses the need to move beyond it, but he is unwilling to move beyond temporality, toward God as creator. He waits on being's unconcealment to "beckon forth," to move *Dasein* beyond the nothing surrounding being to the possibility of being's unconcealment. But no other unconcealment is forthcoming, no further truth of *Dasein*. So, he cannot go. Yet, his waiting is destined to be frustrated since it cannot remain unanswered. To wait is to wait on something. The waiting knows itself to be incomplete. Heidegger appears to experience a mystical connection between the nothing surrounding being and the horizon of the nothing, or God.

Heidegger says that the nothing surrounding being is not the negation of being. Hence we expect him to say what it is. It contains the ground of all logical negation. It surrounds being, allowing it to emerge into appearance. The nothing is not outside being. It is the essence of being, allowing the possibility of being's unconcealment and truth. Being falls into beinglessness without the nothing. Does the nothing point beyond itself? Is the nothing surrounded by a "nothing," is that God? Heidegger does not say so, but the question deserves an answer. Heidegger's lecture, "*The Turning of Being*," delivered at Bühlerhöhe in the spring of 1950, published in the William Lovitt translation (1977) as *The Question of Technicity*, provides evidence for moving beyond temporality. His theme appears earlier in a series of four lectures in Bremen, entitled "Insight Into What Is" (1949). Yet, Heidegger does not make the shift. Is his critique of transcendent, eternal truths too fresh in his mind?

The reduction of being's unconcealment to the horizon surrounding the nothing is not without justification. Earlier, I spoke about the ultimate reducibility of matter to mind as a solution to dualism. I can now elaborate in detail. The reducibility suggests that matter exists because of the nothing or mind (intelligence) that surrounds it. The nothing is not the negation of matter, it is the intelligence behind it. Matter is the intrinsic limitation of mind. This view is evident at two levels of intelligence, human and divine. It signifies human intelligence at the temporal level of finitude where brain meets mind, and divine intelligence as the possibility of a temporal level, where being's unconcealment meets the horizon surrounding it. This view results in panentheism, or the ultimate reduction of being's unconcealment to God. God is in all things as the horizon surrounding the possibility of there being something rather than nothing.

At the first level, the reduction of matter to mind is what gives the person an identity. At the second level, it allows us to intuit God's existence beyond creator. We can recognize the existence of both orders in the psyche. The existence of embodied mind in relationships points to the horizon surrounding the nothing, as the focal possibility of being in relationships. It points to the effects of a divine mind in us, as Eckhart already knows. We know ourselves to be ultimately reducible to the divine intellect, although the insight is frequently buried deep in the layers of our unconscious. However, the study of the psychological principles that accompany how we think reveals our God-consciousness. It is brought out in special spiritual moments of insight.

The epistemic awareness of God's existence is played out in two scenes. First, the nothing that surrounds mind points to the possibility of knowing ourselves as beings in relationships. Second, it points to the possibility of being's unconcealment. These two moments of phenomenal experience form a unit. Our psychic awareness points toward the ontic reality of God. They are not separate movements, but notes in a single melody of existence. Thus, God is seen to be creator of the natural order, while the reality of God exists beyond the natural order. Eckhart's God exists beyond being at a place where the possibility of being's unconcealment is rooted. His lament, "God, free me from God," is an attempt to move beyond temporality, or the creator, to the deepest reality expressed in the psyche. But is this possible? Can we move beyond the nothing surrounding being to the horizon surrounding the nothing? The evidence of a human life suggests that it is possible to do so if something within us, as rooted in the natural order, points toward the timeless.

The oxymoronic character of death suggests that this is indeed the case. The person is simultaneously this-worldly and other-worldly. We know ourselves as being both temporal and eternal. No dualism exists in an oxymoron. The person is both dependent and independent of being. We exist in the likeness of God. This is what Hick sees. Our representation of God is also oxymoronic. Jung puts it differently, but expresses the same idea when he says that God is the ultimate source of good and evil. Mind as temporal requires being to operate, but God also requires being to exist as creator. Mind as temporal can refuse God as a being toward evil, but mind as eternal–our being toward good–recognizes that the possibility of the refusal is rooted outside itself. We are a dynamic interplay of both processes in the person-making ritual of human life. Thus, the denial of a creator negates itself, moving into a higher synthesis of God-consciousness. This is perhaps the cause of our existential restlessness. Our eternal being recognizes that the possibility of being is rooted in God. God is temporal and beyond time as the ultimate source of time in us.

How can God be timeless and in time? This is a complex question. Serious scholars such as Paul Helm (1988) have already struggled with the problem. An answer is contained in our own person-making nature. The oxymoron is not a logical impossibility. Like God, we appear to be temporal and above time. Spiritual enlightenment arises as a process of discovering the presence of the eternal in the temporal. To affirm that we are made in the likeness of God is to recognize and affirm the connection between these two orders of existence. The person-making process is one in which we move toward morality as dialectical (or dialogical) process on the arms of these opposites. The propositions of morality are seen to arise as a process in which the absolute descends to meet the particulars of circumstance, while the particulars ascend to meet eternal truths.

God as immanent in the natural order, or creator, marks the possibility of the nothing that surrounds being. God as transcendent, or reality beyond the natural order, marks the horizon that surrounds the nothing. The God beyond creator is unknowable as such, but God as the nothing that surrounds being is known as the ultimate cause of there being something rather than nothing. This is why the world makes sense. Eckhart's God is the God that surrounds the nothing of being, or the horizon of the nothing. It provides an instance of God at work creating the possibility in which being exists as unconcealment, bordered by nothingness. But the nature of God beyond this work is unknowable in itself, although the human heart sees God as a loving presence. This representation explains the longing of the human heart to be one with God, the source of all availability.

The existence of God beyond the natural world would remain problematic without the inclusion of the eternal in our own temporal way of seeing the world. In materialism, the belief is expressed that we cannot know anything beyond the natural order, since we are natural beings. The argument has a certain appeal. A finite mind cannot use finite processes to recognize itself as being infinite. How, then, does the mind know this? The simple answer is that the intellect's thirst for truth is insatiable. The insight points beyond itself to the awareness of our own Jobian insignificance standing in the presence of the Almighty. We are a spark that transcends itself. We are like the creator. The insight, since it arises beyond the level of intellect and sense, calls for a renewed Kierkegaardian leap into the arms of the divinity. God's loving invitation takes us places where reason cannot go.

The reducibility of being's unconcealment to the creator and subsequently to God parallels our own reducibility of matter to mind. Thus, to become aware of the divinity in psyche is to recognize the possibility that God also exists as the horizon of the nothing surrounding being. God's temporality encompasses the whole of the cosmos or the nothingness of being, while God's timelessness transcends the natural order, or the nothing. Although cosmos is reducible to God, as matter is to mind, the God beyond the creator is the horizon surrounding cosmos, containing the possibility of the nothing.

What if an additional layer of intelligence exists beyond the horizon of being's unconcealment? That cannot be the case since an endless chain of subordinate causes does not provide a sufficient reason for being's unconcealment. We exist in truth, seeking explanations. Although the principle of sufficient reason cannot venture beyond temporality, or identify an uncaused cause, the principle points beyond logic to the ultimate ground of being rational. That search animates mysticism. The experience suggests that God is the uncaused Horizon of being, the I Am who Am, as Scripture teaches us.

To experience the nature of God's presence in being, we focus on the things of our experience. Our world is bordered by nothingness. The nothing surrounding us defines the cosmos. It marks the boundary or form of existence. There would be no cosmos without the nothing. Since God is the horizon that borders the nothing surrounding being, cosmos is intelligible because God is the ultimate possibility of the nothing, of something rather than nothing at all. But God is not cosmos. God is present in the world without being identified with it. This view is not pantheistic. It is panentheistic: God is both immanent and transcendent. At the macroscopic level, God is the horizon of the nothing that borders the cosmos. There can be no cosmos without God.

The experience of mysticism allows us to see the existence of God in all things. It is a presence that is unintelligible without sense or intellect, although it exists beyond sense as the possibility of sense. The experience of encountering God in being overwhelms us. It cannot be adequately expressed through language. We use words to point to a place that exists beyond the word. We write poetry about the experience, but not the perfect poem. Eckhart sees this as he recognizes that any representation of God is a limitation. He looks beyond the creator to find God. But Heidegger prefers to wait. He waits on the source of the nothing to illuminate itself. He deals with it by letting it deal with *Dasein*. But the truth of the nothing's unhiddenness or unconcealment is not forthcoming. It remains unaware in his psyche. This is not surprising. Heidegger is bruised in the round with eternal truths. The struggle to liberate *Dasein* from eternal truths is fresh in his mind. *Dasein* is forced to remain rooted in temporality. Yet, the unconcealment of the nothing haunts him, pointing beyond itself. Heidegger peeks and no doubt sees, but says nothing. His view is at an end.

4. God as Abba: The Lord's Prayer, Then and Now

So, the evidence suggests the existence of the divinity in psyche, other human beings, and now in the horizon of being's unconcealment. The person-making process is executed in this trinitarian relation, as we freely pursue the good and evil inclinations of psyche. The person-making process is free since it is animated by the profound love, or "letting be" God has for us.

The intensity of God's love for persons is expressed in the Aramaic text of the Lord's Prayer, although the King James translation does not convey the prayer's original mystical fervor. Below is Neil Douglas-Klotz's (1990) interpretation of the Aramaic text. It appears in his powerful book, *Prayers of the Cosmos: Meditations on the Aramaic Words of Jesus.* This section is a commentary on that text. The book's Foreword is by Matthew Fox, Founding Director, Institute of Culture and Creation Spirituality. He praises the book's practical nature: "This is a book that allows us to experience the Scriptures once again through the heart, which means through the body, which means on earth, the source and origin of our bodies." The earthy character of the prayer is significant since it supports the suggestion that the creator might in fact be God.

Douglas-Klotz locates the ways of the divinity in the human heart, in accordance with the teachings of the major world religions. To experience Scripture "from the heart" is to draw on the mystical elements that lie at the core of the teachings of Jesus within us. The function of prayer is to empower us toward this release.

The Lord's Prayer invites us to meditate on the nature of God as person within us. The response to the invitation prepares us to dwell in the unhiddenness of "*Abwoon*" or God as Abba. Douglas-Klotz suggests "body prayers" as a means of enhancing our discovery of the divinity within (p. 15). The phenomenological analysis of the text yields insight into the richness of Aramaic and of Jewish mysticism. It conveys the urgency of divine love for us. The prayer is earthy, full of the practicality of every day living. While adhering to the spirit of the translation, the following commentary is my own interpretation of spiritual processes. The *King James* English form of the Lord's Prayer (*Matthew,* 6:9-13) appears in parenthesis for comparative purposes. Here, then, is the Aramaic version of God's love for us:

O Birther! Father-Mother of the Cosmos,
(Our Father which art in heaven)

Focus your light within us—make it useful:
(Hallowed be thy name.)

Create your reign of unity now—

(Thy kingdom come.)

Your one desire then acts with ours,
as in all light, so in all forms.
(Thy will be done in Earth, as it is in Heaven.)

Grant what we need each day in bread and insight.
(Give us this day our daily bread.)

Loose the cords of mistakes binding us,
as we release the strands we hold
of others' guilt.
(And forgive us our debts, as we forgive our debtors.)

Don't let surface things delude us,
(And lead us not into temptation,)

But free us from what holds us back.
(but deliver us from evil.)

From you is born all ruling will,
the power and the life to do,
the song that beautifies all,
from age to age it renews.
(For thine is the kingdom, and the power, and the glory, for ever.)

Truly–power to these statements–
may they be the ground from which all
my actions grow: Amen. (P. 41)

The prayer opens with the Hebrew "*Avenu shebashamiyim,*" a phrase that has been used for millennia to start prayers: "O Birther! Father-Mother of the Cosmos." The reverence characteristic of the person humbly standing in the presence of God is evident in the exclamation "O." This powerful experience is seated in the recognition that God is Birther, or creator, the source of all life, the Horizon surrounding the nothing of being. God is seen to enter into relationship with us and cosmos at a personal level. No experience is more sacred than standing in the presence of our "Mighty Birther."

The reference to "heaven" is an invitation to search out cosmos within the human psyche. Heaven is a cosmic, psychic force within us. It cannot exist outside of us since God is the All inclusive reality of existence. The prayer's purpose (and the goal of religion) is to facilitate reconnecting with that inner place. That view is consistent with systems theory in which we know ourselves to be part of a cosmic process of becoming. We are one of the strands in the web of interlocking cosmic systems. The religious connection provides an opportunity for a spiritual awakening, or birthing experience. We experience birthing in parenting, gardening, nurturing, and by entering into relationships with other cosmic threads that make up the whole of creation. The reference to God as "Birther" points to our own experience of giving life. God the "Birther" teaches us how to pray, using references familiar to us. The line lays the foundation for the conception of the other as an extension of the divinity within our own psyche, as the child is an extension of the parents. The prayer is not an invitation to a confrontation between femininity and masculinity, but a recognition that they are the twin perspectives of our own birthing psyche. In Chinese culture, for instance, personality arises as a dynamic interplay between the yin (feminine), and the yang (masculine) of a person. This view seems to have been forgotten in our patriarchal culture. The *King James* translation focuses only on God as Father. The narrowing is perpetrated in religion whenever the feminine within us is assigned a secondary role.

The *KJV* suggestion that Heaven is a place that exists outside the human psyche is unacceptable since it invokes dualism or separation of the person from God and the cosmos. The tradition is guilty of seating God (and cosmos) outside the human heart.

In the second line of the prayer, we plead with God to "Focus your light within us–make it useful": The process of focusing light contains a reference to being's unconcealment as we discover the existence of eternal truths in history. The line is familiar to Jews as the first line of the *Kaddish*, or the Mourner's Prayer. We yearn to reconnect with the source of all possibilities. The mystical tradition celebrates the person's total dependence on the truth of God. God is the horizon of all things, or the nothing that surrounds our experience of being. This is the place of Eckhart's God beyond God. But we know God through our own framework of spatio-temporal, psychological particulars. We know God as Birther or creator. The mystic is aware that the unconcealment of being is rooted in a deeper, more profound truth of God's love for us–the horizon of creator. This is what Heidegger appears to sense, but does not express. The reference to making the love useful also conveys our responsibility to plant the seed of love in our own relationships with others and the environment through informed social action. We too are birthers. Social action grows out of respect for the existence of the divinity within us, the other, and nature. Divine light radiates through us toward others and the environment. We are not persons because of our *a priori* knowledge of eternal truths, since we co-create their outcomes in history. God is known through the creator's effects on us.

In the third line of the prayer, "Create your reign of unity now–," we experience the unity that characterizes mysticism. The line from the Jewish "*Aleinu*" prayer is said at the conclusion of every prayer service, and in the important *Mussaf* service on *Yom Kippur*. It expresses a faith that good shall ultimately triumph in the struggle between good and evil. But the realization of the divine telos depends on us, since we are assigned a positive role in co-creating cosmos. We hope evil shall not divide us. However, our experience of the world is often broken, stirred by want, greed, and the need to control being's unconcealment. Issues of pain and suffering as often as joy and ecstasy surface.

The prayer extends an invitation to move beyond discord by acting toward the good expressed in psyche. The divine telos centers on the outcome of the person-making process of human life. Evil frustrates the divine telos since it introduces division. In the beginning, the cosmos was intended to be whole, but the forces of evil continually invade the righteousness and justice of the cosmos. If division occurs in either of these two pillars, creation becomes off balance.

The fourth line of the prayer, "Your one desire then acts with ours, as in all light, so in all forms," expresses one of the most profound parts of the prayer, namely, that God's one desire, or telos, accords with our own desire to do good and avoid evil. To say to the other "your one desire be done" is to unconditionally express a desire for the good of the other. Love is a process of moving out of our own selfish concerns by placing the good of the other ahead of our own interests. Mature love is not an attempt to dominate or control the other, but it is a "letting be" of the other. To say to the other "I love you" is to voice an unconditional concern for the well-being of the other. The concern is not inauthentic or problematic. To affirm a desire for the will of the other is to express (and risk) trust in the other. The loved one can abuse or refuse the gift.

The trust we have for others (in love) is framed in the next line of the prayer, beginning; "Grant what we need each day in bread and insight" as a request for the wisdom required to know Creator as God. The term "bread" emerges as the ontological ground of loving relationships. But we are frequently unaware of the love God has for us. In Christianity, for instance, the death and resurrection of Christ is profoundly significant. Yet, the cross remains a mystery; why would the Christ God die for us? The Lord's Prayer invokes the wisdom required to make sense of the dying to self that exists in loving relationships. Emotivism stands in sharp contrast to love, since it affirms the divisive primacy of my own will, or best interest. The request for "bread and insight" is recited in the first paragraph of the Jewish Grace After Meals prayer, "*Hu nosain lechem l'chol basar*." God is a person of whom qualities such as wisdom and power are predicated. We ask that these be given us. We cannot be human without these gifts. They are the most important gifts we can receive, although God's ways are not always clear to us. Perhaps no better expression of the person-making challenge is found than in Reinhold Niebuhr's (1892-1971) *Prayer of Serenity*: that we may possess the wisdom required to distinguish between those aspects of life which can and cannot be changed. Serenity is the acceptance of what cannot be changed, while courage changes what can be changed. Wisdom is intelligence having matured beyond the realm of reason and logic. The wise person possesses the insight of self-control: we cannot change others, but we can change ourselves. We can then empower others to find their own empowerment within. We then exist as one, in divinity. Since nothing is outside of us, we adopt an unselfish attitude toward the world, a non-confrontational way of framing things.

The line also implores God to feed and clothe us, as the birds are fed and clothed. We plead with God to originate the root of the possibility of doing so. We ask for the blessing required to function wisely as co-creators of the world. But we lack wisdom and do not always act responsibly.

We make mistakes and ask to be forgiven; "Loose the cords of mistakes binding us, as we release the strands we hold of others' guilt." The prayer issues a plea for a deep letting go of our mistakes at the psychological, ethical and metaphysical levels of existence. The request is repeated many times in *Yom Kippur* prayers to be allowed to return to the original state of choosing between good and evil, a state that precedes the decision to act toward evil. But God is forgiving. Once we become aware of God's forgiveness, then our hearts are freed to forgive ourselves, others, and the environment. The forgiveness of others emerges at the ethical level of existence as a letting be of others. We empower them as we ourselves are empowered by forgiveness. The letting be is also executed at the metaphysical level as a plea to be *Dasein*-like toward the environment or being's unconcealment. It invokes a disclosure of the unconcealment of being in us, that we might dwell in the house of truth.

Forgiveness is accompanied by a change of attitude in which we are no longer deceived by the surface appearance of things; "Don't let surface things delude us." We receive the gift of framing reality differently. Although being's unconcealment is offered equally to us, the attitude we take toward it is one of good or evil. The prayer says that our failure to move beyond the superficial level of things arises as a willingness to be deceived by the superficial attraction of evil. It asks for enlightenment that in our person-making processes we might be able to discern the existence of a deeper, sacramental level of being's unconcealment. We are asking to be freed "from what holds us back."

Scholars do not agree on whether the next line, "For thine is the kingdom," was originally included in the prayer. The Jewish phrase "*L'cha, adoshem*" translates as "the greatness and the power and the glory." The prayer is recited in a Sabbath morning prayer just prior to the reading of the *Torah* in the synagogue. Douglas-Klotz says that the legitimacy of the line "revolves around how old and authoritative one judges the Aramaic *Pershitta* version to be" (p. 38). Matthew's version includes the line, but Luke's does not.

The return to God as creator completes the cycle begun at the prayer's opening. This interpretation is consistent with a view in which all things are said to emanate from God, only to return to God at end times. The sense is that the person-making process comes to an end in God. But in coming to an end it achieves a new beginning. The victory of good over evil is the final triumph of the person in becoming aware of the sacramental level of being's unconcealment. The enlightenment moves the person away from selfish concerns toward the original sense of cosmos as blessing, forever and ever "*L'dor va'dor.*"

God exists in timeless eternity. We can only identify God through God's attributes. The reference to God as "Birther" allows us to name God by reference to our most sacred experiences, to see God in a personal way. We give birth to both good and evil. Although God is beyond good and evil, the creator sets the metaphysical stage for the person-making process. We dwell in the house of eternal truths unfolding in history, truths that are found at the deeper, sacramental level of being's unconcealment. But we can also live in the world of Plato's shadows by fixing on secular goods.

The *Book of Job* raised the important issue of God's responsibility for evil. We concluded that God as creator is responsible for the limitations or imperfections of the created world, but not for moral evil, since the person-making process cannot take place without a struggle. Creation cannot be as perfect as God since it follows after God, and thus is necessarily limited. But it allows for the possibility of becoming God-like, or cleansing ourselves of the limitation within psyche. The fact that an All Powerful God chooses "Birthing" rather than not birthing also gives us assurance that we shall receive the gifts required to move toward the good. God gives us gifts (not to be misled by the surface appearance of things), namely, love, wisdom, reason, free will, knowledge of the distinction between good and evil in the human heart, a way to pray. These gifts anchor the possibility of the person-making process. While the world of appearances is not necessarily evil in itself, it becomes so when we mistake it for the sacred order of existence, or refuse God's gift of discernment. The greatest act of ignorance is selfishness or pride, placing the puffery of an ego above the primacy of divine patterns or laws.

The Aramaic text of the Lord's prayer contains a powerful mission statement. Unfortunately, the *King James* version reads as an anemic offprint of the original Aramaic text. It bears the imprint of a church culture steeped in dualism and the patriarchy. The reference to "Father," as well as to the division between heaven and earth, reflects a long history of dualism and male domination in the Church. The *KJV* does not give adequate expression to the insight required to distinguish between the world of appearances and the sacramental order of being's unconcealment. Further, it contains no appeal to the feminine character of relationships or to the unity between heaven and earth as sources of empowerment within us, for others, self, and cosmos. But it does show how easily we can be deceived by the surface appearance of things.

Nine

FRAMING REALITY: KNOWLEDGE AND BELIEFS

While the previous two chapters have traced the connection between matter (B) and God (G), the present chapter examines the secular (materialist) approaches to reality. Subsequent chapters (Ten and Eleven) examine the epistemological foundations of secularism in the work of two Rationalist thinkers, Descartes and Meyerson, and the making of the technocratic mentality.

Two fundamental ways of standing in the presence of being's unconcealment, or framing reality, exist: the one at the level of appearance, the other at the sacramental level of reality. In our day, the distrust of metaphysics reflects a tendency to stand before being at the level of appearance. We are easily deceived by the false ideology of a materialistic culture. We celebrate money, power, control, dominion over nature and people. But our deep-seated anxiety about our future, the impending sense that something is wrong with the world, signals a dissatisfaction with the loss of ethical values. The inability to see beyond the superficial level of being's unconcealment is deeply ingrained in the technocratic mentality. The Aramaic text of the Lord's prayer provides us with an ethical perspective to move beyond the emotivism and relativism of secularism into the mystery of standing in the presence of being's unconcealment. The sacramental order of being contains an invitation to the discovery of the sacred in temporality. It exists as the horizon surrounding the possibility of being. The awareness of the sacramental perspective of being is salvific since it saves us from the consequences of embracing materialism. The possibility of standing in the presence of being as gift leads to the awareness that we freely choose our attitude toward being. We can act toward being as evil, or act toward it as good. The possibility of framing being is not only the result of something we do or fail to do, however. It is characteristic of our finitude. But in our response to finitude we can either deny or affirm the primacy of the sacred. Being is already there for us before we develop the attitude. The attitude is the result of framing being or limiting being's unconcealment in some particular way. For as long as we live, being's unconcealment is rooted in the garb of space and time. We see being as through the refracting property of a medium that can distort our perception of the world. Things that exist necessarily, appear to exist contingently. Thus, we often forsake the sacred in pursuit of the secular. But the awareness of existence as gift leads to appreciation of the blessed "Birther." Although the gift of life is reclaimed at human death, it is not annihilated. On the contrary, it seems possible to suggest that being's unconcealment will continue. A belief in the sacred order is not an illusion. But how do we know this?

We are back to circularity or the problem of the wheel. I need a criterion to determine if things really are as they seem to be. The Hindu word for appearance is "*maya*." This suggests an underlying order or structure that empowers "*maya*" to manifest itself. Husserl develops phenomenology as a method for laying bare the nature of the implicate order. But he questions himself over and over again on the possibility of the reduction. The problem is that structure is attained as a reconstruction of "*maya*." We cannot know which properties of "*maya*" are true. Both Hume and Kant came face to face with the problem. While history teaches us that they did not show us the right path, they do teach us where the path is not. The path toward enlightenment is not found in skepticism, and it is not found in the synthetic *a priori* propositions. It might be found in a reverse ordering where the individual emanates from the universal.

Analytic philosophy suggests a useful distinction between knowledge and beliefs; we should only say we know something when we attain knowledge that is certain. But a belief is provisional since it carries uncertainty. Our beliefs are true or false. But knowledge is always certain. The individual that knows something expresses it with conviction. Knowledge as such is not true or false. For instance, when I claim that the noise I hear is loud, I cannot be mistaken about it. But when I say the noise comes from a particular source, I can be mistaken. I need to uncover the evidence to support my claim about the source. Once I find that evidence, I can support my claim and my belief will have been shown to be true. But perhaps I am deceived into believing that something is true when in fact it is false. The ability to discover that a proposition is false is indeed what leads me to abandon certain beliefs about reality. But I am not mistaken in my knowledge that I am sitting at a desk, or that the noise is loud. This is the strong sense of knowing something. The knowledge of absolutes is of that nature. Yet, science can show me that I was mistaken about my beliefs concerning the source of the noise. In that event, I would say that what I thought was knowledge was in fact a belief, which science has shown to be false. But the possibility of doing science is not relative. It is a given. Thus, it is not true that everything is relative to context. If I claim (p), then, the claim can be proven true or false. But the knowledge that I can verify my claims is not itself relative. The ability to distinguish between truth and falsity presupposes the existence of a constant within reason. How else would I recognize falsity? Thus, at least one belief cannot be proven false. This truth is inconsistent with being a skeptic.

The skeptic has knowledge, or at least one absolute that cannot be contested. That being the case, skepticism is a belief shown to be false. In order to avoid the dilemma of Humean skepticism, we need to prove that some of our claims are knowledge claims. The application of theory to practice confirms the view. The fact that we can survive implicates the non-relativistic convergence of reason and reality. In our practical work, we act as if the absolute exists. Although everything in science seems to be limited and approximate, Capra (1992) says: "scientists very often act as if there were absolute truths" (p. 150). Scientists never question truths such as the possibility of doing science, although some scientists such as Einstein wondered why nature should conform to our thoughts. He was expressing an awareness of being's unconcealment as a gift. This is knowledge. He knew himself to be standing in the presence of the creator. The contradiction of skepticism is a reminder of our fundamental insignificance. Having entered into the house of doubt, we sense our own frailty. We are forced to exit skepticism as wounded warriors, in submission to the existence of eternal truths. However, the existence of the absolute is discovered in history, specifically in the history of our relationships. We discover that no relationship is possible without the absolute. The lesson learned from skepticism transforms the defeat of reason into the possibility of insight. It provides the authentic justification for a Kierkegaardian leap into the risk of knowledge. Having risked himself in knowledge, he gained certainty. Other risks are also worth taking: We can know, for instance, that the existence of being is given in a theory of direct perception. We do not need to prove the existence of the world, as Heidegger and Wittgenstein already know. Our being-there in the everydayness of things is already upon us. We can also risk jumping into the arms of God since it legitimates the possibility of being's unconcealment. Being is already upon us, she engulfs us. How, then, do we characterize the attitude of standing in the presence of being, if not through the awareness of standing in the sacred presence of an absolute?

The perspective of reality as sacramental is not one in which we sink away from the surface of being. Our openness toward the engulfing of being exists in the human heart as an expression of the divinity in us and in others. It is voiced as the possibility of dwelling in truth. The pursuit of the ultimate good is a process in which we willingly participate in the presence of mystery.

Once we artificially split the Heideggerian atom, we discover the authentic attitude of the *Dasein* dwelling in being's unconcealment. The moment of phenomenal experience opens into the presence of the sacred. Heidegger sees our being there as a precious moment of conversation in being's unconcealment. The text suggests more "unhiddenness" is forthcoming, but in the end, Heidegger does not completely allow being to engulf him. This is surprising. Heidegger's notion of truth is taken from the Greek "*aletheia*" meaning that truth deliberately unhides itself, it lights itself up. Yet, his work contains darkness. Perhaps the attitude reflects his own way of framing reality. The project begun in *Sein und Zeit* could not be completed without the leap into the arms of a creator. This is a truth Kierkegaard knew. But it is a truth Heidegger would not disclose.

Ten

DESCARTES AND MEYERSON

Although Canadian winters can be charming, ice storms in the Ottawa, Montréal, and Québec City regions in the late Winter of 1998 remind us of our need for protection and survival. The triumphs of science and technology allow us to predict and control nature, even if only some of the times. We learn from past events to better prepare for the future. But the need to survive carries a second principle affirming the inherent worth of nature. The age of pure analysis, however, overlooks the worth of nature, as well as the hegemony of scientific research in which interrelated systems such as culture, society, economics, and politics all play a part. As a consequence, the Rationalist attitude places the survival not only of the planet but of all life forms at risk. In our day of systemic thinking (as opposed to piecemeal), developments in science and technology move out of a profound respect for the nature we are seeking to control. We know that to exploit nature is to exploit ourselves. Yet, this belief was not always evident. This section examines the work of two Rationalists in some detail in order to highlight the consequences of framing the world into constituent parts such as atoms or elementary particles. The evidence that this road goes nowhere exists in the fact that Descartes and Meyerson *are led to conclusions they would rather not accept*. The irony is that their attitude continues to threaten the planet. While this chapter discusses the epistemological foundations of the age of analysis, the next chapter examines its application in technological developments. Science and technology are but two sides of the same cultural coin.

The work of Meyerson is an attempt to recapture the structural world that underlies the world of appearances. He is guided in that effort by Descartes's mathematical method, and by Kant's focus on the *a priori* structure of reason. The fact that this structure leads Kant to the conclusion that reality is noumenal or unknowable does not surprise Meyerson. He appears to welcome it. He says (1933): "Nothing about Kant's idea of reality as being essentially unknowable leads us to think he was wrong about it" (p. 21, my translation).

At first brush, there appears to be some inconsistency in that position since the whole of his work is an attempt to refute the Positivistic claim that description is the only business of science. The whole of Meyerson's work revolves around the central theme that a concern for ontology or structure cannot remain foreign to science. Yet, the unknowability of that structure is a recurring theme in his work. That view is expressed in *Du cheminement de la pensée* (1931), and again in *Essais* (1936). The concern for structure is manifest each time we think because thought is identificatory. Although this remains the single most disputed issue of his philosophy, he leaves no doubt that identification is at least part of the thinking process, if not the whole of it. Meyerson's research into the ways of reason is impressive. His first work, *Identité et réalité,* published in 1908 is the product of nineteen years of research into the psychological principles that accompany scientific inductions. According to him, the whole of science, from its earliest beginnings to its latest developments, uses identifications to explain phenomena. His work is comprehensive. The next book, *De l'explication dans les sciences* (2 vols.), first published in 1921, continues the probe into the psychology of science, while *La déduction relativiste*, published in 1925 is a study of Relativity Physics. Einstein expressed agreement and admiration for what Meyerson says about the psychology of thought. Finally, *Du cheminement de la pensée* (3 vols.), published in 1931, extends the tendency of identification into the realm of everyday language. These, along with *Essais* (1936), a posthumous publication of his major articles (Meyerson provided his own list), constitute the whole of his work. What are we to make of his expressed concern for structure? If we take structure to include, not only the metaphysical foundation of science, but also the objective ground of ethics and positive laws, Meyerson is no doubt right. The critical point remains whether rationalism provides that absolute base, or destroys it.

Meyerson has been acclaimed as one of the most stimulating philosophers of the early twentieth century. The title "profound philosopher" which Henri Bergson conferred upon him in 1909 is well merited. Competent critics such as George Boas, André Bonnard, Charles De Koninck, Joseph La Lumia, George Mourélos, Henri Sée, and Colleen G. Sterling, have each been impressed by his work. André Metz devoted much of his own work to the study of his thought. Jacob Lowenberg (1932) hails him as a new Kant. Whenever Einstein was in Paris, he always made it a point to visit Meyerson. On the occasion of Meyerson's death in 1933, *Nouvelles Littéraires,* a leading Paris publication, announced him as being "Notre plus grand philosophe des sciences." The appeal of Meyerson's work is immense since he is a Rationalist in what is best of the cartesian tradition. He acknowledges his personal debt to Descartes in an interview with Frédéric Lefevre on 6 November 1926, where Meyerson is quoted as saying about him: "the greatest mind ever produced by history, a thinker whom ancient philosophers would have transformed into a God" (my translation). Given this, we might expect Meyerson to rise above relativism, but his thought takes an unexpected turn.

Meyerson's rationalism is excessive, however. He says that the whole of thought is governed by two *a priori* principles which he likens to instincts: legality and causality. The first of these stipulates that we are genetically programed to think of nature "as attending herself with some degree of regularity." The second principle of reason goes further than this, suggesting that we are also programed to search for structure whenever we think. If nature attends herself with some degree of regularity, it is because she is structured to behave in regular fashion. Description cannot be the only business of science. The psychology of our scientific induction proves otherwise. Science exhibits a concern for ontology. Meyerson's focus, however, is not normative, but factual. He is not intent on laying bare the nature of the persistent residuum, whether the atom or some constituent particle within it, but only with the exigency of reason to postulate its existence. The propositions of science (and ethics) are incomprehensible without reference to structure. He draws his evidence from the whole of science, beginning with the early atomism of Leucippus and Democritus, progressing to Aristotelian qualitative theories, including the quantitative theories of rational mechanics, from Einstein's relativity physics to Heisenberg's quantum physics. He even extends the process to the level of common sense thinking. The whole of science, including common sense, expresses a concern for ontology. Yet, something is wrong because his Rationalist insistence on structure deconstructs the possibility of doing science. When the last thought is expressed, and the final word written, we end up without ontology.

The goal of Meyersonian science is to explain reality through successive identifications. The more we succeed in explaining and therefore predicting a course of events, the greater the control we have over nature. In theory, our degree of control is reducible to the formulation of increasingly comprehensive identity propositions. The movements of reason take place in two progressive stages. In the first stage, we recognize that a given consequent cannot be other than it is because reason has identified its cause or sufficient and necessary conditions in an antecedent set of events. Thus, we can forecast that whenever a known set of conditions affect the properties of a substance, a predictable set of behavioral effects follows. The success of science is based on the identification of antecedent and consequent elements of change. The identification of cause and effect, however, means that change must be an illusion. The first atomic theory of matter was developed as an attempt to explain that illusion. Meyerson's rationalism relegates the differences between antecedent and consequent to a spatial rearrangement of properties in the Kantian tradition. His slight shift away from Kant is that we sometimes think of space as being wholly *a priori* when in fact some aspects of it are seen to be determined *a posteriori.* While the progress of change is stopped in the first movement of reason, the second movement goes even further by eliminating time. If no fundamental difference between antecedent and consequent is observed, not only is there no change, but time must also be an illusion since it measures the intervals of change. The process of identification goes even further: If we are led to the observation that the whole of reality is reducible to "cubes" we must now inquire why cubes rather than "globules" of matter? Since all that is left at this point of the reduction is a fundamental particle in space, reason pushes the particle into space through the identification of the two. Space emptied of contents vanishes in turn. Nothing is left. Once reason can no longer identify, it disappears in turn. What has gone wrong?

The Cartesian philosopher has access to reality by having access to his own brain. Reality is known in the absence of the observer. But the brain cannot function without something to identify. Fortunately, Meyerson points out that identification is only a tendency of reason. We do not actually succeed in positing ourselves into non-being because nothing of reality lends itself to the formula of identification.

Sadi Carnot is the hero of science because his pioneering work in thermodynamics published in 1824 as *Réflexions sur la puissance motrice du feu* warns that the goal of total identification is illusory. It costs energy to do work. Thus, the identification of phenomena supposed by rational mechanics is not at hand. At the same time, Carnot's principle possesses nothing that is pleasing to reason. Meyerson explains that it lapses into a period of forgetfulness for thirty years before being discovered anew by Clausius in his own work on heat published in *Poggendorf's Annalen* from 1848 to 1862. The discovery was for a time known as the Carnot-Clausius Law of Thermodynamics, although Clausius recognized that Carnot had established an earlier claim to it.

Meyerson's work takes a turn: Nothing of reality lends itself to the formula of identification. He reserves the term "irrational" to designate places of recalcitrance between reason and reality. In fact the whole of science is now seen to consist of irrationals or places of irreducibility to the formula of identification. He cites impact and transitive action as instances of irrationals. The most basic irrational is diversity. Reason cannot know diversity without reducing it to identity. Thus, the Kantian thing-in-itself is born again as unknowable. The whole of Meyerson's thorough investigation into the psychology of our scientific inductions results in an all-encompassing epistemological paradox. What we do when we think and what we do when we apply theory to practice are two different things. Knowledge is not possible, yet it exists. How can the ways of reason and the ways of reality converge when nothing about reality lends itself to the formula of identification? So Meyerson has a problem. This is the same difficulty that first drew Meyerson to philosophy. About 1900, he was working as a chemist in Argenteuil. A process, sound in theory, failed in its application. Disillusioned, he left to study philosophy.

Does this problem show the error of rational mechanics? Does Meyerson suspect that reality is not reducible to increasingly comprehensive identifications, that the sacred is not reducible to the secular? Not at all. Mathematics is seen to provide the solution to the epistemological paradox. Mathematics, as Descartes knew so well, explains both identity and diversity. Meyerson's reading of Descartes leads to the view that the propositions of science are "plausible," meaning that they can be shown to contain a mix of the *a priori* quest for identity along with the empirical elements of observation. The proposition $7 + 5 = 12$, for instance, means we have identity in diversity after all. Reason continues to pursue the goal of total identification while knowing that it can only achieve partial identities.

Descartes's *Geometry*, published in 1637, together with *Meteors, Dioptrics,* and the *Discourse on Method,* is an important work. It lays the groundwork for analytical geometry as a method for the systematic investigation of known curves, negative quantities. It establishes the idea of continuity which in turn leads to the theory of function and limits. His *Geometry* also contributes to the theory of equations. The essence of the method lies in analysis or the supposition that the solution to a problem is already given in the letters a, b, and c for known quantities, and x, y, and z for unknown ones. Synthesis, on the other hand, ensures that the solution used in analysis is correct. The operation from analysis to synthesis moves through the processes of intuition and deduction. The method was not unknown to ancient geometers, but Descartes was the first to use the technique systematically and fruitfully. Thus, when Meyerson applied the method to the solution of plausible propositions, he was following the natural evolution of Descartes's deductive science. He simply picked up the play where Descartes left off. Unfortunately, the epistemological paradox announced a warning that Meyerson had heard earlier in Argenteuil, but did not heed. It announced that something was terribly wrong with the method. Although the emergence of a paradox is not in itself suggestive of a wrong, the attempt to solve it by reducing it to one of its arms is in error. In this case, he reduced being's unconcealment to the expressions of analytical geometry.

Meyerson carries the seeds of that intellectual sin to their logical term. He is caught up in cartesian dualism. The convergence of reason and reality expresses the unconcealment of being in increasingly comprehensive identity propositions, ultimately stretching reason to the point of non-existence, while their divergence results in the irrationals or the unknowability of being's unconcealment (the Kantian noumenon). The plausible proposition arises out of an epistemological vertigo between these two chasms. The real we encounter in the act of knowing is not the being of things but the result of an identification. Meyerson (1962) says that our belief in the existence of a world outside consciousness is the result of a hypostasis, a problem he finds puzzling:

> But the problem is to know how I was able to take the first step, to conceive even the possibility that something can exist outside of me, outside of my consciousness; how, supposing even that the concept of 'an outside' comes to me from another source, I had the paradoxical idea of placing in it what is my own sensation, what belongs incontestably to me. (P. 358)

Descartes has the same problem. In *The Passions of the Soul,* a work he wrote four years before his death, he wonders how the mind connects to the body—"because it is of a nature which has no relation to extension, nor dimension, nor other properties of matter of which the body is composed" (p. 345).

The lesson of rationalism is worth learning. Reality does not lend itself to the (arrogant) ways of reason. Those who do not learn it appear destined to repeat it in the future. Yet, the ways of rational mechanics animate the technocratic mentality's reduction of the sacred to the secular.

However, one additional point must be made before turning to examine how the technocratic mentality provides us with an instance of cartesianism. On what ground do we reject Descartes's absolute (the *cogito*), but not the possibility of absolute knowledge? The problem with the *cogito*, including the innate idea that God exists, is that Descartes acts as if his abstraction is the reality. But dualism provides no mechanism whereby God or any product of the cartesian mind can descend to meet the empirical particulars of cultural elements. Descartes's God cannot enter into personal relationships with the world any more than epistemology can deduce the existence of the world out of rationalist principles. If the claim to ethical beliefs is justified, God must not only be shown to exist but must be seen to enter into relationships with the cosmos as a condition of His existence. So my critique of dualism is extended to the existence of the abstract deity. God can no more exist without relationships (as a "disemcosmic" deity) than the disembodied self can act in the absence of a body. The ontological argument is based on a caricature of God as abstract being, unable to carry the force of absolute truth into the particulars of everyday life. The God of Descartes is a God without a cause. Yet, the possibility of ethics depends on the discovery of an Absolute that enters into relationships with us. Quantum physics seems to be moving in that direction, given that the creator entering into personal relationships with cosmos is God. But the evidence is not forthcoming in the technocratic mentality where the cycle of dualism is continued, as if the abstraction were the reality.

Eleven

THE TECHNOCRATIC MENTALITY

The Rationalist ambition to reduce reality to increasingly comprehensive identity propositions finds expression in the triumphs of contemporary technology. But the success of mechanization progressively gives way to a growing sense of discomfort, or malaise about the world. Credit is given to modern science and technology for responding to the original Judaic demand to demythologize nature, but the "technocratic mentality" pushes that victory beyond the pale of justice.

From the beginning of the sixteenth century, the march toward the development of increasingly comprehensive identity propositions animates the whole of the scientific community. Francis Bacon (1561-1626) emerges as one of the first theoreticians in this area, providing a modern theory of induction to conquer nature. Using a vicious metaphor he sees nature as a woman, "torturing her until she is made to reveal her secrets." Bacon's inductive science and Descartes's deductive system come together in Newton's *Principia*. From now on, induction and deduction combine in the new scientific paradigm. The Newtonian model imagines the cosmos as a mechanical system in which the parts can be measured and redistributed to suit our best interests. The period is one of rapid expansion and development as one by one the secrets of nature are unlocked. Being's unconcealment is pushed to the limit. But the drive to conquer nature is not always animated by the spirit of the person as a being toward good. Nature is exploited for the bomb and for economic profit. Corruption and greed are evident in our mismanagement of resources and impatience to own things. The age of materialism dis-empowers persons. Economic concerns drive our being toward others and the environment. While our being toward the environment is enacted at the secular level, the other is often viewed as a means toward selfish ends. The multinationals control the markets, while governments sing the praises of increasing economic activity.

As a consequence, the individual is alienated from relationships. The typical disorder in our own day is the lack of affect we display toward others. We do not trust anyone. We become detached, unable to relate to others. We live in an age of emotional suffering. When we turn inward, we find a loneliness that grows out of our loss of power, and when we turn outward we experience the other human being and the environment as a threat. The insecurity we feel toward others is met by denial and unavailability. We no longer share in the lives of others. We react to being's unconcealment by seeking to own and control things.

In our day, positive law has become the ideal natural law. The image of the human as sacred now deconstructed, the legalism of secularism triumphs. We develop non-religious ethics and celebrate our newly found economic power through the courts. Economic might makes all things right, including torture and murder. Having closed ourselves off against the transcendental experience of God in psyche, we have become our own finite Gods. But we lack omniscience: Two

World Wars, the bomb, Auschwitz, world hunger, massive unemployment, torture, increasing domestic violence, the breakdown of family values, the depletion of natural resources, the violation of human rights ... are signs that something is terribly wrong. The problem has been compounding for more than a decade. Kai Nielsen reporting in Davis (1989) provides alarming statistics: 10,000 people die of starvation each day, while 500 million suffer from malnutrition, 800 million live in extreme poverty. We allocate one trillion dollars a year to military spending, while according to the World Food Council, four billion a year committed internationally until the end of the century would feed everyone (p. 21).

Martin Heidegger is one of the first to raise environmental concerns. His testimony parallels my own focus on the sacramental perspective of being's unconcealment. *Dasein* expresses a concern for *"Wesen"* or the essence of being as unconcealment. He does not direct our attention to *quidditas* or what something is in Aristotle's sense, but to the way an entity "endures as a presence." When "weren" is used as verb, the focus is on "to dwell." Being's unconcealment dwells as presence. *Dasein's Sorge* or concern is the letting be of the entity that dwells in the house of being, so that it can endure as presence. According to the William Lovitt translation of his text (1977), Heidegger warns in *The Question of Technology* that modern *"Technik"* or technicity, is not respectful of the being of things. He observes a shift in attitude from traditional to modern technology. The essential character of traditional technology is that it is rooted in a letting be of nature, a process in which energy is simply transferred from nature. But modern technology is invasive since it transforms nature. For instance, in traditional technology, the windmill and the water-wheel stand still in the absence of wind and water. No work is done in the absence of energy. But modern technology stockpiles energy. For example, the modern power plant does not wait on nature to produce work. Things get done in the absence of wind and water. Although this appears as a positive development, the problem arises in the attitude or way we frame being. In our day, stockpiling goods arises out of greed and the desire to control more and more of nature. Being is viewed as a resource in waiting. Being stands in reserve, to be controlled, exploited, stockpiled, hoarded, and harvested by us. The *"Gestell"* or way in which we frame nature does not allow being to endure or come forth as presence. We have lost the reverence we once held for being. Our *"Gestell"* is untiring, unceasing. We are like locust on the land. The hegemony of *"techne"* has shifted from the "letting be" of being, to the control of being. We have shifted our focus from the sacred to the secular perspective of being. Technology has become a symbol of our standing at the ready to exploit nature. Heidegger's work issues a warning, and an invitation to take some distance from this way of framing being since it endangers us. "Enframing challenges forth into the frenziedness of ordering that blocks every view into the coming-to-pass of revealing and so radically endangers the relation to the essence of truth" (*ibid.,* p. 33). He invites us to take some distance from the technological attitude, lest it dominate us in turn.

Heidegger's call to "dwell in the house of being" is issued once again in the early seventies when the Club of Rome, a group of scientists brought together to examine the long-term effects of rapid developments, publishes *The Limits to Growth* (1972). The report warns that the planet cannot sustain current levels of economic development. Given the exponential increase in the depletion of non-renewable resources, in population growth, food requirements, and the pollution of the environment, the earth will not survive into the twenty-first century. E.F. Schumaker's (1911-1977) *Small Is Beautiful* (1973) suggests we study economics "as if people mattered," rather than serve the mistaken illusion that "bigger is better." In 1993, Neil Postman publishes his own indictment of the technocratic mentality in *Technopoly.* The book continues to warn about the "surrender of culture to technology," but *The Limits to Growth* has fallen on deaf ears. That fact is noted by the Club of Rome in their twenty-year follow-up to the original report, and in John Hein's report (1989) on global economic trends in the 1990s. We continue to frame being as resource in waiting and ignore the warning signs. The technocratic mentality is imbedded in how we think. It suffocates the psyche's tendency toward the sacramental perspective of reality.

Twelve

PERSONS AND MORALITY

1. The Problem

The view of person as a being in relationships shifts the focus in natural law theory, science, and technology, from human nature as abstract essence to the person-making process. This process includes the activities of the person as a being toward good, along with other beings toward good, sharing with them a responsibility for framing being at the sacramental level and the construction of a better world. The person-making attitude secures the possibility of being moral. In a sense, this is stale news since the tradition already focuses, not only on the circumstances of the human act, but also on love of neighbor and love of self. The problem with the traditional conception of natural law is twofold, however. First, it is abstract, rooted in universals. But no one actually lives in the abstract, universal world of Rationalist ethics. We are concrete beings, living in a world of pervasive technology. We often become the victims of unanticipated technological consequences. Secondly, our cultural differences enrich the expression of morality. The propositions of ethics are expressed within these two perspectives.

In the tradition, human nature is the expression of the divine law in action. We perfect ourselves by performing acts in harmony with our nature. Positive law is alleged to be moral if it is based on human nature. The just law reflects the eternal law in the human. The *Canadian Charter of Rights and Freedoms* (Canadian Ministry of Supply and Services, 1982), as well as the *Universal Declaration of Human Rights,* contains the expression of our fundamental divinity. According to natural law theory, we have a right to perfect ourselves by performing certain types of acts in harmony with our nature. But the increasing number of Charter violations is unethical for a different reason. We do not have an ethics for our times. Two aspects of the problem come to the surface. The first is a weakening belief in the deductive force of universal principles. The second is the expanding range of inductive consequences brought about by technological developments. Positive law is caught in the middle. The first point is examined through the shift in focus from the conception of the human as fixed essence to the realization of the person as a being in relationships. The second point argues for the increasing relevance of local conditions in the determination of moral behavior.

The propositions of morality arise at the term of a dialectical movement on these opposites. We trust that positive law is grounded in ethics, or that the law is moral. But this is not always the case, as we have yet to make the shift from traditional theory to recent developments in ethics. We have deconstructed human nature, and so we have no agreement or vision of the person as ethical. In the old model, the person has intrinsic value before action. In the proposed model, the person develops moral posture by entering into a systems process of relationships.

The law is an ordinance of persons in relationships promulgated for the common good of society at large, including the good of the environment.

2. Applied Ethics

The basis of transcultural ethics being deconstructed, laws are based on inductive precedent, reflecting the particular contingencies of a given locality. Laws have lost their deductive, transcultural force. The law has become the child of cultural relativism. We do not know how to behave ethically, since there is no unified agreement to secure the vision of being moral. The view of human nature, once held sacred by the tradition, has been replaced by emotivism. Recent developments in biotechnology send a message that being human is not special. Recent experiments using gene transfer technology have shown that at a basic level the genetic or DNA component of human life is interchangeable with any other life form. This leads David Roy (1989) to wonder, "where is the ethics for our knowledge and power?" (p. 113). Roy is right. Alasdair MacIntyre has already made the point. The age of emotivism provides no objective ground of value, no room for ethics. In deconstructing the base of ethics, biotechnology introduces an image of the person that commands no reverence. For instance, we can reach millions of individuals through internet, but we have no ethical rules of the road. We discuss the morality of assisted suicide, but human life has no intrinsic worth. Science and technology are heralded as the new secular religion. These empirical prophets celebrate their sacred genome projects at the political table. Economic viability is the new chant, the mantra of the age. Positive law struggles to maintain respectability. But this is a difficult challenge in the absence of the sacred. A law is no longer said to be just because it protects the rights of the individual to be God-like. In our day, justice is served when the law is properly funded. We do not "trust in God," but we do trust economic growth. The argument for emotivism appears to be winning the day.

With the first appearance of *Vera Lex* in 1979, a global community of scholars and informed social activists have agreed to debate the issues in a public forum. What is the status of natural law in the light of recent developments? One of the issues that seems to be emerging out of this debate is the view that natural law theory needs to be reformulated in the wake of technological developments. The tradition did not have to cope with rapid technological changes, thus it placed undue emphasis on the intuited, universal principles of natural law. But in our day, the second-order consequences of technological developments cannot be ignored. Thus, morality is perceived to be evolving in history. The critics of natural law theory are right to point out that the conception of the human as made in the image of God is misleading. Being God-like is not an event, it is a process. The psyche's thirst for order announces that the propositions of morality cannot be reduced to emotivism.

How shall we frame the new ethics? An ethics that is rooted in human relationships focuses on belonging. We belong to a large network of support systems that define us. We are nothing without them. They enable us to move toward the final perfection that is announced in the human psyche. Although the objective ground of ethics exists in the person's relationships, the morality of a particular course of action arises out of the singulars of local experience. Being moral is the result of a process in which the ethical base of relationships descends to meet the particulars of experience. At the same time, the particulars of experience rise to meet the universal principles of the person as a being in dialogue. The process is dialectical. The formulation of rational principles of conduct originates in the person as a being toward ultimate good, in relationship with other beings toward good. But the specification of the good is culturally based. Thus, the expressions of morality are relative to culture. However, the possibility of being ethical is a transcultural experience, rooted in the possibility of entering into relationships. All the acts of persons converge and diverge in the dynamics of the person-making process. We are the same in acting toward the good. Yet, we differ in our cultural vision of the good and how to attain it. Each human act provides a particular instance of being moral in as many instances of the good as we find cultural perspectives. Thus, our common being toward good and evil, our being toward others, and our being toward the environment provide a focal point to house the rich diversity of expressions that characterizes the pluraculture.

To be ethical is to move into relationship with others and the environment out of a common generic thrust toward ultimate good. It is to empower others and the environment by acting in conformity with the ways of the divinity in our collective psyche. We act toward the promised good, as manifest in relationships. Ethical truths are expressed in our person-making history. The process of becoming moral is dynamic. Although the possibility of being ethical exists in relationships, the realization of the ethical only arises at the term of the person-making process. Thus, while the human psyche hungers for the good promised in the divine telos, it can only be attained through culturally different other human beings. We experience confrontation between the universal and the particulars of experience. The term "confrontation" is chosen to reflect the nature of the moral life. It involves struggles between the rationalism of universal ethical theories, wanting to do universal good, and the particulars of our moral choices. The solution to ethical issues is not found by adhering to universalist theories alone (the human essence as abstract), nor is it contained in the particulars of a local grouping (cultural relativism). That conception fails to accord moral status to the action of groups outside the local community, as every relativist already knows.

Morality as dialectical process is hard won since the universal and the particular do not easily settle their differences. Nothing about the universal is particular. And local circumstances cannot be expressed abstractly. The character of the person as a being toward absolute good is best described as a tendency of the psyche. We always tend toward absolute good, although we never in fact attain that perfection, or agree in the realization of the good life in our own communities. We progress toward it. Meyerson is right about that feature of rationalism. At the same time, the expressions of morality are not wholly "irrational" since they are not reducible to cultural differences. We make moral progress at the transcultural level. But each victory is a hard won battle in the war between rational ethics and the situated values of a local group.

Morality, then, arises as person-making process, fusing the intuited need to enter into relationships with the concrete experience of a lived life. We are moral beings in the making through others and the environment. The process of person-making is dialectical, or dialogical, not the result of an abstraction. Eternal human essences do not exist outside the relationships that make us human. Being human means interacting with people we do not always like, or an environment that is not always friendly. Yet, we become human through others since they function as an extension of ourselves. To dislike the other is to dislike some aspect of the perceived good within our own psyche. To plunder the environment is to pollute our own being. Thus, ethics is not born out of the abstract heart of an individual in isolation, but in the flesh and blood interactions with the other, wanting to be God-like, or wanting to be Satan-like, singing the praises of biocentric ethics, or torturing nature for her secrets. The other is a concrete co-principle of ethical possibility. When two individuals interact, they reduce the psyche's tendency toward good to the actual realization of the good in a locale. Ethics exists at the intersubjective level of everyday life. No ethics is possible without the other and the environment. This is not to ignore our individuality, but to affirm that private thoughts become public action. The possibility of being an individual arises out of the relational character of being a person. The tendency toward ultimate good is concretized through other human beings. In our day, however, the vision of the other is growing increasingly distant. Technology desensitizes us. But the operational character of a human life takes place at the personal level of relationships. How can we be impersonal with ourselves without being ill? When a person is totally cut off from both the inside world of psychic reality and the outside world of interactions with others and the environment, no morally responsible person is there. The feeling of detachment, of being unrelated to others, seems to characterize the age of relativism.

Some critics of natural law theory appear to reject caricatures of being human. They reject a fictional representation of the person as a rational being with a direct line to the divinity. The abstract subject is alleged to be using God as an umbilical connection to the outside world. This seems to be why Heidegger rejects absolutes. He is right to do so. But natural law theory is not expressed that way. Aquinas, for instance, recognizes that the human act takes place in circumstances without reducing morality to situationalism. But he is also a mystic, and so he tends to under describe the significance of local conditions. The character of the ethical person as a being in relationships adds to his vision of being human. In our day of pervasive technology, beginning in fact with the Industrial Revolution, and continuing with nuclear reactors, we are more sensitive to the consequences of the machine on people and on the environment. It provides additional evidence that we are nothing in the absence of relationships. We are now more aware of the second-order consequences of human choices. They cause a ripple effect on the whole of the global community. The belief in a "substantial self" whether as thinking thing or subject of experiences is the product of an erroneous view of self as atomistic center of activity.

In our day, the process of moral decision-making is in turmoil because no global ethics unifies our moral choices. Recent developments in technology compound the problem. In the area of computer technology, we have greatly expanded the range of relationships with other human beings, but have yet to generate computer ethics acceptable to all parties. Issues of privacy, intellectual property rights, censorship, and pornography are some of the problems that affect relationships. The privacy issue is not about information, for instance, but it is about wanting to limit who has access to our relations. The computer is also generating a two-tier class of citizenry, since those individuals that do not have access to that educational resource are being marginalized.

The scene repeats itself in the area of genetic engineering. The Roslin Institute in Edinburgh, Scotland, recently announced that an adult mammal had been successfully cloned. Since the procedure is simple enough, the focus shifts to the feasibility of cloning humans. We can harvest human clones for organ needs, experimentation, or simply to create spare copies of our best human beings. Although human cloning is currently endorsed by few, the fluid state of moral judgments introduces the possibility that it will be morally acceptable to the next generation. This is inevitable, given the lack of agreement on what it means to be human, or given the view that human life has no intrinsic worth.

But some human beings appear to have characteristics that are worth reproducing. Why not clone a few Nobel Peace Prize Laureates, and perhaps a mystic or two? We can stockpile and harvest them as required. In the future, we might enlist the services of mystics and peacemakers to defuse explosive confrontations. But once we move beyond the level of appearances toward the objective base of being a person, it becomes apparent that being human is not only a matter of having a privileged genetic structure or being rational. The process of becoming persons is one in which we enter into relationships at the microcosmic and macrocosmic order of being. What is special about us is that we are the product of divine patterns or laws, striving to become God-like. No other living entity provides evidence of struggling with good and evil in relationships to empower/dis-empower others and cosmos. The first instance of the person as systems process is observed in the human body where the part is seen to acquire meaning in relation to the whole. The part in itself cannot represent anything, but as animated by divine laws it acts primarily for the good of the whole, and only secondarily for itself. The process extends to society and cosmos. Thus, the morality of cloning shifts to an objective base. The issue is not about technologizing *Genesis,* 1:28, or mapping the genetic way of being human; but it is about becoming human through relationships. Does the proposed clone become God-like by entering into relationships?

Morality is a dynamic, evolving issue. In the old model, cloning raises ethical concerns about the deconstruction of human nature. Once we reject the traditional argument for the existence of human nature (as abstract essence), we can revisit in fresh perspective human cloning. The issue takes on a crisper dimension, however, when it is shifted from the abstract category of human nature to the particulars of the person as a being in relationships. The critical, ethical issue now reads as follows: can the clone possess a vision of the divine within psyche; is that vision projected onto other human beings (or clones); and does the clone dwell in truth, or in being's unconcealment? If the answer is yes to all three questions, then not only is cloning ethical, but we might have an ethical responsibility to clone the marginalized. Unfortunately, the issue of cloning arises out of a secular vision of being human, namely, the inductive level of biotechnology, or the reduction of the sacred to the secular. Our primary emotional objective is to generate spare parts for ourselves and unsuspecting warriors for our unpleasant tasks. This view offers no objective belief in persons as process. The secular mentality reduces the human to a chemical formula and the divine telos to selfish beneficence. In that event cloning is not about generating other human beings at all.

Our materialist age could profit from a few more saints, however. But science cannot reproduce human relationships. To make an exact duplicate of an existing mystic is not merely to replicate a physical entity but it is to generate a being that enters into the same intensity of relationships with others as the mystic. How imagine the music of Hildegard von Bingen's *Vision* as an expression of chemistry? For manifestly that is not possible. The mystic psyche moves beyond the range of observation and measurement by waking to ecstasy in the presence of the divinity. Mysticism views the other as an extension of that divinity. It provides the grounding for a divine resonance between individuals. It extends resonance to being's unconcealment, framing reality in sacred perspective.

In mysticism, a spontaneous consonance arises between the existence of the divinity at the psychic level and the horizon that surrounds being's unconcealment. The union raises the person above the particulars of experience into the realm of the absolute. The mystic can see the face of God in a tree. Can a clone do that? The mystical experience arises at a place beyond sense and intellect, since the existence of God is not discerned empirically. As Saint Paul says, spiritual things are spiritually discerned (1 *Corinthians,* 2:14). Being human is about being spiritual. Meeting the divinity raises us to ecstasy. The traditional language of the mystical union is modeled on that of the sexual union of two lovers, completely absorbed in one another. The mystical *Song of Songs,* is struck beyond the pale of quantitative analysis where cloning takes place.

The dialectical nature of our moral judgments can also be illustrated by the nature of death as process of entering into relationships. At the biological level, human death is the death of the whole brain rather than the death of the part. Research at the cutting edge of neuroscience confirms that the mid-brain and brainstem continue to function after the death of the cortex. This only makes sense if it is known that the part functions primarily for the good of the whole. The cortex continues to fulfill its primary purpose in the absence of measurable activity or higher thought processes. As David Lamb says in Cockburn (1992), personal identity is not reducible to consciousness or cortical activity (pp. 43-56).

The Sue Rodriguez case illustrates the wider spectrum of human relationships through which moral judgments are expressed. Her case is documented in a *Senate of Canada Committee Report* (1995) on euthanasia and assisted suicide. Rodriguez, suffering from a degenerative disorder of the central nervous system, amyotrophic lateral sclerosis (ALS, also known as "Lou Gehrig's disease"), petitioned the Supreme Court of Canada for the right to obtain aid in dying. In 1994, I argued in an article published in *Policy Options* that although the Court did not grant her motion, her request has strong emotional appeal. The case is interesting since it pushes our ethical and legal imaginations to the limit. In Canada, for instance, suicide is not against the law. So, if a patient is able to directly administer her own death-causing action, even through the assistance of a robotic arm, the matter is lawful. But let a physician, or some other human being, offer aid in dying and the individual commits an offence under the *Criminal Code of Canada* (Section 241). Sue Rodriguez argued that the law preventing her from killing herself was discriminatory, since some individuals cannot commit suicide without assistance. Section 15 of the *Criminal Code* specifies that "every individual is equal before and under the law and has the right to equal protection and equal benefit of the law without discrimination and in particular, without discrimination based ... on mental or physical disability." Yet, in a narrow five to four judgment, the Supreme Court ruled against the request.

In traditional natural law theory, the debate centers on the distinction between letting die and directly causing death. We cannot ethically and legally cause the death of another human being. In some cases, however, it is ethical to let a patient die when continued treatment appears to be impractical or causes great suffering, given that the agent's intention is honest and that the good effects of the act precede the act's evil effects (death). The ethical and legal point of these cases turns on the interpretation of quality life. When does the quality of a person's life deteriorate to the extent that continued treatment is deemed to be heroic rather than the norm? And how do we measure quality of life, if not with the traditional view that all human life is sacred? One of the problems is that the traditional representation of human nature is too narrow. The view of the person as a being in relationships, or dialogue, holds more promise.

The strength of Rodriguez's argument is, in part, that she felt spiritually well with the request for aid in dying, while seeking to spare her son the unnecessary embarrassment that would follow if her own suicide became public knowledge. This view introduces two relationship criteria: first, the psyche's movement toward God, second, the dialogue with other human beings. The criteria illustrate the nature of our moral decision-making processes, of ethical principles meeting the particulars of a case. The matter is complex, but the stage is set to begin the exploration into the characteristic of the relationships. The decision to seek aid in dying arises in a given cultural setting. Each culture has the right to give relative weighting to the variables that enter into the stream of a relationship. In Western medicine, the emphasis is placed on personal autonomy or being in control, while in other cultures, the sanctity of life is the overriding concern. In our materialistic society, the need to be in control of events, including when to die, seems to dominate the decision-making process. Rodriguez is no exception.

At one level of the decision process, for instance, we examine the authenticity of her spiritual claim. When is spirituality inauthentic? Can it be falsified? We can look to a client's psychological history to determine if the request is in her best interest. Does the evidence suggest emotional problems? Is there a hospital career or history of emotional suffering? Is the request for aid in dying informed? Has the client been counseled? Rodriguez was in fact an articulate, bright, courageous, and compassionate person, fully aware of the consequences of assisted dying. Her decision is culturally defensible at this level, since she believed that her search for aid in dying was spiritually sound.

But we must consider other variables, such as her relationships with existing social institutions. This ethical criterion operates at several levels. First, what medical model are we using? The physician-patient relationship merits special attention, since it exists at the front line of the debate, providing a possible source of conflict with established guidelines. The relationship has shifted from the paternalism of an earlier day to a contractual model that encourages broad autonomy. In this model, a true sharing of responsibilities between physician and patient occurs. Should conflict arise in a proposed agreement, the contract is not made, or is broken. The contract is made in accordance with existing laws and the goals of medicine. Thus, the decision moves beyond the doctor's office to include a network of standard reporting practices to a medical board or medical advisory committees. In Canada, those committees report to provincial medical boards and to a Provincial College of Physicians and Surgeons. This is not relativism, but an open dialogue.

The fundamental ethical issue here is whether the request for aid in dying empowers or dis-empowers others. The reference to other human beings is specific. In the Rodriguez case, it includes her son and his relationships. But the matter does not end here. It also affects other ALS victims. Does the precedent discriminate against their right to life? Will it put them at risk?

As the matter stands at present, assisted dying is not sanctioned by law. Yet, some individuals obtain aid in dying through the services of a medical underground.

In that event, the act is not deemed to be moral, or legal, although it might be ethical, since the decision arises dialectically. But there is still more to consider.

At the level of the person as an entity toward being, the focus shifts to a fair allocation of scarce medical resources. Do we have the medical technology required to assure our patients a reasonable quality of life? What about costs? Unfortunately, limited resources require us to prioritize our choices. We cannot allocate resources to the treatment of every imaginable case. If we decide to make ALS relief our first priority, then, we do so at the expense of some other priority. Further, what sorts of safeguards can we put in place to protect the rights of innocent victims? Could a law that legitimates assisted dying discriminate against the frail elderly? So, the issue gets more complicated.

The medical model in place in Europe, the U.S.A., and Canada favors the young for humane reasons since their lives are still ahead of them. The decision to allocate scarce medical resources also turns on a cost-benefit analysis in which younger patients receive first priority since they are expected to live longer, thereby maximizing return on investment. In our day, however, our moral decision-making is often governed by economic considerations. We have lost sight of other equally important issues in the person-making process. Some of these factors are culturally based.

The fact that ethical action is rooted in a local culture does not reduce morality to relativism. At first blush some moral practices are difficult to appreciate. What moral value exists in female circumcision? How do African and Arab nations legitimate the behavior? What about the practice of raising a dowry through prostitution? Does that have moral worth? In some countries, cannibalism is morally acceptable, while elsewhere female embryos are aborted. While these practices can be legitimated in a cultural setting, they appear to lack universal moral merit. Cannibalism is against the law in most countries of the world. So, how can we have a unified moral theory? Christine Pierce and Donald Van De Veer (1995) ponder the issue:

> some people do believe in and practice polygamy (Africa, Asia, Utah), polyandry, cannibalism, slavery, bride-burning (for 'insufficient' dowries in India), animal and human sacrifices for religious purposes (the Aztecs at one time, the Santerian religion in Florida), eating horses and dogs as a routine part of the diet (Korea, France, China), routine clitoridectomy of young nonconsenting females (Africa) and infanticide of normal female infants (India), routine coercive extraction of bribes to do business (the Near East); many do not. (P. 470)

Still, moral relativism is not only compatible with the existence of universal ethical principles, "but is actually *implied by* this form of moral absolutism" (*ibid.*, p. 473).

While we ascribe different moral value to human acts, depending on cultural settings, they spring from a common ethical base of the person as a being in relationships. This is where we need to search out an answer to our question. What is the purpose of the act? Does it treat the other as a means or as an end? Is it spiritually significant to the individual? Seeing ethics in the light of relationships widens our focus to include a richer appreciation for the range of moral expressions that characterize the pluraculture.

On the macrocosmic scale, we also participate in giving birth to the cosmos through our choices of person-making processes with both the other and the environment. When our relationship with other entities is based on love we empower them to action. The letting be of being allows regeneration, while empowering others enlists their support in the God-like process of becoming human. We enter into a birthing process with the divinity as co-birther of the cosmos whenever we enter into authentic relationships. For as long as we act out of a principle that is guided by the presence of the divinity within psyche, we choose good and contribute to the construction of a better world, or realize the divine telos. To act toward the ultimate good of the whole is to bear the stamp of a divine birther. To act toward evil is to champion disorder and the destruction of the unity that binds us. Thus, the ethical base of action is the attitude we carry into relationships. In fact, we cannot suppose that we can act amorally or as non-ethical beings. To be human is to be ethical, although we might not always behave morally. The ethics is rooted in the possibility of the action. Thus, we always act, whether consciously or unconsciously, for either order or disorder. The unity of a human life is a unity of relationships. The greater the unity, the greater the harmony of the person-making process.

The conception of the human as a being in relationships striving to become God-like provides positive laws with the moral foundation required to establish a current of true and fresh values. The ethical principle that animates positive law originates deductively in a vision of the person as a being toward Divinity, and inductively, in the particular cultural relationships of human action. Positive laws are not relativistic since the local particulars ascend toward the universal divinity principle as expressed in relationships. While the objective precepts of law are transpersonal and transcultural, the statements of law are always the expression of a culturally sensitive morality. Although the interpretation of right conduct is seen to shift from one culture to another, the movement toward good is not reducible to emotivism. The strong element of chance that determines the expression of our moral beliefs is itself rooted in an objective foundation. As John Hick (1976) says:

> A person born in Egypt or Pakistan is very likely to be a Muslim; one born in Burma or Tibet is very likely to be a Buddhist; one born in most parts of India is likely to be a Hindu; one born in Britain or the U.S.A. is likely to be a Christian ... in all of these streams of religious beliefs there is a conception of the transcendent Eternal. (P. 31)

While the expressions of morality are dynamic, voicing the changing beliefs of different cultures, they meet in the ways of the person-making process.

The cultural dimensions of the human act are recognized in the discipline called Religious Studies. The current practice is to conduct the study of a religion through the study of sociology and anthropology since these are the repositories of culture. The measure of a society's attitudes, values, and beliefs goes a long way toward providing us with an insight into the empirical differences between the world religions. At the same time, a more complete understanding of religious experience necessarily includes insight into the transcendental realities that secure the foundation of religion, or the person-making process. This is what unites the world faiths. Seen in that light, positive law is a two-edged sword; it derives its ultimate authority from the realm of the transcendent, but it is promulgated in accordance with the cultural differences that exist among nations. Thus, positive law is by nature an evolving dynamic process that is based on the discovery of God in history rather than being fixed on some eternal, immutable vision of the ultimate good.

Thirteen

THE SCIENCE, TECHNOLOGY, SOCIETY MOVEMENT

In the 1970s, the science, technology, society movement, or STS as it is known in the literature, grew out of the realization that rapid developments in science and technology generate unanticipated and undesirable consequences in society. Technology is not value free, since it is the result of our interventions. It mirrors our goals and objectives. But the problem is that people with power can determine the kinds of technological developments that are implemented. The poor are often marginalized because of the social and political nature of technological developments.

Neil Postman (1993) writes in *Technopoly*, for instance, that technology has transformed the art of medicine or healing from a personal encounter between physician and patient to a reliance on the objectivity of the machine. America loves gadgets, he says: "Machines eliminate complexity, doubt, and ambiguity. They work swiftly, they are standardized, and they provide us with numbers that you can see and calculate with" (p. 93).

The introduction of medical technology has radically transformed the health care model. It has made it cumbersome, expensive, and impersonal. It creates an artificial distance between physician and patient. In today's society, the machine replaces the patient's personal testimony. Not only are the machine's measurements thought to be more reliable than a patient's personal witness, but they also protect the physician in the event of a malpractice suit. The high cost of medical technology also forces a physician to see more patients than before. The time spent in consultation with each patient is reduced. The critical role of relationships in the life of a human being is undermined.

The consequences of technological developments can be identified through their effects on six main interrelated areas of concern: resources, environment, economy, culture, polity, and society. The ethical issues that arise in the allocation of scarce medical resources can be examined from the perspective of these systems. From the perspective of the economic system, for instance, we wonder whether everyone has equal access to the newly found powers of medicine. The high cost of medical technology seems to favor allocating scarce medical resources to younger patients because they are expected to live longer, thereby creating a better return on investment. This is how economic factors can control the politics of allocating medical resources.

The British National Health Service does not provide renal dialysis to those aged 65 or more. Yet, by the year 2000, 12.8 percent of the population of Britain will be over 65. How do we justify the hard ethical choices confronting us in the allocation of scarce medical resources when a society cannot afford them all? We cannot treat everyone. Helga Kuhse and Peter Singer in Cockburn (1992) endorse a radical formula first developed by Alan Williams (1985), a British health economist, in which two main factors enter into play. One is life expectancy, the other is the quality-adjusted life year, or QALY.

> The essence of QALY is that it takes a year of healthy life expectancy to be worth 1, but it regards a year of unhealthy life expectancy as worth less than 1. Its precise value is lower the worse the quality of life of the unhealthy person. If being dead is worth zero, it is in principle possible for a QALY to be negative, i.e., for the quality of someone's life to be judged worse than being dead. (P. 14)

Using this formula, a patient in irreversible coma is experiencing a negative QALY or a condition worse than death. Similarly, most of Kevorkian's assisted-suicide cases can now be legitimated on an economic basis. However, the formula turns on the definition of quality life. Kuhse and Singer do not think that human life is an intrinsic good in itself. At first blush, that view appears to support the primacy of relations. But the quality of such relations is poor. Life becomes good as a precondition to other goods and values such as "the existence of pleasurable states of consciousness, the satisfaction of preferences and desires" (*ibid.*). The volume for life must be of value to the person whose life it is, in this case the pursuit of certain preferences and desires. But many individuals who pursue the good life do not seek only their own preferences. Thus, QALY operates on the basis of emotivism.

Can such a law be ethical? If the law is designed to protect the best interest of the individual, it must be seen to do so because the patient's relationships are deemed to be sacred. Personal autonomy ranks high on the scale of patient rights. In the event that a patient is unable to express his or her best interest, the courts may appoint a legal guardian to do so. This suggests informed consent, namely, that the patient (or surrogate) is fully apprized of the consequences of a treatment choice. But this is not always the case. Some patients, for instance, are pleased that their wish to be euthanized was not carried out. A partial explanation of the behavior is that in the old ethical model, the patient's level of wellness is viewed atomistically. This mechanistic representation of illness tends to favor an emotivist, self-interest approach to the quality of life. It betrays our systemic roots in relationships, or the characteristic of the person as a being toward self, others, and the world.

The issue of allocating scarce medical resources creates serious ethical responsibilities for a culture. On occasion, we must decide which of two patients has priority in the allocation of health care resources. At that point, the age bias of QALY emerges. The formula favors the young, which is not acceptable. Kuhse and Singer conclude their paper with the following remark: "some rationing of health-care services to the aged can be justified ...[we can] divert some of the savings into palliative care and seriously consider the question of active euthanasia" (p. 19).

Although they admit that these are not pleasant scenarios, rationing is already taking place in many countries and is likely to become more prevalent. A recent study commissioned by the Canadian Senate (1995) recommends palliative care for the terminally ill rather than assisted suicide. The decision-making parameters of the Senate committee are wider than QALY.

While it seems true to say that a human life does not possess "intrinsic worth" in itself, that is so because no human life exists outside relationships. The point is not that "what is there" has no value, but rather that nothing exists outside relationships. Consciousness and life expectancy are but two of a wide range of characteristics that describe being a person. Thus, QALY cannot define what it means to be a person, although a person's relationships always exist in conditions such as QALY. Kuhse and Singer substitute a condition of human life for the essential nature of being a person. This is reductive and unacceptable. In ethical science, all life processes are judged to be of inherent value. This deductive principle descends to meet the particulars of circumstances, as we have seen, while the outcome of a proposed course of action is assessed in light of the person's relationships. A just, ethical decision to allocate scarce medical resources is not only the expression of economic conditions. The ethical parameters need to be widened to include the whole of our relationships.

The "Loving Resistance Fighter," to borrow a title from Postman's last chapter in *Technopoly*, is raising an ethical flag. The decision to secure moral choices on the basis of economics and self-interest is a consequence of "technopoly" or what was described earlier as the technocratic mentality. The conception of QALY as being an antecedent causal condition of our ethical choices reflects the secularism of our age. In our day, we seek to maintain a position of absolute power and control over human life. This is an extension of the Rationalist control of being. QALY is not so much a solution to a problem as it is an indication of the mentality of the age. The problem facing us is that the empirical conditions in which ethical choices are made are not seen to include the whole range of human relationships, such as the person's being toward ultimate good as well as the person's relationships with others and the environment. We need a change of heart to begin moving in that direction.

Our present attitude toward the mature management of resources is that it must lead to sustainable developments. In essence, the United Nations view of a sustainable society is one that satisfies its needs without diminishing the prospects of future generations. Guarded consumerism suggests that unless we put back into the environment what we take from it, future generations will not be able to meet their needs. But the gross domestic product (GDP) is based on economic concerns rather than on the availability of resources. Lester Brown of the *Worldwatch Institute* in Washington says that the world is fast running out of usable land, as urbanization fills open spaces with housing, shopping malls, and parking lots. The problem is that we ignore our own finitude. But the availability of water, nitrogen, and carbon is limited. Our forests are decreasing by 17 million hectares a year, while desert areas are increasing. Air quality is also decreasing. An increase in greenhouse gases is contributing to global warming. The Prime Minister of Denmark Gro Harlem Bruntland says in her report on the environment (1987) that we are worse off today than we were fifty years ago. What we need is not only a more efficient way of managing resources, but a change of heart. "The changes in attitudes, in social values, and in aspirations that the report urges will depend on vast campaigns of education, debate, and public participation" (p. xiv). Heidegger and Postman join Bruntland in that mission.

The change of heart moves away from the old absolute view of resources toward the interdependence of all life forms. We spend approximately 1.8 million U.S. dollars an hour on military armament, while every hour 1,500 children die of hunger-related causes. We live in a world that celebrates war, not children. Hans Küng's (1991) assessment is sobering: "Every week during the 1980s, more people were detained, tortured, assassinated, made refugee, or in other ways violated by acts of repressive regimes than at any other time in history except World War II" (p. 2).

The world is growing increasingly violent. Every day a species becomes extinct, while every year an area of tropical forest three-quarters the size of Korea is destroyed and lost. The loss adds to the burden of an already staggering Third World debt of more than 1,500 billion dollars, a debt increasing at a rate of 7.5 billion dollars a month. Yet, Küng optimistically expects that our world religions will generate the required change of heart in us. Religion is our last hope for a global ethics to preserve the "integrity of creation."

We live in an age of pervasive technology, an age in which the character of the person's relationships is radically transformed. But our relationships with being's unconcealment are invariably expressed in the monosyllabic language of cost-benefit analysis. We do not focus on personal growth, but only on the useful. This explains high global unemployment, possibly 500 to 600 million worldwide, in an age where work abounds. Matthew Fox (1983) suggests we suffer from misemployment. For instance, he says we can reduce unemployment by 15 percent through the development of non-useful activities (p. 14). In our day, the attitude of economic power and control pervades the whole of the six systems. The profit motive is imbedded in North American culture. Although the balance of power is beginning to shift toward the East, China, Japan, Korea, Hong Kong, where is the prescribed change of heart? In the global arena, the person functions primarily as a being toward the stock market. The profit motive continues to control us.

The ideology of technological domination is not based on good science. It is proved false by the increasing number of anomalies in deep ecology, human suffering, global crimes, injustice, and global disunity. They announce the need for a paradigm change. The "loving resistance fighter" invites us to look at the world through another vision, one in which the person emerges as a being in relationships.

The change of heart mentality does not suggest that the old theories of science and technology are false, but only that they are incomplete. For instance, the transition from the Newtonian world view to quantum mechanics did not prove the Newtonian view wrong. But it did prove the need to reassess that way of framing reality in order to move toward a deeper level of being. Science is a reflection of cultural values. Computer technology, for instance, mirrors us. It is a product of our science and technology. But the software programming is written by culture. Thus, there will not be a shift in computer ethics until we have a shift in the culture that supports it. At present, for instance, pornography is a seven billion dollar a year business. We can only expect that future internet sites will carry more of this junk, unless we experience a change of heart.

In our day, the beginnings of a shift in attitudes is emerging. The feminist movement, for instance, is leading the awakening of the person as a being in relationships. The patriarchy has dominated the stage for 3,000 years, deciding what role women shall and shall not play in human affairs. It might be an oversimplification to suggest that the patriarchal attitude has brought about solutions such as QALY, but it is not inappropriate to suggest that it has framed the person from an economic perspective. Feminism replaces a male logic of interrogation with a logic of dialogue in being. It issues an invitation to awaken to the ways of the feminine that exist in the human psyche. The change of heart attitude moves us away from the addiction to stockpile nature, toward the celebration of the divinity within human relationships. But the psychology of modern technology—the incessant addiction to power and control—extends beyond nature to include people. Violence abounds in the world. While some Third World countries appear to resist the intervention of North American technology, cruelty toward others abounds in most countries of the world. Biocentric ethics suggests that if a single stream is polluted, the cosmic cost is incalculable, but if a single person dies of malnutrition or torture, then what is left is not a world minus that person but a qualitatively different world. The loss marks a victory for evil in the person-making process.

How do we maintain an appropriate balance in our approach to technological developments? Wisdom suggests that the management of information requires a balance between the know-how (technology), the know-what (science), and the know-why, or spiritual dimension of human existence. Science and technology are preoccupied with results (technicism), but results can only be evaluated as ethical when they are aligned with a celebration of the divine telos within psyche. Otherwise, technological developments turn on themselves to control us. The point is readily made with the invention of the clock, a classic instance of the gadget controlling the human life. The clock tells us when to sleep, rise, wash, eat, and so on. The spiritual "change of heart" does not take place in a world without clocks, but it seeks to avoid dependency or addiction to the power and control of the clock. In my philosophy classes, for instance, some Mi'kmaq students remind me that time is relative to culture, as they invariably arrive ten to fifteen minutes late for class each morning. In this instance, the know-what of science is not aligned with the know-why of native spiritual experience. Yet, the work gets done. Heidegger's focus on the letting be of things comes in handy.

Aboriginal spirituality also provides a model to guide us in our relationships with the environment. The focus is on a deep ecological "letting be" of nature, or biocentric ethics. It enlists a hegemony of fundamental respect for the being of things. In that model, being has inherent value, or worth, not in service to us, but in itself. We need to respect the standing value of the environment if we are to survive.

The conception of being as possessing "standing rights" is not based on the love of nature, but on respect for nature. An individual organism exhibits characteristic properties as teleological centers of life pursuing its own survival in its own way. Organisms resist destruction and evolve by becoming better suited to an environment. Human beings have only recently made an appearance on the stage of biotic life. Paul Taylor (1994) expresses that insight:

> If the time that algae have been here (600 million years) were represented by a football field (300 feet), then the period during which sharks have been swimming in the world's oceans and spiders have been spinning their webs would occupy three quarters the length of the field; mammals would cover the last third of the field; hominids ... the last two feet; and the species Homo sapiens the last six inches. (P. 25)

Aquinas's views on the transcendental properties of being anticipate biocentric ethics, although they function at the level of the speculative intellect, providing additional insight into the mystery and richness of nature. First, being resists destruction; it is characterized by unity or integrity. The parts of a being cling to themselves, acting for the good of the whole. Second, being is intelligible, meaning that being's unconcealment or self-disclosure is a gift to us. We stand in relationship with that which lets itself be known. Being participates in clarity or truth to the extent it manifests itself. Third, being is good since it is pleasing to an appetite. This is the quality of being as harmonious. Finally, being possesses beauty to the degree in which it exhibits unity, truth, and goodness. Our failure to recognize the inherent value of being is reducible, not to anything in being, but to our way of framing being. It arises as a manifestation of the psyche as being toward evil.

Once the inherent value and fundamental rights of the biotic community are recognized, however, it seems but a small step toward granting legal rights to being. We suspect that being's best interest will continue to be represented in the courts, as evidence that our "change of heart" is underway.

Finally, the STS attitude or resistance to the superficial allure of power and control brought about by technology leads to informed social change in what Paul Durbin (1992) terms the "Social Worker Thesis." Since education is at the heart of culture, his point is that all education should be delivered as social work, assigning responsibility to students for moving materials beyond classroom walls to the community in which they live. Informed social action includes a knowledge of scientific, investigative skills, as well as a knowledge of how policy-making bodies operate, good communications skills along with a clear focus on what has to be done. The interdisciplinary character of the learning experience is one of the hallmarks of STS education. Being human includes an obligation to enact certain responsibilities in informed, multidisciplinary, and cultural perspectives. For instance, the lesson learned from the current debate on the allocation of scarce medical resources is that dilemmas such as the QALY proposal will continue to arise as a consequence of our reductive quest for economic power. The current ideology is little more than an attempt to legitimate economic efficiency as the panacea of human existence. The debate is not settled at the academic level only, or in scholarly books, but in the application of theory to our grass roots communities.

What sort of social action should we initiate? The materials we study in the classroom cluster around three main levels of relationships that characterize being a person. First, in the area of the psyche or mental health. Second, in our relationship with others through religiously inspired social action. Third, in our relationships with the gadgets of technology, since they represent the industrial way of framing being. The academic treatment of the person in relationships is paired with a practical applications component in which community assignment figures prominently. In my own STS classes, for instance, the action focus is worth 30 percent of the final grade. It is not enough to discuss injustice; we do something about it. We can begin with a simple action toward the plight of the elderly in our community, followed by a reflective essay on the results.

First, we can focus on our dependence on technology in order to recognize that a technological solution is not always in our best interest. Although our dependance on technology is not in itself always negative, the unreflective consumption of resources destroys human freedom. Taking some distance from technology through a simple act like unplugging the television for a week allows us to gain better sense of the hold technology has on us.

The problem lies in our attitude toward being. Technology arises as a way of framing being, an orientation that carries our intentions into nature. While medical surgery saves lives, for instance, we have a tendency to overdo a good thing. We tend to over prescribe surgery, so technology defeats the original intention of saving lives. In a chapter on medical technology, Postman (1993) makes a bold, but not surprising observation: "it is no exaggeration to say that American hospitals are commonly regarded as the most dangerous places in the nation. It is also well documented that, whenever doctor strikes have occurred, the mortality rate declines" (p. 105).

Second, it need not be the case that all relationships with others are conducted on the basis of the profit motive. Our society is placing increasing importance on volunteer work. We can choose to incorporate social action as part of course content in most subject areas. For instance, there seems to be increasing pressure to include social action in courses in religious studies. Our students in world religions courses can be encouraged to move beyond the classroom to apply theory to practice, thereby meeting the real needs of the culturally diverse citizenry. Why is Confucianism as organized religion losing ground in China, if not through a failure to meet the needs of the people? Alternatively, a course in theology can enlist the support of students to visit the sick, the housebound, the lonely, the depressed, the bereaved–people in crisis of any kind. Liberation Theology seems to have had its humble beginnings in such grass roots movements.

Third, the focus on religiously motivated social action is an important feature of the religious institution as a community of like-minded individuals in action. For instance, the development of parish justice and peace groups to counter violence in the world, or the development of action groups to focus on overseas aid. These recommendations are only suggested for illustrative purposes since the possibilities are unending. The challenge is issued to educators to meet society's need for reform through informed social action. Education is at the heart of culture; the transmission of values shapes the citizen's attitude toward the world. If education does not soon bring about the required change of heart, we might experience an ecological meltdown, including an irreversible shift in the relationships that define us. In that event, our recovery might not be possible, since the meaning of being human will have undergone an equally profound paradigm change.

The STS awakening does not merely move us toward a deeper level of reality, flog rationalism, vilify secularism for the disharmonious state of the planet, or bemoan the fleetingness of relativism. The change of heart that accompanies the STS way of framing being is not merely a revolt. The awakening taking place in systemic thinking is an awareness of the interdependence of all things. But the focal point about belonging to cosmos is that we trace our beginnings to the nothing that envelops it. Here lies at least one absolute truth–the nothing of cosmos provides a sufficient and necessary condition for the gift of existence. The change of heart is brought about because the question why something exists rather than nothing is answered. The hegemony of technology as "letting-be" merges with the sacred perspective of nature as unconcealment. The critique of the technocratic mentality is at an end. To science goes the credit for moving philosophy to the next level. The merger between physics and metaphysics is discussed in the next chapter.

Fourteen

A NEW PARADIGM: THE MERGER OF SCIENCE AND RELIGION

So, we have identified the need for a change of heart and for a focal point in which the person as a being in relationships functions at the center of technological developments. That view transforms the traditional representation of the person as abstract essence to the complex of associative relations that make us who we are. At the psychological level, our being toward good and evil carves the attitude of secularism or sacramentalism we carry toward others and the environment. The attitude of secularism, or economic control of nature, generates the undesirable consequences of technological developments. The STS awakening taking place in the pluraculture is an indication of the ongoing struggle between good and evil in the human psyche. It suggests that a change of heart is underway. This section examines the evidence for such a change in the merger of quantum physics and religion. In our day, science and religion are cultural allies, raising the view of human existence beyond the pale of secularism.

In our day, war, hunger, violence, and injustice, along with the environmental disasters facing us, force a change in the meaning of being human. The illness that threatens to engulf us reflects the many faces of the secular attitude toward other human beings and the environment. We are eco-psychological, ethico-psychological beings in distress. The various strings of our defining relationships are interdependent, sending an urgent plea for an STS recovery. They hang together on an epistemic mobile in which the part and the whole are in dynamic relationship. Whatever affects nature causes a ripple effect in the whole of living systems, including us. Thus, religion joins science as psychology meets ecology to orchestrate a plan of action. The failure of mechanism or scientific reductivism arises because science is discovering that nature, like any living system, is in relationships. The relations include us since we cannot observe nature without observing our own attitude toward nature. The failure of world religions is that they have not cooperated to generate a common transcultural theology of the eco-spiritual. We need to move beyond religious territoriality and scientific reductivism to recognize the fundamental interconnected and interrelated character of all existence. The work of science and religion collectively functions in the fashion of liberation movements. While science might not call its work salvific, or religion call its work eco-spiritual, they are both in the grassroots business of healing.

This connection is not always in evidence. The search for truth is like an ocean in which science and religion are two modes of dialogue. For a long time, science (Eastern and Western) worked side by side with religion. During the first millennium following the death of Christ, the Roman Church awaited his second coming. Technological development floated at the superficial level of the ocean, largely irrelevant to our well being. That attitude continued into the thirteenth century. Aquinas's treatise on the *Division and Method of the Sciences*, for instance, is only a study of science as speculative activity. Earlier, Plato warned against the illusions of the phenomenal world, while Aristotle developed his qualitative view of science. Science did not receive the (Western) attention it merited until the sixteenth century when Bacon's inductive theory and Descartes's analytical geometry merged to move us beyond anthropomorphism. However, the new scientific activity cast religion (and Eastern science) out of the waters of truth. Auguste Comte (1789-1857) introduced Positivistic epistemology as the final stage of human thought. In our day, Heidegger and Wittgenstein completed the process of rejecting the illusion of traditional metaphysics, including eternal truths, or absolutes. Western science became the new religion. The Newtonian model of physics reigned until the early twentieth century when the study of sub-atomic physics produced a quantum leap in the number of Meyersonian irrationals facing us. Walter Heitler (1963) says that the increasingly mathematical representation of reality undergirds the shift toward quantum physics:

> The individual atom cannot even be pictured in space and time. Even a bare description of it demands profound mathematical concepts. So it can hardly be thought of as something of a purely material nature; its 'mathematical aspect', that is, its non-material aspect, is even more strikingly prominent than is the case with an object of classical physics. (P. 53)

As the limits of classical physics become more apparent, the culture of quantum physics moves toward religion as if to reclaim "a lost inner child." Quantum science initiates a prodigal return to Eastern science and religion. Today science and religion merge to focus on processes or relationships rather than on immutable truths and fixed atoms. They share a common horizon standing in the presence of being's unconcealment, witnessing the interdependence of all living systems. How does life begin? F. Alan Wolf (1997) states the accepted view of contemporary science when he says:

> The vacuum state continually froths up matter and antimatter, then gobbles it up again. Ten to twenty billion years ago, the vacuum formed a primordial point from which space, time, and all the matter and energy that fill our universe burst into existence through an explosion that physicists call the Big Bang. Nothing created something then, and this process will continue for 20 billion years, until the universe collapses back into the primordial point through a process known as the Big Crunch, where space, time, matter, and energy end. (P. 46)

Wolf's view rests on the belief that the universe is growing apart–an observation first made by Edwin Hubble in 1929. Hubble discovered that the light from distant galaxies is growing redder because the universe is expanding in all directions. But if the universe is growing bigger, it must have been very dense at some point in time. In fact the farther back we go, the more the universe approaches infinite density. One eventually approaches a point in infinite density from which the universe began to expand, called a singularity or the Big Bang origin of the universe. The explosion must have taken place outside of time, space, matter, and energy in what can only be called a nothing. When all the distances separating us are shrunk to absolute zero, we are confronted with the amazing awareness that the world and all things in it comes from nothing at all. We are not outside that process but integral to it. Science now sees us as the output of that creative activity.

Quantum physics and religion meet in several areas to plot a common healing strategy. The nothing surrounding the Big Bang origin of the universe is not merely the negation of everything, but is the condition out of which something (rather than nothing) emerges. To the scientist, the entire universe is enveloped in a background of microwave radiation. To the philosopher (including Heidegger) the nothing is surrounded by a horizon, but to the faith community the horizon is God or a creator in personal, loving relationship with us. So at a basic level, science, religion, philosophy, and faith connect with God in being's unconcealment. Science traces the sufficient reason of the nothing surrounding the Big Bang origin of the cosmos to a creator, while religion moves beyond creator to God. Science tells us how the universe began, religion tells us why. Both views emerge out of our response to being's unconcealment–a place where God's transcendence and the creator's immanence connect. The one is secular, the other sacred. Both views are holy. In contemporary science and religion (a mix of Eastern and Western science), reality is non-dualistic, or holistic. The distinction between religion's transcendent God and science's immanent creator dissolves. The propositions of science rise above the natural order to encounter the creator, while the God of the supernatural order descends to meet the creator. The statement that the creator is not God is unacceptable because it springs out of dualism, or worse, bad science. In systemic thinking, science and religion construct metaphors in which all existence reconnects with the creator-God. God and creator are distinct perspectives of the same reality, but not separate entities. God is the creator entering into loving relationships with us, the creator is God or the horizon bordering the possibility of relationships.

The Christian religion uses metaphors such as the cross to express the experience of encountering God. Science uses its own metaphors or conceptual models of the universe to make similar connections with the creator. Scientific theories are validated in those models. Newtonian physics, for instance, used a mechanical model to represent nature. But the model proved to be incomplete. The discovery that the earth is a living system (the Gaia hypothesis) led to a revolution in our way of thinking about nature.

The outputs of science and religion are rooted in a common human concern for salvation, the one at the terrestrial level, the other, respectively, at the supernatural level. They join forces to find solutions to pressing social issues because fewer than ten percent of us live at a decent level. The ecological welfare of the planet as a living system is also much more complex than we first imagined. Science learns to respect the being of things, allowing nature to heal herself. At the same time, religion discovers that eternal truths are not handed down from time immemorial, but that they are discovered in history. Science and religion become allies in the search for dynamic spirituality.

How is science spiritual? We can have religion or cultural movements without spirituality and we can have science without spirituality, but eco-psychology is spiritually based since it is transformative knowledge, or praxis. In the process of introducing the observer into the equation, quantum physics includes the cultural attitudes, beliefs, and values we have about reality. This includes our most intimate moments of conversation with the divinity in us, other human beings, and the world. We not only see nature, but also see ourselves in dialogue with nature along with other human beings in dialogue with nature. Deep ecology includes a concern for all the relations that define us.

Quantum physics expresses a new way of thinking about our place in the world. It arose to displace Newtonian physics because there were simply too many things wrong with the old model. The theory of quanta was first used by Einstein to explain how light travels through space. However, at first blush, Einstein's theory of general relativity (the study of the very large) and quantum physics (the study of the very small) seemed to contradict. A quantum is a packet of energy or light that an electron emits as it moves about the nucleus of an atom, jumping from energy level to energy level. It is both a particle, and a wave, depending on the observer. The new connection between religion and science is based on the attempt to bridge the gap between these two orders of being. The experience generates a spiritual awakening. Science and religion are fed by the common insight that the observer stands in a sacred space in the cosmic environment. We do not enter into cosmic processes only as observers, but arise out of them. The awareness springs out of being very small (shrinking ourselves to absolute nothing). Whereas religion establishes its connections with a cosmic God, quantum physics meets the creator in the observations of very small matter. At first, the same divinity is viewed differently because the approach to the immanent and the transcendent is different. Recent developments in science, however, suggest that the small mirrors the large. The same patterns or laws at work in the origin of cosmos are at work in our observations of the sub-atomic world of matter.

The propositions of quantum mechanics articulate the limits of human understanding through a paradox in which matter is simultaneously real and unreal. Religion formulates its own paradox through the view of the person as temporal and eternal. They share common ground before the mystery of being, although science might not call the being God, and what religion calls ecumenical, science calls ecological. The person is infinitely small, but infinitely great as belonging to cosmos. The metaphors of science and religion express a common belief in the interdependence of all phenomena. This is systems theory.

For many scientists working in the area of quantum mechanics, the reconciliation of science and religion is not only a possibility, it is already at hand. Fritjof Capra, and F. Alan Wolf (1997) are two of the researchers at the cutting edge of the merger. Wolf won the American Book Award in 1982 for *Taking the Quantum Leap*. He also authored *The Dreaming Universe, The Eagle's Quest*, and *Parallel Universes*. Capra's *Belonging to the Universe* (1992) is examined in some detail in this chapter since the book records a series of productive exchanges between himself as physicist and the theological perspectives of David Steindt-Rast and Thomas Matus. Their discussions took place at the Esalen Institute, California, from 1990 to 1992, in "beautiful surroundings that bring us to witness the Gaia hypothesis, the intermingling of God and nature" (*ibid.*). The merger of science and religion is a familiar theme to Capra since it was expressed a decade earlier in his *The Tao of Physics*.

The connection between religion and science is born at the primitive level of our experiential encounter with being's unconcealment. The quantum physicist and the theologian arrive at the same conclusion; one starting from the inner realm where the psyche connects with being, the other from the inner world of sub-atomic particles where the person enters into the equations of physics. The unconcealment of being emerges as the root of the possibility of both encounters. The realization that nature is intelligible, or governed by laws, is a startling discovery. It serves as a focal point where religion and science meet. We might theorize about the sorts of events that need to occur for life to begin, but as Einstein once remarked, how does the universe know that? The question generates the experience of standing in the presence of divine patterns, or laws. When the laws of reason and the laws of the universe meet, we see ourselves looking at ourselves. And the cosmos is experienced as a living system.

The Gaia hypothesis recognizes the fundamental interconnectedness of matter and consciousness. The conception of matter as being fully alive explodes the billiard-ball model of the atom. Persons and matter are both seen to be struggling for survival. We form part of an interconnected whole. The feeling of awe that arises in the face of our encounter with being's unconcealment makes us profoundly grateful to be a part of the living system. We stand in the presence of a gift from the divine observer.

The theologian calls the gift faith, while the scientist thinks of it as an experiential knowing. Einstein was aware of the gift. He saw that science without spirituality is lame. But spirituality without science is blind. Our *Gestell*, or way of framing reality, is rooted in the belief that science and religion are co-dependent. They are both addicted to God, one as loving creator, the other as sufficient reason of the natural order.

Authentic wonder enlists the divinity. The dependence on God is present in Aristotle's telos, or final cause, as in all great works, including Descartes's mathematicism. But it was reduced to functionalism during the cartesian era, leading to the denial of the creator, the STS awakening, and quantum physics. The indeterminacy principle is a reminder that matter and mind are both aspects of self-organization. The insight into the dynamics of the whole allows us to understand the properties of the part. It brings empirical confirmation of what mystics knew all along but could not express in the language of science: matter is reducible to mind, mind to being or cosmos, cosmos to the creator, and the creator to God. The characteristics of God as transcendent and immanent merge. We are part of an interdependent, interlocking system. We belong to the cosmic community. We recognize the interconnection of all processes in divinity, and celebrate the sanctity and uniqueness of all life forms.

The experience of oneness shows that we cannot decompose the world into independently existing atoms or subjects of experience. In the Newtonian paradigm we dominate and control nature. That paradigm is still useful within its range of applicability. But when we moved beyond Newtonian physics to the deconstruction of absolutes, we generated a way of framing reality that continues to haunt us today in the undesirable second-order developments of technology. The exploitation of our being toward self, others, and the environment generates global chaos. We are forced to reexamine the human mission statement. It forcibly reminds us, for instance, that the characteristic property of femininity that accompanies our spiritual enframing has lapsed into a period of forgetfulness. Yet, it must be awakened once again. It supplants the (masculine) logic of domination and control of nature by an awareness that we are in dialogue with the sacred order of existence. In quantum physics, science is in dialogue with matter. How do we converse with electrons?

In 1913, Niels Bohr published his basic theory on the structure of the atom. That theory contained the elements of the dialogue between persons and electrons. The first hurdle was to assign an identity to the particles of matter. Every element has a kind of fingerprint that identifies it. Scientists can identify a particle by analyzing the kind of light that is produced when an electric current passes through it. Bohr was able to predict the kind of light that would be produced by different materials. Divide the atom and it is no longer the same material but something else. However, we do not always move in the right direction. Splitting the nucleus of uranium produces the release of a tremendous amount of energy, leading the male in us to the production of the atomic bomb.

The introduction of the observer suggests that we cannot simultaneously determine the position and velocity of a particle because our observation changes the direction and momentum of the particle in unpredictable ways. Thus, the uncertainty principle can be formulated as an instance of the person as a being toward matter. Simply put, matter assumes different modalities of existence, wave or particle, depending on the environment in which it is observed. Thus, being's unconcealment invites us into a web of relationships with living matter to co-create cosmos. We exist in virtue of such relationships. In creating cosmos we create ourselves. But in Newtonian physics, our role is to conquer rather than create, that is, we reduce matter to increasingly comprehensive atomic bits of data, or identity propositions. We act as if nature stands at a distance from us. Bertrand Russell's logical atomism continues the Newtonian, reductivist tradition. He says the world is composed of atomic bits of information. The function of language is to mirror these data into atomic and molecular propositions about reality. But the failure of the paradigm at the sub-atomic level is being's way of asserting her ultimate primacy. We belong to being as spiritual life process. This is a net gain, not a loss. Belonging to cosmos creates a new sense of freedom because nothing is outside us. In fact, the properties of being can only be understood in terms of our own place in the network of interactions.

What if that place changed, would the nature of the observed also change? It seems possible to suggest that we will undergo profound changes as our own place in the cosmos shifts. The transition from death to the afterlife provides an instance of such a shift. Perhaps the divine observer sees us one way in this environment and a different way in the afterlife? The belief is not illogical. It is consonant with the ways of quantum mechanics. Furthermore, that view maintains our personal identity because the same matter is at one time wave or particle depending on the environment. Thus, the same person is individuated with characteristics appropriate to the environment. The same person can appear one way on earth and a different way in the afterlife. The model also allows us to make sense of God's timelessness. Since nothing exists before the Big Bang, the creator must have acted in timelessness. The creative act began the movement of matter and energy in space and time. Further, since the universe is expanding indefinitely, points ahead of us are the not-yet of space and time. And if the universe expands forever, the not-yet of space-time is in timelessness. We move from the not-yet of space and time into the not-yet of timelessness. This is God's telos unfolding out of the laws and patterns governing being's unconcealment.

But how is a person like an electron? This representation is consistent with the reducibility of matter to mind, although science might call matter wave or particle, and religion might call the divine likeness mind, or soul. The contribution of philosophy is in the analysis of being's unconcealment. In particular, the changed environment can be explained through a shift in being's unconcealment. It seems logical to suppose that while being's unconcealment appears one way in the natural order (God as creator), it might exhibit different characteristics outside that realm (God beyond creator). We can think of the shift as a mirror image of being's unconcealment. This view is consistent with systemic thinking, or the rejection of dualism.

In the event of human death, being's unconcealment is sustained in the afterlife, as is our role in cosmic processes. Continuity is always presumed in logic. The divine gift of life on earth forewarns us that the gift must be extended to the afterlife. Quantum physics now proves what the human heart already knows. However, the moral life includes a refusal of the gift, much in the same way that a scientist can choose to do bad science.

In quantum mechanics we never speak about being without, at the same time, speaking about ourselves as entities toward being. However, the processes of reconnecting with being are highly ambiguous, in science as well as in religion. When Max Planck, Einstein, Bohr, Werner Heisenberg, Erwin Schrödinger (1887-1961), and others penetrated the sub-atomic level between 1900 and 1930, they found that much of their experiences of the familiar world proved to be inapplicable. In the world of the infinitely small, for instance, matter does not exist. Roy Woods in Cockburn (1992) traces that line of thought through Rilke, Heidegger, and Zen (pp. 108-142). Reality exists as a pattern of interconnected energy rather than as object. Matter seems to spontaneously come into being, but like the Cheshire cat in Alice's wonderland adventure, it disappears when things start to make sense. We can draw some conclusions about that behavior. The first, and most obvious, is that dualism is plainly in error. The observer necessarily enters into the equation with the observed. There can be no subject-object dichotomy since they form a unit. The new physics also precipitates the meltdown of Newtonian physics at the level of the infinitely small. The religious parallel is that the denial of God leads to the no-person theory. If there is no God, there is no God in us, and consequently no self or creative act–contrary to current scientific belief.

The development suggests that the split between science and religion only appears at the superficial level of being. Matter and persons are fully connected at the sacramental level of interactions. The electron becomes an extension of the person, and the human mind an extension of the electron. It confirms that matter is reducible to mind. If we artificially stop the moment of phenomenal experience, once again we note that persons and electrons are probabilities. This brings out the obvious: persons and electrons are both dependent on the divine observer, or creator, for their existence. In other words, the grace of God is what saves us from extinction, both in this world and in the next.

The human observer and the divine observer are connected, or in relationship, much in the same way as God and creator are connected. It is no more difficult to imagine that we owe our being to a divine observer than it is to imagine that the properties of matter trace their characteristics to the presence of a human observer. In fact, this reality underlies the person-making process. We are made in the likeness of a divine observer, as matter is made in the likeness of the human observer. The view does not infringe on human freedom, but gives it added significance. We are charged with the responsibility of co-creating cosmos. Systems theory views freedom as integral to the person-making process. The whole of cosmos is in a process of becoming more free through relationships. The view provides a glimpse of the religious experience, a moment of intimate reconnecting with cosmos.

The world of sub-atomic physics provides confirmation that this is the case. The existence and inexistence of the same particle of matter gives evidence of a yin and yang process of becoming. With relativity physics, we know that to be, and to be in motion, are interchangeable terms. The velocity of particles is seen to slow as we approach absolute zero. But if the energy level drops to zero, the particle ceases to exist. And so the energy level of systems oscillates between positive levels and zero, thereby spontaneously popping in and out of existence. This is a second view of the Big Bang origin of cosmos. At first blush, the issue is perplexing since it means that the universe could have come about as caused or uncaused. If the universe is uncaused, the connection between science and religion is obscured.

Two views on the origin of matter turn on the acceptance and rejection of the law of universal causation. One view states that quantum mechanics proves universal causation to be false. According to the theory, some events do not have causes. How is that possible? The law of causation says that every event has a cause that lies in an earlier event. But since the Big Bang is the first event of time, it is uncaused, meaning that no earlier event takes place. Have we overstepped the limits of the principle of sufficient reason? It seems not to be the case.

At some point in time, the entire universe was no larger than an atomic particle of infinite density. Douglas P. Lackey says in James Huchingson (1993): "The behavior of a universe of such small size could be as spontaneous as the decay of a radioactive atom" (p. 194). The argument is based on the evidence that the energy level of particles in quantum physics can never be precisely measured, as we saw. They oscillate between certain levels. Particles passing into existence (as the energy level increases) are usually called virtual particles. They appear to be uncaused since they come into existence from a vacuum or nothing. Thus, matter shows a tendency to exist and not to exist, depending on probability. Under certain conditions, matter pops into existence. But is this a proof that some events are uncaused? No. We need to go behind the scene to recognize that matter obeys certain laws, or patterns of existence. How do particles know to pop back into existence as matter, or obey such laws?

The smallest particle is said to be infinitely dense before it pops into existence. But how can a particle be infinitely dense? According to W.L. Craig and Q. Smith (1995): "infinite density is precisely equivalent to nothing." No object can possess infinite density for "if it had any size at all it would not be infinitely dense" (p. 43). Thus, if the quantum physicist's smallest particle is infinitely dense, the universe must have come into existence from nothing. Yet, the nothing is not nothing at all. The universe comes into existence obeying the patterns and laws of such a particle. This suggests that the universe is the creation of a mind analogous to our own. If that is the case, the particle moving out of the void is not a random event. It must be seen to follow the law of universal causation. As Aquinas points out in the *Summa*

Contra Gentiles (Book 2, ch. 37), the universe cannot exist without a sufficient reason. He traces the explanation to the divine exemplar, or plan. So, the uncaused cause creates the cosmos out of nothing, directing it to behave in accordance with divine laws. "In the beginning God created heaven and earth" (*Genesis,* 1:1).

It turns out, not that we witness uncaused events, but that sub-atomic particles are indeterminate. Where does matter go when it is not being perceived? That question was already asked by Berkeley. He seems to have been right, not only about this world, but also about the next one. Quantum physics confirms Berkeley's insight. It is simpler to imagine that matter is conserved in existence by an observer (divine and human) than to support the view that matter is annihilated. But quantum physics adds a fresh spin to Berkeley's argument, since it suggests that matter moves in and out of the void. Thus, the void must be something real after all since it is governed by laws, or patterns. How else would matter (coming out of the void) know it should behave according to laws such as the laws of expansion and contraction? Thus, the human observer is a witness to creation. We see the creator's plan in action whenever we observe matter pass in and out of the void. This suggests that the creator enters into relationship with us. We are co-opted into the creative process whenever we observe the behavior of sub-atomic particles. Science tells us how matter comes to exist (the laws of matter), but religion tells us why, since observers (like us) are required to specify the nature of matter as wave or particle. So, the scriptural creation story is doubly amazing for we are created to create in turn, or be God-like (made in the likeness of God). We are active participants in the marriage of religion and science to beget matter. We stand in the presence of the divine psyche at work. But how should we create?

The distinction between virtual and real particles can be compared to the yin and yang opposites of Chinese philosophy. Both are manifest in the struggle of existence. Two modes of insight correspond to yin, or feminine, and the yang, or linear mode of thought. The yin is characterized by a vision of the world as a network of interrelated and interdependent systems. Yin insight is a spontaneous, pre-discursive, intuited vision of the right-brain type. Yin is the proper starting point of science and religion since it generates spontaneous consonance with nature, or the moment in which the person as an entity toward being's unconcealment is the most vivid. Our relation to being's unconcealment is yin-like rather than linear, or dualistic. We do not progressively move out of psyche toward others or the environment since we are one with all things. Relationships characterize the three faces of being a person. We only focus on this or that face of being human by artificially freezing the phenomenal moment of experience.

Descartes's method of analysis is an instance of a yang or left-brain insight, although it is introduced as an intuition. He provides the account in his *Rules for the Direction of the Mind:* "the conception which an unclouded and attentive mind gives us so readily and distinctly that we are wholly freed from doubt about that which we understand" (Rule 3). The focus is on reason. While his view has its place in the propositions of Newtonian science, the model is inadequate at the sub-atomic level, since it introduces a deep division between humans and nature.

Yin insight abhors dualism. The yin not only postulates the existence of a continuum between all living systems but also introduces feelings and emotions in the life of reason. Intuition has a "logic" of its own, one which reason might not understand. Yin and yang insight form a unit. Intuition is not irrational, although it grasps the whole before grasping the nature of part. Intuition is non-rational. Descartes's use of "intuition" is synecdoche. He follows Euclid in providing a starting point for mathematical deduction. However, like the Chinese *Tao*, it introduces only one of the modes of a person's being. The yin opens on a more comprehensive vision of reality. It provides an awareness of the interconnection between all life forms. The realm of yang, however, is characteristic of rational insight. Our rational language obeys the tightly articulated rules of logic to arrive at true beliefs. Good technology, a technology that respects the being of things, is animated by yin-yang insight. We need to be rational, but we also need to be tolerant, compassionate, and less self-centered because we enter into relationships that define us. We need notes (yang), but we also need a melody (yin).

Science and religion stand in spiritual awe of the same mystery of existence. They view the sacramental order of existence, giving witness to a common expression of awe, compassion and gratitude to God. Philosophy's most fundamental question, "Why is there something rather than nothing?", is now answered. God chose to create. We see ourselves moving out of the void into existence as we gaze on the horizon of the nothing surrounding being's unconcealment. Science's sub-atomic world and religion's inner world connect as we see ourselves looking at ourselves. The question, "Why is there something rather than nothing?", reveals us at work. We discover the presence of timelessness in our own temporality.

The discoveries of quantum physics also provide fresh insight into the nature of death as such, since we are seen to be beings toward the eternal. Science calls it the laws of the void rather than the eternal, while religion views us as beings toward God. So, the eternal and the temporal converge in the scientific-religious propositions of a human story. The oxymoronic character of a human life in which the temporal and the eternal roost side by side is explained. The person is a being toward death, but also a being toward immortality. I stand in the presence of the temporal, but I also stand in the presence of the eternal. It depends on my environmental perspective, or how I frame being's unconcealment. In science, the property of an electron also depends on the environment it interacts with. The electron does not have any intrinsic property independent of its environment. Capra (1992) confirms what we have already noted:

The properties it shows, particle-like or wave-like, will depend on the experimental situation, that is, on the apparatus it is forced to interact with. We find that we cannot define this dual aspect of matter simultaneously. The more we emphasize one aspect, the more the other becomes uncertain. The relation between the two is given by the uncertainty principle. (P. 68)

The solution to the paradoxes of science and religion is found in a synthesis of perspectives rather than in the attempt to reduce one to the other. Religion discovers the presence of the eternal in the temporal by framing the temporal in light of the eternal, while the probability statements of quantum mechanics (the indeterminacy principle) reflect the oxymoronic infusion of the environment in the observed, or the reducibility of matter to mind, as discussed earlier. Both pictures are required to give an account of the whole person. The more we emphasize one aspect, the more the other becomes uncertain. For instance, overemphasizing the temporal or secular perspective in Western culture makes the existence of the eternal uncertain. Placing undue emphasis on the eternal makes the value of the secular world uncertain. Religion, like quantum mechanics, requires both orders to give a full account of the human experience.

The person, like the electron, only has meaning in relationships. They are not substances or entities that exist in isolation from an environment. Persons, like electrons, are beings in the making. Each interaction can give rise to the unexpected. The creator gives us the gift of existence, but we might not know why God chooses to enter into relationship with us. Religion calls the gift love. Our indeterminacy is apparent at the metaphysical level where we confront our finitude. Maritain notes that only God can know us in the way we seek to know ourselves. We also meet the indeterminate in our loving relationships. First, because the other is an extension of the unknown within us, or what Marcel terms mystery (secondary reflection). Second, human indeterminacy arises at the level of standing in the presence of being and the *via transformativa* of the mystical experience. We explode in the presence of the divinity, not knowing exactly (clearly and distinctly) how love scatters throughout the universe. Persons, like matter, are governed by an uncertainty principle, as Kierkegaard's subjective thinker already knows. We would revert to the void but for the creator's sustaining love.

Our relationships are always indeterminate at the sacramental level since they are sustained by the mystery of being God-like. We stand before being's unconcealment filled with the wonder of existence. Why do life, death, suffering, evil, and good exist? Yet, the experience leads to the discovery of the world as blessing, providing an answer to our questioning. Existence is the gift of the divine observer, although there is no guarantee of continued existence. Given that insight, science and religion humbly give thanks for creation.

A further kinship between sub-atomic physics and religion exists in their way of unfolding truth. Religion, when it is informed by science as well as sacred texts, discovers the presence of eternal truths not in a repository of eternal truths but in history. Truth is an historical process in the making. Heidegger is right to the extent that God does not dole out quotas of truth at the start of the earthly banquet. But Heidegger did not see that God brings gifts during the banquet because he would not venture into the horizon surrounding the nothing. The discovery of eternal truths takes place in the processes of civilization or kingdom building. The world is "brought forth" by science and religion. Does Heidegger's mystical turning see us co-creating with God? He cannot share his insight without rethinking the place of the absolute, however. Thus, history allows the unfolding of untruths as well as truths.

We abandon old paradigms when we recognize their falsehoods. In our day, the anomalies brought about by the second-order consequences of technological developments announce the beginnings of a new paradigm change in our relationships with being. We have discovered the need for an ethics of peace toward others and nature. The discovery of being's woundedness points to our own finitude. That discovery sparks a change of heart in us so that we now frame being as sacred. No doubt, being has been sacred all along. But no one knew that truth until it was discovered in history. The vision of being's unconcealment, specifically of the horizon surrounding Heidegger's nothing, explains the possibility of being's unconcealment. The awareness shows us how the eternal is discovered in history. God as immanent to cosmos (the creator) is the observer in the Heisenberg environment. God as transcendent, or supernatural, is the Horizon surrounding the void in the pre Big Bang and post Big Crunch modalities of cosmos.

The new paradigm in religion is also announced in the celebration of cosmic spirituality. In the old Christian paradigm, spirituality centered on the fall/redemption condition of the person. The person was thought to be born fallen from grace, but redeemed through the death of Christ. The recovering human heart is epitomized by Saint Augustine's tears of contrition. Once forgiven, the repentant continued to frame the person's existence as a guilt-filled, worm-like process of pleasing God, less he be cast into the depths of a Jobian Hell. But in the new paradigm, human existence is seen to be cause for celebration. Life is an original blessing, as Fox maintains in *Original Blessing*. Christ is not a judge, but an ally. Our relationship is not based on guilt (the Fall), or fear of reprimand (Hell), since it is founded on acting as divine birthers. We belong to the cosmos, although we can act toward good and evil. Polluting the environment is an instance of choosing evil.

Capra tells the story of opening his course on spirituality by giving his students a paper bag with the instructions to go clean the environment. The lesson teaches us much about values in the new millennium. The choice of evil (pollution) only corresponds to one of the possible choices facing us in the person-making process. The selection of good also corresponds to the individual's free choices. But the range of choices facing us in creation-centered spirituality is wider than the fall/redemption paradigm. Countless numbers of individuals are involved in the new eco-spirituality. Planting trees, recycling, soil conservation, land reclamation, social action, each adds to the dimension of traditional prayer forms. Liberation Theology, for instance, is a grassroots movement that seeks to liberate the people from the oppression they encounter in daily life. The development of co-operatives originates as a response to some individuals' economic hardships. Capra's spiritual lesson is also liberating since it redeems us from acts of oppression against the environment.

Küng's informed book *Global Responsibility* (1991), looks to the world religions to provide leadership, although they have not provided it in the past. However, the new paradigm offers fresh hope for reconciliation. One of the obstacles to dialogue in the old paradigm is the cultural differences that separate us. For instance, the religions of Semitic origin (Judaism, Christianity, and Islam) are predominantly involved in religious confrontation. There have been more holy wars launched in the name of the divinity than for any other cause. We seem to enter into relationship with the sacred through war. A clear divide exists in that respect between the wrathful God of the Hebrew Scriptures and the loving God of the Christian Testament. The teachings of the Koran also suggest that Islam is the only true religion. This, too, is exclusive. Unfortunately, there does not seem to be much room for compromise. The religions of Indian origin are supported by a mystical mood that is unacceptable to Westerners. The early Indian religions of the Upanishads, Buddhism, and Hinduism focus on an inward journey that is only recently finding its way into Western healing, or medicine. Eastern medicine assigns an important role to the patient's feelings, for instance, while the West does not. Western medicine is only now beginning to abandon the reductivist view of the body as a machine. The religions of the Chinese tradition, Confucianism and Taoism, are characterized by the search for harmony within psyche. But Confucianism is not a religion as such. China's new economic pragmatism does not make room for it. Confucianism is more comfortable with the political China of the pre Deng Xiaoping era.

We live in an age of reform, however. The new paradigm teaches us that the cultural differences between world religions are to be celebrated. They add to the plethora of possibilities for entering into relationships with the sacred. Although all religions join in the goal of person-making, we recognize that many roads lead to the same goal of salvation. The problem of our blindness toward cultures different from our own is tempered by the unity of compassion and respect we experience toward the divinity. Our religious tolerance of the differences among us is heightened by quantum mechanics. Religion, as we saw, is a process of making connections: as the same particle of matter is seen to vary with its environment, so the expression of religious belief varies with its cultural setting.

The differences among us need not lead to cultural relativism. Paul Badham makes the point that while early developments in quantum mechanics seemed to dispute the law of causation, this is no longer the case. In his unpublished article, "Religion, Science, and Philosophy," Badham gives full weight to Aquinas's causal argument. Aquinas's belief in the objectivity of causality (the uncaused cause) is supported by the evidence of quantum mechanics. Since the energy level of the smallest particle of matter oscillates between a level of zero and some finite number, the patterns or laws of matter must exist in the void, providing a sufficient reason for the Big Bang origin of cosmos (the nothing surrounding the creator).

Aquinas's view is an argument rather than a full proof that God exists. Yet, the existence of laws or patterns in the pre Big Bang void provides a necessary and sufficient reason for the existence of the world. His argument points toward the proof given in quantum physics. Once we move away from metaphysical dualism, the religious argument suggests that God is at least the creator and possibly much more. The patterns or laws of the universe make clear that the creator enters into personal relationship with us. This is the sense of a loving God. Christians believe that Christ is God. But in Jewish thought what matters is the covenant between God and Israel. What matters for Islam is the belief that God reveals the eternal truths of the Koran through the prophet Mohammed. However, the world religions speak in single voice whenever they praise God as the "Mighty Birther" of the world and all things contained in it.

God invites us into the birthing process, although a finite observer views the properties of matter as being paradoxical. In 1905, Einstein discovered that light can be regarded as a stream of particles, as Newton had observed, but it can also be regarded as a wave motion. He was confident that the contradiction would eventually be explained. This was in fact the case two decades later when de Broglie and Schrödinger produced a conception of the world in which matter could be regarded as wave or particle depending on the observer. This meant that time (and space) was detached from the rigid structure of the past, since it is relative to the observer. However, our new found ability to "play with time" is a profoundly spiritual thought. Because we play an active role in the determination of the characteristics of matter, we co-create matter. The term co-create is chosen carefully. Quantum mechanics does not suggest that the person alone creates matter. We are left with the challenge of explaining how both wave and particle motion pass from the nothing of the void (virtual size) into the something of observation. We need to know where the patterns or laws of matter originate and enlist the Creator God as a necessary and sufficient explanation.

Badham cites Paul Davies (1992) who says somewhat tongue-in-cheek that nowadays "science offers a surer path to God than religion." Divine causation is the most probable explanation of the patterns of existence. In Big Bang cosmology an incredible tension exists between two competing forces of the early universe. One is expansion, the other is gravitation. While expansion drives matter apart, gravity pulls it back together, allowing the world to form. These two forces are so closely balanced that they differ from one another by just one part in 10^{60}. John Polkinghorne (1993) marvels at the accuracy. "If I took a target an inch wide and placed it on the other side of the observable universe, eighteen thousand million light years away, and took aim and hit the target, then I would have achieved an accuracy to 10^{60}. Remarkable!" (p. 238).

The evidence of a world so finely tuned that human life can arise from it suggests that the creator cares about us. That too echoes Aquinas's design argument. Stephen Hawking (1993) also finds that the original state of the universe must have been carefully chosen. For example, according to Hawking (1988) the heat of the universe one second after the Big Bang could not have been other than it was.

> (Heat) had to be exactly as it was because a decrease of heat by as little as one part in a million million would have caused the universe to collapse ... . (Furthermore) Electro-Magnetism and gravity had to be correct to one part in 10^{40}, the rate of expansion to 10^{55}, density to 10^{60}, and the smoothness of expansion to 10^{123}. (P. 127)

Although Hawking is reluctant to appeal to God as creator of the universe, an alternate model must explain the origin of the universe. Hawking must argue that the singularity of the Big Bang does not proceed out of the nothing. He seeks to accomplish this by assigning a role to imaginary numbers at the earliest stages of the universe, thereby unnecessarily complicating the process. So, the universe would have formed out of negative time rather than from nothing. But the problem is that imaginary numbers cannot explain real events. He commits the fallacy of misplaced concreteness. On the contrary, Davies (1992) says that the odds against all of the above variables coming right together to explain the origin of the universe are at least one followed by a thousand billion, billion zeros (p. 203). This is solid evidence that the creator wrote us into the universe in a significant and highly elaborate way. If any of the prescribed conditions were absent, human life would not exist. Davies's evidence firms up the belief that "creator entering into personal relationships with us" is another name for God.

William Lane Craig's article (1998) "Scientific Confirmation of the Cosmological Argument" describes the characteristics of the Creator-God in greater detail;

> Since He created the universe from nothing, we know that He must be enormously powerful, if not omnipotent. Since He brought the universe into being without any antecedently determining conditions and fine-tuned it with a precision that literally defies comprehension, He must be both free and unimaginably intelligent, if not omniscient. Moreover, the fact that the entire known universe, from the smallest elementary particles to the most distant stars, was designed in such a way as to be a suitable environment for the existence of human life on Earth suggests the astounding conclusion that He may have some special concern for us. These properties constitute the central core of what theists mean by 'God'. (P. 40)

Further, the person-making process is also subject to the forces of expansion and gravitation. Although science does not call the forces of matter and anti-matter good and evil, the expanding universe depends on them to mutually annihilate one another. But there seems to have been a slight inequality in the parts generated by the cosmic explosion, perhaps one part in a billion, and the cosmos formed. Persons also spring out of the cosmic soup (God's inner court), in tension between the forces of good and evil. Spiritual leaders like Buddha and Christ generate gravitational force on us, giving a slight edge to the good. This lends hope to the belief that the person-making process shall culminate in the triumph of the good.

In particle physics, the force of gravitation creates clusters such as planets, stars, and galaxies. In theodicy, the force of our good and evil tendencies underwrites the person-making process. But for the good in us, we would scatter toward non-being or not move toward the realization of the divine telos. Our defining relationships would remain sealed in the void. Given the good and evil tendencies of the psyche, however, the person-making struggle is possible, empowering us to cluster toward good or become God-like.

The psychology of the outside world–the psychological processes that accompany how we think about others and the environment–mirrors the psyche. The propositions of quantum science, as well as the imagery of the social self, arise in the likeness of the psyche. For instance, elements of the psyche, such as the unconscious, the a-causal process of synchronicity, the collective unconscious, and archetypal imagery–to borrow from C.G. Jung–find expression, not only in the characterization of the social self, but in the propositions of quantum science. The process of becoming human beings or being God-like arises as these elements, discovered in history, emerge out of the darkness of the unconscious psyche into the light of awareness. The view of the inside world provides a map, not only of our origin in Creator, but heralds the future of developments in science and religion

Fifteen

A POSSIBLE ESCHATOLOGY

1. Overview

The term "eschatology" is from the Greek word "eschaton," meaning the last end, or the doctrine of the last ends. The first objection raised by the skeptic is that we cannot venture beyond the realm of natural phenomena, or experience, without lapsing into a world of theory and conjecture. Yet, the merger of science and religion allows us to move beyond the natural order. Standing in the presence of being's unconcealment, or the pattern of laws that exists in the universe (the horizon surrounding being's unconcealment), we can view death in light of those natural laws, namely, that the person is ultimately reducible to such laws. Death, then, is not something we do. or fail to do, but a reclaim in the patterns governing being's unconcealment. That being the case, perhaps being's unconcealment emerges anew in the afterlife. In that event, being's unconcealment should rise to absolute unhiddenness.

The connection between immortality, persons, and God introduces several possible eschatologies. One can believe in God, for instance, but hold a materialist view of the person. In that event, we might survive death as energy and emerge as conscious beings in a second Big Bang in eighteen thousand million years or so, or simply become extinct in a Big Crunch. Voltaire (1694-1778), for instance, believes in God and the design argument, but rejects immortality because of his materialistic view of consciousness. So, what is the point of surviving as energy? Some reincarnationists believe in rebirth without believing in God. If the universe obeys the laws of thermodynamics, however, all energy might come to an end, including us. A sustained belief in reincarnation is difficult to support in the absence of a second Big Bang. But the belief in reincarnation poses even more serious problems to the Western way of thinking.

David Darling (1996) in *Zen Physics* appeals to quantum physics to provide scientific validation of the Eastern belief in reincarnation. His argument moves along two interdependent lines of thought. The first is that the objective character of Newtonian physics breaks down in the realm of the very small. The second is that the subjectivity of observation enters into the equations of quantum physics. Darling integrates the subjective (sensation and consciousness) and the objective qualities of matter such as size and number into his theory of reincarnation. The argument appears to mirror Berkeley's objection to Locke's epistemology. Locke had separated primary and secondary qualities, but Berkeley (and now Darling) move beyond the subjectivity of secondary qualities to incorporate primary and secondary qualities in the moment of experience. Darling reasons that matter and consciousness are homogeneous ways of belonging to cosmos, as is ultimately evident in the reconciliation of the subjective and the objective approaches of science. We do not stand as objective observers of the cosmos but see ourselves looking at ourselves whenever we theorize about the nature of cosmos. So far so good. His rejection of dualism has a certain appeal, but at what cost?

First, his unification theory is grounded in materialism. He rejects the existence of the human soul, or speculative intellect. In effect, Darling's rejection of dualism fails even to distinguish between mind and body. How, then does matter become aware of matter? Second, he explains personal identity by explaining it away. The fact that we are matter now appears inconsequential as we complete the process of identification with the whole of matter in the afterlife. The loss of personal identity is not one of Darling's concerns. Eastern science has long taught that once the tendency to cling to self disappears, it matters little that survival is impersonal because enlightenment is a state in which the loss of self is a desirable goal. Third, as a consequence of this view, he underdescribes the moral character of a human life. But can we tolerate injustice, torture, and the violation of human rights as being a transitory state of persons who have yet to move out of their ego? Although Darling is not suggesting we do this, the point is, his eschatology leaves no room for moral issues. In my opinion, his defense of reincarnation undermines the critical importance of the person-making process, or the salvific nature of relationships. Still, if Darling is right and the relationships of the afterlife are impersonal, the loss of personal identity could be in our best interest, lest Divine justice hold us accountable for the failure to develop a moral life.

Yet, the merger of science and religion also suggests the possibility of personal immortality. Since relationships individuate us in this life, we expect that an analogous stream of relationships shall converge to individuate us in the afterlife. For that to be the case, our defining relationships at the psychological, ethical, and metaphysical level must continue beyond death. How is this possible?

Although the existence of God is not self-evident, we can know something about God's attributes through the effects of God on us. The evidence supporting the existence of a creator suggests that God entered into relationship with us some fifteen to twenty billion years ago when the patterns or laws of the Big Bang appeared and gradually enacted the emergence of conscious, human life three or four million years ago. The fact that God the creator is seen to enter into personal relationship with us confirms that God must care about us. The presence of a tendency toward God in the human psyche suggests as much. However, we cannot know anything about the divine essence outside such relationships. To be made in the likeness of God suggests that God is Relationships. It seems logical, however, to suppose that God the creator will wish to maintain relationships with us in the afterlife, but it is difficult, if not impossible, to imagine the nature of God (I Am who Am) beyond the creative role of relationships. We can only conjecture that the divine plan to create the universe must have been eternally present to God, although only recently manifest to us. The creator must be in relationship with God to function. And the afterlife stage of human development seems to contain a divine invitation to rejoin the God beyond creator and time for some new type of co-creative relationship, perhaps the beginning of a fresh journey in the infinite God of love.

The proposed study of the eschaton unfolds in three consecutive movements. First, being's unconcealment continues to play a focal role in our personal identity. While being's unconcealment ceases during the final moments of dying, we have reason to believe that a reversal in unconcealment carries us into the afterlife, along with the relationships that characterize us. In that event, the person-making process is transformed, although our personal identity is sustained. Second, from the psychological perspective, death offers us an opportunity for a final decision in which we irrevocably side with good or evil. Third, the afterlife state must include a continuity in our social relations, since they define us on earth. What do we do in the afterlife? The reversal in being's unconcealment must provide the metaphysical ground in which we begin a new life process, possibly the infinite journey in God. What about our bodies? The patterns or laws that caused us to emerge as conscious physical beings must accompany us in the afterlife. Thus, our afterlife arises in a mirror image of being's absolute unconcealment, or patterns of human existence, in which we press the relations formed on earth into a fresh round of relations with the divinity. Persons as evil might refuse such relations or enter the heavenly void.

2. The Reversal in Being's Unconcealment

The distinction between dying and death allows us to suggest that while dying is the absence of consciousness, death is the removal of ground in which the possibility of consciousness arises. Death is not something we do, or fail to do, since it is a concealment in being's unconcealment. Death is a concealment in the possibility of human existence. At human death, being's unconcealment refuses "to be," or make itself manifest to us. But what becomes of us? We are maintained in existence, if the reversal occasions a mirror image of being's unconcealment. The scientific experience of matter and anti-matter suggests this possibility.

We have seen that a person is not a soul or a body, or even an amalgam of body and soul since the person does not exist in the absence of relationships. Our study has focused on three levels of relationships. They must be seen to continue in the afterlife, if that is to be us that survive the death of the body. The first evidence that this is the case exists at the psychological level. For as long as we live, the psychological aspect of our relationships takes place as a dialectical movement on the arms of good and evil within psyche. But the desire to pursue the divine good within psyche is a promise of its attainment in the next life. For those to whom God is a reality, say Paul and Linda Badham (1982): "no basis could be more secure" (p. 123). The presence of the divinity in psyche is a strong argument for survival. The desire for survival has a long history. Kierkegaard views it as proof of the afterlife state. The afterlife is a recurring theme in the teachings of Christ. The belief is expressed in biblical revelation. If we passed out of existence at death, it would contradict the love God has for us. According to Christian belief, we are remembered by God in death: "I will never forget you. See, upon the palms of my hands I have written your name" (*Isaiah*, 49:16).

In Christianity, human death is the final point in our struggle with good and evil. It marks the end of the person-making process as we know it, resulting in a final synthesis or choice of the good. The choice of evil is not maintained in death since it refuses the divine telos. In order to safeguard our personal identity, we exist as finite beings in the afterlife, although the psyche's tendency toward the good continues in timelessness. The new beginning continues the divine telos, or infinite journey in God.

The divine telos maintains our relations. It seems reasonable to expect that what is freely given here is maintained in the hereafter. For those who may doubt the existence of an afterlife state, the view of the afterlife presents no greater difficulty than a belief in the existence of reality before death. The existence of the temporal world is indemonstrable. Yet, no one but Descartes and a few skeptics doubt the existence of this world. In fact, Descartes's doubt is only methodological. He knows a great deal more than he says he does. The belief in the afterlife condition, craved by psyche, can only be realized if being's unconcealment continues beyond our death. The fact that it is continued for the living, and that we are intimately connected to them (through love), suggests continuation for the dead. Continuity is always presumed in logic. Thus, at some point, being emerges to a fresh round of unconcealment for the dead. The evidence supports this belief.

How can the psychological tendency toward wholeness survive death? The presence of the craving in us is an implicit promise of its fulfillment. We cannot logically suppose that God could have made us struggle between good and evil without bringing closure to the matter. For as long as we live, the struggle between good and evil is ongoing. As reason and will mature in relationships, the human act expresses itself through moral choices. Virtue is attained on the installment plan. The decision to pursue evil arises out of our misdirected psychological choice for good. We are largely unaware of the consequences of choosing evil, and can be controlled by such choices as we witness and learn from their unfortunate effects. The moral life matures in death. Death is the end of the person-making process, leading to a final choice between good and evil. Since the final choice cannot be executed in this world, there must be an afterlife where such a choice is possible. This safeguards our personal identity at the psychological level of relationships. Of this, more later.

The psychological relation is immersed in our social existence. The person is seen to be a being toward others, as we freely choose to empower or dis-empower other human beings. This grounds the possibility of ethics. Persons become God through others. Our relationships with others are based on the projection of the divine in us toward them. This act of love contains an invitation to self-effacement.

It fuses the person into a social self. Ethics is the study of that bond, or the God connection between two or more psyches. Our ethical relationships with others grow out of an authentic, selfless love of the other for the sake of the other. That love defines us. In Christian belief, for instance, the death of Christ personifies selfless love; "Yes, God so loved the world that he gave his only Son" (*John*, 3:16-18). We become more loving by being more God-like. God became human in order to show how every human could become God-like: "to make clear that his deeds are done in God" (*ibid.*, p. 21).

Although morality arises in a cultural setting, our world is moral because of the ethical connection between us. The immoral act dis-empowers others, or views them as an extension of our own being toward evil. To behave unethically toward others is to prevent them from seeing the good within their own psyche. This attitude is described in Sartre's *No Exit*. To define the other is to restrain the other, preventing their growth. While Sartre's characters are assessed through imaginary deeds, real evil abounds in our world.

In the course of a human life, our social relations harden. The attitude we have toward others accompanies us in the afterlife, since others are an integral character of who we are. Marcel's philosophy of participation suggests that the communion of lovers continues in the afterlife. Love bridges the gap between temporality and timelessness. The love is evident in the survivors, and must exist in the deceased since together we form an I. The experience occurs at the level of secondary reflection, a place irreducible to the ways of the technocratic mentality. It seems possible to suggest that those individuals who do not express a desire to see God through loving relationships on earth will, however, lapse into non-existence at human death.

The Apostles' Creed affirms the belief in a "communion of saints." Although some uncertainty surrounds the precise formulation of the phrase, J.N.D. Kelly (1960) suggests it appeared "in the resolutions of a Gallican synod held at Nîmes [694 kilometers south of Paris] in 394" (p. 389). So, what exactly is the nature of this communion? According to Mary Douglas (1997), in ancient Judaism "there is nothing that the dead can do for the living or the living for the dead" (p. 20). This is not surprising since the focus is on (Marcel's) "having" dimension. In ancient Judaic texts, the anthropology of death suggests, not that the dead commune with the living, but that the possibility of communication ceases at death (death as absence). Douglas views the separation as a ploy to ensure that the living can go about their business without (political) interference from the dead. The rejection of a cult of the dead "has to be seen in a modernizing context of national rebuilding and religious reconciliation" (*ibid.,* p. 23).

However, a new element surfaces in the Christian era, namely, a creedal belief in the "communion of saints," or fellowship of the living and the dead as Church. The focus shifts to (Marcel's) "being" dimension where fellowship exists at the sacramental level, integrating both sides of being's unconcealment into a single voice. Death must be other than absence. It seems possible to imagine that the dead can intercede in the prayer intentions of the living, as they might have similar experiences as the living. But what can the living do for the dead? Since most Christians have abandoned the belief in purgatory, they cannot claim that prayer eases the suffering of the dead. Thus, the risen dead must function as an extension of the good within ourselves, reminding us of final victories in the struggle between good and evil. Our psyche as a tendency toward good is one in fellowship with them, one in the divine psyche. In that sense, we empower the dead, as they empower us.

The third level of relationships characterizing the person is that we are in relation with being's unconcealment, as the work of Heidegger makes known. Our communion with being's unconcealment continues in the afterlife, given a mirror image of unconcealment. In that event, my imprint on being carries over into the afterlife. The essential characteristic of the human body is not the quantitative allocation of body parts as such, but the principle of embodiment, as we saw earlier. What counts about physicality is the pattern of physical laws that governs us. Without the presence of fixed laws to govern human relations, we would not exist. Nor would anything else. We emerge out of divine relations as embodied entities. The information contents of my embodiment are what persist in the afterlife. Polkinghorne (1993) says, "It does not seem in the least irrational to suppose that the pattern might be reconstituted in a new environment of God's choosing" (p. 243).

The expression "I am my body" means I am the physical, visible manifestation of those laws. I arise as the nothing surrounding extension. I am, in fact, like God, the horizon surrounding the nothing of space. This is the meaning of being God-like. The whole of me emerges out of that environment. My metaphysical presence delineates being's unconcealment. My bodily unconcealment in the afterlife is analogous to the behavior of the wave becoming particle in a changed environment. This view preserves personal identity since I am not a disembodied soul in the afterlife. My individuation undergoes the metamorphosis of matter in a changed environment. The reduction of matter to mind illustrates the simplicity of the representation.

The person arises at the intersection of an infinite number of relations. We have only discussed three such instances. They are contiguous in space and time, although the character of the person as correlate of being's unconcealment appears to exhibit a temporal priority. Our temporal existence is the manifestation of God's love for us. God so created the laws or patterns of the universe that we would emerge into conscious life. That condition begets the possibility of entering into the person-making process. The existence of God, manifest in psyche, the social self, and the patterns of cosmos, provides assurance of our ongoing relations in the afterlife.

The argument from design is a powerful refutation of relativism. Science now provides us with the mathematical precision required to trace our origins to a carefully chosen beginning. We cannot explain the origin of the universe through the principle of chance. We are directed to enter into a network of interactions with the universe, forming an intricate web of systemic relationships with cosmos. The existence of the divinity in psyche is the divine imprint in us. However, the imprint is not an event, but a process in which we become more God-like. We unfold the divine plan in history through our informed choices. We are entrusted with the role and responsibility of co-creating the world. The process takes place in our free choices of relationships. Our tendency toward good and evil manifests itself in the two primordial ways we frame things. The fact that we often frame relationships at the secular level, pretending that truth is relative to context, leads to the problems of pervasive technology. In the technocratic mentality, our social and eco-relations are inhumane, refusing the good of our own psyche. They result in acts of manifest self-destruction of the social self as well as of the planet.

The person's tendency toward good, when it is celebrated in the person-making process, takes on the full responsibility of co-creating the world, framing relationships at the sacramental level of existence. The clearest evidence of the sacred exists at the level of *"den enkelte"* social action, an action that springs out of a purity of heart to meet the ordinary struggles of life. We unselfishly, spontaneously, act toward the good of the global family-at-large, but develop the virtues required to maintain that vision.

We suspect God will wish to maintain such relationships since they arise out of the guidance of a divine telos. To put it bluntly, our survival is in the creator's best interest. The quest toward the sacramental or sacred perspective of reality allows us to see things the way God does. But when secular relationships take place without the vista of the Eternal, they frustrate the divine telos. We have no argument for their continued existence in the afterlife. The secular mentality breeds divisiveness and chaos. It continually interrupts the harmony of creation. What becomes of our being toward evil in the afterlife? We suspect it is scattered into the non-being of the void.

For as long as we live, the process of person-making is one in which we freely choose to create ourselves. We act toward good or evil to empower or dis-empower others, framing being's unconcealment as sacramental or secular. The human struggle is played out on the arms of these opposites. The opposites do not result in an either/or confrontation of choices, however. We never become totally good or evil since to do so is to become other than what we are. We perdure as the product of dialogical choices between good and evil. The synthesis is rooted in finitude. Thus, our final state is somewhere between good and evil. This justifies the possibility of beginning anew in the God of the afterlife.

Our temporal habits prepare the way for the afterlife. The person's struggles in psyche, in others, and in objects individuate the moral life. The propositions of morality arise as the good and evil tendencies within us descend to meet the empirical particulars, framing others as good or evil, and things as secular or sacred. At the same time, the empirical particulars of our cultural experiences ascend to shape the psyche until it hardens into a fusion of hard-won virtues at death. We cannot exit life as completely good or evil, but only as good beings that still could do evil, and as evil beings that still could do good.

The formula of the person as a being in moral synthesis lends itself to the view of a reincarnation and the continuation of the dialogical process at some other level. If the eschaton includes reincarnation, God's design for us must be seen to regenerate evil out of the void of non-existence, and plunge us into a fresh round of person-making processes. However, if the eschaton completes the person-making process, there must be a final judgment in which our moral choices harden, or come to an end. The choice of belief in reincarnation, or resurrection, is culturally based. The view of the person as relation is factual, not normative. The religious or cultural expression of immortality varies, however. Chance determines whether the religious view is Christian or Buddhist, although the presence of the divinity in psyche arises by design, as we saw.

Reincarnation eschatology suggests that a number of rebirths are necessary to purify the individual before the attainment of enlightenment or freedom from suffering is possible. The afterlife continues the stage of purification attained in the earlier life. When no progress is made in one form of existence, the individual returns as an inferior life form. Thus, the whole of life is an object of reverence. The Buddhist process of purification is a demanding, disciplined, hard-won struggle with human suffering. The journey ends in the elimination of the ego-state, the principal cause of human suffering. We achieve peace beyond comprehension. But to Western reason, there is one main problem with the view. For as long as we exist, we cannot imagine the person as enlightened. It is not a characteristic of being human. Epicurus might have said that for as long as we live, we are not enlightened. And when we are enlightened, we are no longer human. Thus, enlightenment is nothing to us.

In Christian eschatology, the expectation is to make the final exit as finite beings, less than perfectly good. It seems reasonable to expect, however, that the afterlife does not enlist the struggle between good and evil. It seems possible to suggest that human death begins a new journey in God as infinite love. This view is internally consistent with what has been said, since death stabilizes the psychological and moral condition of life, or state of love expressed by us. If death is the beginning of a fresh journey in the infinite God of love, reincarnation and resurrection theory meet here. The individual's relative state of "enlightenment" is characterized by a final solidification of the moral life.

It is counter intuitive to think of death as being the end of existence when our psyche craves immortality. A first objection to survival arises at the epistemological level. The popular view of death is that it is the absence of consciousness. But that opinion is plainly in error since consciousness is characteristic of the living. It has nothing to do with death as such. Most articles and books on death and dying do not always make this simple distinction. If death were the absence of consciousness, or sensations, we might ask how it feels not to feel, or what sort of consciousness exists in the absence of consciousness. This is absurd. The view of death as arising at the place of concealment in being's unconcealment avoids that epistemological nonsense.

We exist in the familiar world. No proof is required. But we can freeze the moment of phenomenal experience for a closer look at being's unconcealment. The suggestion that death arises on the occasion of being's refusal to be for consciousness allows us to distinguish fully between dying and death. Death is not the absence of consciousness or the absence of life, because it is the removal of the possibility in which absence or presence exists. It was suggested above that death is a concealment in being's unconcealment, giving way to a fresh round of unconcealment at the level of the divine observer. Being, on occasion of human death, emerges to absolute unhiddenness. We exist in the afterlife in relationship with a mirror image of being's unconcealment. Being shows itself fully to the dead, as it is in itself, from itself. The dead frame being's unconcealment through a finite, hardened attitude gleaned in the temporal life. In the afterlife, the person's dialogue in being continues the processes of relationships begun on earth.

Perhaps the first objection to this view is that the body is seen to rot in the ground. How, then, is personal survival possible without the body? It seems that the patterns or laws of cosmos no longer apply to us at death. Our continued physical existence is no more difficult to imagine than that sub-atomic matter also exhibits contradictory characteristics. It can appear either as a wave or as a particle, depending on the environment. The solution to the apparent contradiction emerges in the insight that we are faced with a both/and choice rather than an either/or confrontation of opposites. Thus, the patterns or laws of cosmos must be maintained in the mirror image of being's unconcealment. The appearance of matter as particle gives way to the emergence of wave characteristics in a changed environment. No one doubts that the human body also obeys the laws of matter. The reduction of matter to mind is but a special feature of being a person. But if we suppose the existence of a divine observer, can we not imagine that the person exhibits the same characteristic as any other finite entity? It is not contradictory to imagine the same person appearing one way in the temporal scheme and a second way in timelessness. The term "resurrection" conveys the sense of that belief, although it has been misinterpreted to suggest an interim state of disembodied existence. We cannot be disembodied in the afterlife since death continues the processes begun on earth and ensures our individuality. In a human life, we place our fingerprint on the environment through our attitude toward being. Remembering that a Niels Bohr arc identifies matter, the production of a divine arc in us might also generate an identifiable light of who we are and what moral decisions we bring to the next world.

Perhaps we already appear as a both/and contradiction of wave and particle to a divine observer since human death is a paradox to us. The oxymoronic character of human death suggests the presence of the eternal in our temporal existence. How else explain that the phenomenon of human death is both timely and untimely, personal and impersonal, a source of inspiration and a source of despair? We know ourselves to be mortal, yet death is not an experience. We lack the empirical evidence to document a belief in our own mortality. Further, the nature of thought is such that we cannot imagine ourselves coming to an end. In our more lucid moments, when we are immersed in the fire of intuition, we know that we partake of the eternal because we cannot imagine ourselves as coming to an end. Maritain (1954) takes the argument a step further in suggesting that we "preexisted in God before receiving our temporal beginning" (p. 72). The intuition is supported by the logic of the heart.

For as long as we live, an aspect of our relationships remains unknown to us. The clearest evidence of this dilemma is contained in the experience of loving the other. A spouse, for instance, can love a child of the relationship without being able to explain why. An aspect of human love moves us beyond logic, beyond the discovery of necessary and sufficient conditions. The ability to understand love is also beyond the range of a child's intellect. Yet, the love between parent and child goes on. So the Schrödinger phenomenon applies to our own behavior as it does to the behavior of subatomic particles. Perhaps it applies equally to a divine observer since our condition is not fixed until death.

3. Persons Are Free Correlates

The strongest case for persons as free correlates is made from the perspective of our reducibility to the divine existence. We mark the intrinsic limitation of a creator entering into loving relationships. Since we know God through our participation in the creator's activities, it follows that the person-making process is ultimately rooted in divine existence or freedom. But our claim to metaphysical freedom is not self-evident from the point of view of epistemology. It seems that divine omniscience includes a knowledge of all possible outcomes. Some clarifications are in order.

In the first instance, the freedom of being human is seen as a gift from the creator. It legitimates the possibility of entering into the person-making process. The gift of freedom allows us to make moral decisions on both sides of being's unconcealment.\For as long as we live, the process of becoming God-like, or not becoming God-like, depends on our free choices. We can act toward good or evil.) Does God know the outcome of a human life before it is fully played out? God's omniscience does not include the knowledge of our final ending. This view respects the gift of freedom. To lovingly set an individual free is to be unaware of the sorts of choices the individual will make. If we already know that the individual will choose x rather than y, is not the individual acting under the *illusion* of freedom? To the objection that our freedom is an illusion because God's omniscience includes a knowledge of outcomes, two replies are given. The first is that we do not exist as substance or eternal essence. Nor do we exist as only matter or energy. We exist in relationships. We become persons through a dynamic process of entering into relationships with others. This is how we build and sustain community. But the task is not completed on earth. Thus, how can God know that which is not yet complete? Necessarily God cannot know the nature of a non-existent outcome. Secondly, the principle of divine omniscience is safeguarded by recognizing that it extends only to the range of possibilities, or probable future choices of the person. Thus, the divinity might be aware of the wide range of choices that exist before a person at any given moment of time, without actually knowing which choice a person will make. The realization that the person can freely choose to co-create cosmos with God, or seek to frustrate the divine telos, makes our role and the gift of freedom more valuable. God's love for us is unconditional. And we surprise God by our moral choices. The belief that God is not omniscient with respect to our future choices does not diminish the necessary existence of the divinity. On the contrary, it carries the sense of a dynamic process of creation, one that lovingly enlists the person-making process in a co-creative role. In that light, our freedom arises as something in the making; it fluctuates in the highs and lows of the person-making process, along with the highs and lows of God's "inner court."

4. Death: Moment of Final Decision

The process of making ourselves in the likeness of God continues to the point of death. On the occasion of human death, when being's unconcealment enfolds, the person makes a final decision to irrevocably side with God or evil. In this fashion, we freely decide the nature of our own *post-mortem* world. Two main reasons lead to this conclusion. The first is that we cannot explain the obstinacy of the dead without supposing that they are given such a final choice. But the decision cannot be taken in the absence of the data required to make a decision irrevocable. For as long as the person lives, the possibility of receiving new data and acting differently exists. But the condition or obstinacy of the dead is eternal. Thus, something must happen at death. If the dead are obstinate it must be because they lack no data. Thus, death must be an occasion for data input. This view is necessary since all of the data required for a final decision are not available in this life. Once the decision is made, the dead do not repent because they lack no data. Their condition or nature is congealed by a final decision. The influx of data brings closure to the person-making process and to the tendency toward good and evil, eternally fixing the dead in the condition of temporal choices. The final decision marks the beginning of a new phase of relationships in the afterlife.

The metaphysics of the final decision is as follows: On the occasion of human death, being's unconcealment arises anew in the full disclosure of absolute revealedness. The dead lack no data because the whole of reality emerges to absolute unhiddenness for them. For as long as we live, our decisions are clothed in the garb of temporality. We make mistakes. But it seems that there is no room for the possibility of ignorance and making mistakes in the afterlife, unless death continues into rebirth. The relativity of observation hardens at death. Thus, what is relative to a human observer, including God, is fixed or made immutable in death. We will know ourselves fully in timelessness, as God will know us, since the human project will have reached completion. Our attitude and God's attitude converge in human death. We will judge ourselves in conformity to the degree in which we become divine-like. This interpretation of events is fully consonant with the Thomistic belief that habit "persists in the soul of the dead" (*Summa Theologica* 1. 64. a 2), adding the condition of a reversal in the relationships that individuate us.

Our moral habits carry all the properties of our conscious life into the afterlife, including our beliefs, desires, feelings, thoughts, and the whole range of experiences that constitute personality. According to William James (1983), nothing we ever do is lost on the brain: "down among the nerve cells and fibers the molecules are counting it, registering and storing it up to be used against him when the next temptation comes" (pp. 77-78). That being the case, it follows that all the data stored in the brain (the whole of our relationships) accompany us in the afterlife because brain is ultimately reducible to mind, as we saw earlier. The view of death as being the moment of final decision is also expressed by P. Glorieux (1932), and by Ladislaus Boros (1965). Although Aquinas does not opt for the final decision as such, he thinks it unlikely that God would impose a burden on us that was not imposed upon angels. He says that the angel's final decision is made in the light of all the data required to make it irrevocable. The view of a final decision and data input is required to make sense of the obstinacy of the dead. There can be no final state without a final decision. This view does not diminish the significance of our temporal existence. This life is what prepares us for it. Death solidifies our existing perfection by raising us to final perfection. Temporal habits, virtues, vices, and the change of heart mentally underwrite the final decision. They pour the mold for the obstinacy of the dead; as the die is cast so the metal hardens. So, death is a final hardening of the attitude, secular or sacred, through which we frame our relationships.

This view does not suggest that the dead roam through the corridors of the afterlife hoping to cut their best deal before deciding on a final state. Since the data are intuited, the decision is spontaneous. The last moment of death and the first moment of the afterlife coincide. Time ceases to exist after time, although duration exists in timelessness.

Although this view expresses a consistent transition from thanatology to eschatology, problems remain. For instance, how do infants and aborted zygotes make a final decision? They come to an end before reaching maturity, before having the experiences required for a final decision. The reply to the objection arises beyond the level of appearance. The final decision is not made on the basis of reason or the activity of a speculative intellect, but on the basis of relationships. The zygote and the infant both enter into a complex web of relationships with self, the other, and the environment. The zygote begins at the cellular level of relationship with the mother's uterus and environment. Although the range of such relationships appears small, they are fully commensurate with being a zygote. They accomplish the divine telos, or person-making process, intended for zygotes, although this fact is sometimes only appreciated by the parents. The value of the particle in the environment is relative to the divine observer. The following simple analogy suffices to make the point: A thimble and a large container are equally full when completely filled; the infant that dies at birth and the adult that dies after a long life are both in relative processes as the outcome of anterior conditions. Perhaps the divine pattern is the essential thing, not the actual life of the individual. If it has taken eighteen thousand million years to produce me as zygote, is that not the essential thing rather than my brief history of biological existence? Furthermore, the final decision is not taken at the end of time, or even by some measure of duration existing beyond time, but intuitively in timelessness. It is possible that everyone exists in God from time immemorial before receiving a temporal existence. In that event, even the longest possible biological life-span would not register on an infinite scale. While it is true that the person-making process can hardly take place without a human life, there is a sense in which the metaphysical event of life is more basic than the epistemic process of life-making. Further, it is logically possible to suppose that the main play of human existence takes place, not on earth, but in the infinite journey in God that begins at death. Perhaps we enter the afterlife as infants, ready to begin a new journey in God.

[The final decision is taken as the data of temporal existence are made eternally available to us. The temporal dimension is only relative to us. The past, future and present exist simultaneously in timelessness. In death, we will see ourselves as God sees us from God's eternal present. Thus, our temporal framing collapses into the present, into the eternal now of existence. The present cannot have duration since part of it would lie ahead of itself, or behind itself, which is absurd. Temporal events such as death and resurrection occur simultaneously in timelessness. Given this view, the belief that the body of the deceased is in the ground and not in the ground at death is not contradictory because matter is relative to the observer. To a divine observer, the "resurrection of the body" (by this I mean the patterns of our physical existence), occurs simultaneously with the death of a person. We do not wait in timelessness as disembodied souls, or in limbo, before deciding our fate. Thus, the apostle Paul has not been waiting 2,000 years for his body. The final decision is not taken at a time after time. It is made in duration beyond time, the here and now of timelessness.

One further point needs to be explained. All temporal, person-making processes cease at human death. So, what do the dead do now that their state is fixed? Their state is only fixed from the perspective of a congealed tendency toward good and evil. But the outcome of the person-making process predisposes us toward a fresh round of activities in the afterlife. We participate in eternal life in the measure of a final solidification of temporal habits. The tendency toward good vanquishes the tendency toward evil. This is to fulfill the divine plan or law of existence. What sorts of activities toward the good take place in the afterlife? We can only suppose, not that no activity exists in the afterlife, (death as such is not absence) since death is preparation for new growth, but that the activities of the dead are qualitatively different from the activities of the living. The difference between them is not one of degree, but one of kind. The death of a human being does not result in a heaven-plus-one relationship story, but in a qualitatively transformed environment.

What sorts of relationships occur in the afterlife? In order to maintain a consistent belief in the final decision theory, we must suppose that the epistemic process of knowledge reverses itself. On the occasion of human death, we experience a Copernico-Kantian reversal in our epistemic activities. This is said to explain the suddenness of the final decision. In this event, the brain does not wait to be informed by sense experience to generate ideas, but itself transforms the senses. The movement is spontaneous as the sense immediately conforms to the beliefs the human formed on earth. Kant might have been wrong about this world, but he was right about the next one. Since the data intuited in a final decision must be comprehensive (to explain the obstinacy of the dead), the body will literally glow from the flame of spiritual enlightenment. Thus, we enter the afterlife fully formed from the temporal life, justifying belief in a fresh round of innate ideas. To be fully formed is to be fixed in place by the final decision.

That state or condition of mind allows us to participate fully in the contemplation of the divine within psyche. We see the divine face as we have trained ourselves to frame the world. And the divine face, or the horizon surrounding the nothing, shows itself to us in the measure that our moral habits allow. That is, we receive God in the measure of our awareness of God in psyche, others, and the world. Since the divine face unfolds in timelessness, our participation or action toward the face of God must begin an eternal journey. Death opens the door to the infinite journey in God.

How do we communicate in the afterlife? Communication can arise through a spontaneous consonance among similar states of enlightenment, passing from one person to another without the use of the neural pathways of the brain as process. What Descartes saw will come about as the concept and the idea exchange seats in the heavenly epistemic house. The brain might function as the repository of solidified habits. We can imagine the divinity as a Loving Presence in communion with us through telepathy and clairvoyance. In simpler terms, the community connects through the presence of divinity in the *post-mortem* psyche. But the problem with this imagery, as with any discussion of death as such, is that we verify the theory in our own experiences. Since we do not have experiences of life after life, verification is limited. However, once we recognize why we cannot understand the nature of death as such, we can advance an explanatory view, one that looks to being's unconcealment as containing the possibility of consciousness, while being consistent with the available evidence. We think that this has been accomplished.

It seems possible to suggest that the final decision separates the good from the evil tendencies of psyche. Thus, the culture of the afterlife is wholly spiritual. We know, for instance, that language cannot be separated from a cultural setting. Thus, the person acting toward evil would not be comfortable in a spiritual culture, or be able to communicate with the good.

The human, then, is given the person-making capacity to become a finite force for good or evil in this life. The condition of the dead in the afterlife is a hardening of the relationships begun on earth. In fact the full force of the person-making process as becoming God-like suggests, not only that we become like God at human death, but that God becomes more fully personal in the eschaton. This seems to be central to Jung's *Answer to Job*. However, I do not wish to populate the afterlife with a stockpile of fallacies from earth. So, it is best to proceed slowly in this area. The infinite journey in God means that the relationships of the person begun at the trinitarian level of self, others, and being are solidified by death to continue endlessly in eternal life. Let us review the case.

The matter of the person as a being toward good and evil is settled for all eternity in human death, as we become immutably, obstinately good or evil. If, depending on temporal habits, we decide for the good, then we become congealed in our God-like condition or nature. But if we become like God, God must also be seen to become like the good in us. In other words, the presence of God in the human heart must emerge to absolute unconcealment, no longer expressed in the unconscious voice of psyche. The divinity shall emerge in full disclosure at the level of timeless conscious light. This is probably what Aquinas intends to convey by his idea of a "beatific vision." No wonder the "risen" body is said to glow. God will empower us as we empower God. The divine existence will arise from the darkness of the human heart to transfigure the whole of our environment. In brief, our own epistemic, Kantian reversal is accompanied by a reversal in the metaphysical expression of the divinity.

The unconcealment of being will arise fully to light up being's unconcealment. We will move, not from being to God, but from God to creation. Scripture says that the body of the risen Christ was transfigured. His body assumed different properties and capacities such as shining brightly, walking through solid objects, and bi-location. His body was not subject to the conditions of other bodies in space. This seems to be the sense of Saint Paul's "spiritual body" (Paul, 1 *Corinthians,* 15). Mary Magdalene was the first to see Christ, but she did not recognize him until he spoke (*John,* 20:1-2 and 11-18). Possibly our bodies or physical properties will likewise change in the afterlife since the patterns or laws of cosmos will exist outside space and time as we know it. These laws will be seen to emanate from the divinity. The experience is profoundly spiritual (and transformative) since it takes place in divinity, beginning the infinite journey in God. Persons will emerge to absolute spirituality since they exist in a changed environment. This view avoids the problem of personal identity. We saw that in quantum mechanics, the properties of matter vary with the environment. Matter is not only wave or particle but spiritual.

But what about the evil ones? Are they saved in the eschaton? To be evil is to frustrate the eschaton. It is to say no to the divine telos. To do so is to arise in the darkness of the void as totally other than God. At that point our relationships will come to an end and return to the cosmic vacuum, as we existed before the divine observer made a decision to create rather than not create. We will cease existing rather than continue to exist as beings toward evil.

Although the doctrine of Hell has been with us since the time of Augustine, can we imagine an infinitely loving God casting a person into a state of eternal, horrible suffering? This is not to suggest that frustrating the divine telos goes unnoticed. We expect divine justice. Perhaps the evil in us devolves into the realm of the void. Contemporary theology seems to support this principle.

For as long as we live, evil is an integral part of our finitude. It characterizes our mode of individuation. Once the struggle between evil and good is played out, and the final hardening of the good or evil takes place, there will be no place for evil in the heavenly environment. It will have fulfilled the necessary condition for which it was struck. Thus it will cease to exist, not only because God's infinite goodness leaves no room for evil, but because it shall have reached its teleological end. That being the case, God must plunge evil back into the void where it no longer controls us or causes injury and suffering of the innocent. The good ones become fully aware of the evil. Let me explain. In depth psychology, it is alleged that what we are unaware of controls us. So in order not to be controlled by evil, it must be brought out to full light. This is the sense of casting evil into the void. While God cannot annihilate the work of the creator, an aspect of the creative activity ceases to exert influence on creation. Evil continues to exist as a metaphysical entity or aspect of finitude, but it ceases to function as a psychological tendency of being human. It is raised out of the realm of darkness or the unconscious to be plunged into a state in which all possible consequences of evil choices become manifest. At that time no further activity toward evil is possible since all is unconcealed.

The social self is also an important characteristic of being dead. This view suggests that the dead bring something of the living into the afterlife. How can that be me in the afterlife without my loving relationships? But the living are generally unaware of this. Where is the empirical justification of this belief? Although parapsychology offers a wealth of detail on this matter, for my own part I am largely skeptical about the suitability of this approach to death. We cannot support the belief that our empirical communication with the dead is authentic. What mediums report about the dead is so trivial and general that the information is worthless. No one has ever returned from death to tell us about the nature of death as such. But some individuals claim to have lived past lives. Are they to be trusted? The simple answer is no. A ten-year-old child does not give evidence of the wisdom acquired in a previous life. Children's reports do not stand up to critical scrutiny. Furthermore, reincarnation does not satisfy the criterion of personal identity, given that the ten-year-old possess a different brain or body than the deceased.

The problem with studies of the paranormal is that they fail to document such experiences. They confound the empirical facts of dying and death, failing to distinguish one from the other. The whole brain definition of death, for instance, suggests that the "near-death experience" or NDE is an experience of the dying brain, not of death as such, since it occurs before the whole brain is dead. Once we move beyond cortical and mid-brain death to include the death of the brain-stem, as specified in the biology of death, the NDE reports become conspicuously absent. No one comes back to report about their own brain-stem death. Why, then, do we think that the NDEs have an experience of death as such?

Since the first appearance of Robert Moody's book *Life After Life* (1975), the experience of the dying brain has been documented in scores of studies. Those patients who survive the event report similar stories of moving through a tunnel toward a bright light, surrounded by love, seeing deceased parents and friends. The experience is profound and transcultural, often leading to a fresh spiritual awakening. So, the dying do experience something, although it cannot be death as such. The simplest explanation is that the experience is chemically induced. It might be due to a lack of oxygen in the dying brain (anoxia), or perhaps the brain creates its own hallucinations through the release of endorphin at a critical point in the dying process. Susan Blackmore (1993) concludes her own in-depth study of the NDE phenomenon with the observation that the hallucinatory experience of being outside the body can be explained by the brain's release of endorphin. That production is associated with the intense feelings of joy and peace so characteristic of the NDE (p. 112). Since Blackmore is also a string-theorist, she describes the joy as a movement out of ego concerns, becoming one with cosmos. The experience is mystical.

In the most favorable scenario, the NDE is euphoric and a right frontal lobe (yin) predisposition to immortality. The view is not illogical, since we are beings toward immortality. Death is not an instantaneous process. So, the dying trajectory might trigger some genetic biological mechanism in preparation for death. We have known about the non-logical ways of right-brain thinking for about eighty years. But the problem is that such a predisposition cannot be quantified. Although the somatic condition of the NDE is reversible, confusion arises because we cannot measure the brain's activity at that point. We, then, mistakenly equate the absence of measurement with the condition of being dead. Indeed, premature burial was a source of concern before the introduction of modern embalming techniques. At the turn of the century, we did not possess the technical expertise required to distinguish fully between dying and death.

In our day, the problem of prematurely pronouncing death is compounded by the precision of medical technology. A report of the Hastings Center published some 25 years ago dwells on some of the consequences of rapid developments in medical technology. The same individual, for instance, can be pronounced dead or alive in different parts of town, on the same day, depending on available technology. That condition is made worse by several human factors, such as time of day and age of patient, including the perceived status of the patient. We are only human. At some point the decision is taken not to pursue heroic measures. And the patient is left to die. Yet, we continue to fear death. The fact that belief in the NDE is widespread at the popular level might simply reflect our own death-denying culture.

However, Gabriel Marcel's philosophy provides the best evidence that some persons are in non-natural communion with the dead. Marcel's experiences of the paranormal are not meant to be explained empirically, since they take place at the level of love. The skeptic replies that the experience is not genuine. We are reproducing memories about the likeness of the deceased in us. Yet, the survivor's experience of death is no less vivid. The experience takes place at the level of mystery in a realm where things do not have to be visible to make sense.

Marcel uses the term mystery to signify that the communication with the dead takes place at the level of relationships. But a relationship of this nature doubles back on itself to reconnect with the psyche. Obviously, the living walk away from the grave, the dead do not. But the activities of the wounded psyche confirm that something paranormal is taking place. An aspect of us dies with the loved one, while an aspect of the loved one lives on in us. This is to experience the afterlife. Marcel's suggestion that communication is raised to a higher level is confirmed by our experiences. The relationships I form with others is essential to being a person. I am less of a person without my relationships. In fact, if all my relationships came to an abrupt end, there would be nothing left of me. This is why survivors often soon follow loved ones in death after a long and loving relationship. They lose the sense of being a person.

Loving relationships undergird ethics. Ethics is the measure of our enactment of the good within us toward others. To be ethical toward others is to say to them, "You shall not die." We lovingly empower them out of the divinity that exists within our psyche. That empowerment exists as the root of the possibility of being moral. It is an absolute, without which there could be no universal drive to love or care about people. Our ethical relationships meet in the divinity. They exist in and through God. The survivor and the deceased remain connected through God. This is what is felt in the psyche when a loved one dies. They resonate in us as we meet them in the divine heart. For as long as we live, we interact ethically because of the divine love within. Thus the divine heart provides a focal point for ongoing relationships in the afterlife.

Although matter is ultimately reducible to mind, patterns or laws of matter govern mental life. How is this characteristic of being human continued in the afterlife? The ontological laws of human relationships emerge to a fresh round of divine-making processes in the afterlife (person-making having been brought to fruition), governed by the horizon of being's unconcealment. Thus, the divine law emerges in characteristic mode proper to an environment that exists beyond the natural order. Although we do not understand anything about that environment, we can suggest the sorts of things that need to be in place to explain the reality of the afterlife.

At human death, the relationships that characterize us solidify through a reversal in the nothing surrounding being. This is a place where being's unconcealment functions as the intrinsic limitation of God, or is ultimately reducible to God. This view allows us to make sense of the "beatific vision." The dead see God face to face in being's absolute unconcealment, as they view the horizon of the nothing surrounding the natural order without the limitations of temporality. For as long as I live, my dialogue in being's unconcealment is incomplete since it is characterized by contingency. I live out my relationships toward the good on the installment plan, focusing, as I often do, on the world of appearances. But each act of genuine care that is expressed at the sacramental level of existence is a payment of rent on my final decision to irrevocably side with the unity, truth, goodness, and beauty of God. My attitude as a being toward God, others, and the environment generates my metaphysical fingerprint on the horizon bordering being's unconcealment. That imprint is the signature of my God-talk on earth.

If I harden toward evil on earth, flowers might appear dull, and children dumb. But if I harden toward good, then there is beauty in simplicity, God in a child's laughter. My metaphysical print on being is the sum of my interactions, my vibrations on being's unconcealment. The print is carried over into the meta-unconcealment realm of being's disclosure. The flower carries my attitude into the afterlife. Nothing I do is lost, since nothing exists outside God.

I have no doubt that some Wittgensteinian scholars are growing increasingly weary of my rhetoric. So perhaps I can redeem myself. In order to write non-religious epistemology it seems necessary first to recognize that the conception of the individual as a being in relationships provides a fresh perspective for both metaphysics and ethics. In our day, metaphysics seems to be taking a new path. In the past, we focused on substance or essence before proceeding to a study of the properties of a substance. This was to fulfill the Thomistic promise, "*operation follows nature*." Metaphysics was said to be the judge of epistemology: Descartes's "critical problem," for instance, arose through a process of mistaking the idea for the concept, while empiricism focuses on properties without expressing a concern for the substantial core that underlies the possibility of properties. My own sense of this history is that metaphysics is overextended. The critics are right but for the wrong reasons. Although the Thomistic distinction between the concept and the idea provides a safe house for the objectivity of knowledge, it also promotes an artificial distance between the natural law and being a person. Aquinas's view plants the seeds of dualism. The view of the disembodied soul is as deficient as the no-soul view.

The problem is avoided by moving from the conception of the person as abstract substance to a view of the human as a being in relationships. David Cockburn (1990), for instance, suggests that what we first express toward others is an attitude, before knowing who they are. Thus, he proposes to construct the metaphysics out of the epistemology. I do not think he would object to the suggestion that we do so because the attitude we have toward others is a reflection of the good or evil that exists within us. And if this belief is true, it seems but a small step to add that the ways of the heart also frame the way in which we direct ourselves toward being's unconcealment. The sum of all our attitudes forms the cluster that expresses who we are. Our attitudes direct us to react spontaneously to other human beings. We also react spontaneously to the presence of evil in others, and to the degradation of the environment.

I react spontaneously to evil and suffering in the world. I cringe at the sight of violence and the suffering of other human beings, including animals. Some of the nature shows on television are horrifying. The other day, for instance, I saw a documentary on the nasty habits of the lion devouring a living zebra. I react spontaneously. Something is terribly wrong with our world. Why do innocent animals suffer? As a philosopher, I need a logical explanation. My spontaneous attitude leads to the development of metaphysics, ethics, and social action. I do this because I care about my world. Since I believe God enters into relationship with us, God must also care about the world. Thus, I cannot write ethics without God. The spontaneous attitude leads to the discovery of an absolute in history.

Ethics is present in the ways of the psyche as an attempt to make sense of life through our relationships. But it also points beyond itself to the transcendent presence that exists beyond the natural order. When the mystical Eckhart prayed God to rid him of God, he saw that our temporal perspective generates an impoverished view of God. Yet, the natural order is the intrinsic limitation of the supernatural order, as the creator is the intrinsic limitation of God.

The attempt to write non-religious ethics ignores the character of person-making as an infinite number of strings or associations formed with the world. It ignores our spontaneous attitudes toward things. One of the most basic strings is the God connection in psyche. Why should we seek artificially to reduce the moments of person-making to one string and not the other, if not as a reflection of our own will to power? Unless some universal constant exists to unite the strings of being a person in relationships, the universality and absoluteness of ethical obligation is without foundation. The existence of God at both ends of the spectrum, the infinitely small of the human heart and the infinitely large of the cosmos, provides an absolute that is desperately needed in an age of relativism.

So, when is the end-time? The simple answer is that it will come to pass when the divine telos is realized, or the person-making process reaches full maturity. For as long as our being toward evil wins the day, no final end is in sight. But the triumph of our tendency toward good signals the end of a process.

5. Heaven on Earth

We have examined the sorts of things that need to happen to survive human death. But what are we in the afterlife where the person-making process is no longer? The afterlife place is termed "heaven," signifying the beginning of a new process in God. What is heaven like? The exploration of the question is limited by our experiences of the divinity in us, in other human beings, and in being's unconcealment. The human processes of becoming God-like having reached a final end, the person's condition or nature irrevocably hardens, or assumes final shape. It predisposes us to begin the infinite journey in God in a fixed way. We now participate in the heavenly process in the measure of our having become God-like on earth.

In the course of this discussion on immortality, we have yet to land on Socrates (469-399 B.C.E.)–"the wisest man in Greece," according to the Delphian oracle. So it is fitting that we should examine his view of death and immortality, since it might contain an insight into the nature of heaven. His work does not contain a solution to the problem of the nature of death as such, although he has much to say about it. He tells us in the *Apology* that the fear of death is misplaced, since death is good, "either death is a state of utter nothingness and utter unconsciousness, or, as men say, there is a change and migration of the soul from this world to another" (p. 211 b). Although the *Phaedo* argues for the immortality of the soul, this tells us more about Plato's theory of ideas than about Socrates' beliefs in the afterlife. Plato was intent on providing a home for the soul before birth and after death. Aquinas takes their views a step further by making the religious connection between immortality and living in the state of grace.

Socrates' goal was to define, through ceaseless questioning, the nature of the (good) soul. Thus, he is in no way dogmatic about immortality, leaving the question open. "For is not philosophy the study of death?" (*ibid.*, p. 232d). At his trial, for instance, the condemned Socrates could have used his wits to gain acquittal, but did not choose to do so. He could hardly convince his audience that philosophy is preparation for death by betraying his own calling. But in what sense is the philosopher not afraid of death, if not that the soul finds shelter in personal immortality? Is not death the separation of the soul from its opposite–the body?

The question is highly relevant, since in our day philosophy functions more as a service industry than as an end in itself. The practice of philosophy today generates clear and distinct syntax in the rhetoric of living a human life. Wittgenstein rightly abandoned philosophy when he saw it come to this end. How can philosophy be a human activity in the absence of wonder, love, and values? Where is the consolation of philosophy if not in the preparation for becoming more divine and thereby more human? It turns out that Socrates' greatest concern is not the fear of death as such, but the fear of hating argument. This provides an important clue to the nature of philosophy. His attitude toward death rightly views philosophy, not as a means to an end, but as an end in itself. According to Ann Hartle (1986), "Socrates is doing battle against the greatest evil [to hate argument]. The battle against the fear of death is secondary" (p. 53). And there lies its greatness, not in the strength of proofs for immortality, but in the activity of doing philosophy as if it matters to the gods.

My critique of the tradition is raised in this spirit, not to move beyond it, since far greater thinkers have already attempted this task and failed, but to move within it. Socrates' lesson is that the consolation of philosophy is in making sense of the present by valuing those sorts of deeds that contribute to the good life. The reward is in the pilgrimage itself. My critique of the tradition is that Socrates ought not have separated the soul from the body. Death is not the opposite of life (dualism). The fact that the soul does not depart without the body (the laws or patterns of existence) at death means that the creator of the natural world necessarily meets the supernatural God of the afterlife in a single, non-dualistic, compassionate voice of existence. So, the discovery of the divine in our psyche, other human beings, and the environment continues in the afterlife. My reflection on the nature of life after death is a projection of those sorts of processes, or relationships, on earth that characterize the good life, or the person-making process. In brief, heaven must be a lot like earth. Heavenly persons continue to act toward the good, although the tendency to do so remains tempered in finitude or limitation of created existence. This view safeguards personal identity in the absence of evil.

Heaven must be governed by patterns, or laws, reflecting the wisdom of the divine Creator. Our final judgment is a measure of the degree of harmony between the divinity in us and the divine law. Our moral beliefs will more adequately conform to the ways of divine law, since the culture of heaven is populated by persons that express a similar interest in acting toward the good.

Anthony de Mello (1982) tells the story of "The Perfect Apple":

Nasruddin had barely finished his discourse when one of the scoffers in the crowd said to him, 'Instead of spinning spiritual theories, why don't you show us something practical?'
Poor Nasruddin was nonplussed. 'What kind of practical thing would you want me to show you?' he asked.

Pleased that he had mortified the mullah and was making an impression on the crowd, the scoffer said, 'For instance, show us an apple from the garden of Paradise.'
Nasruddin immediately picked up an apple and handed it to the man. 'But this

apple is bad on one side,' said the man. 'Surely a heavenly apple would be perfect.'

'A celestial apple would, indeed, be perfect,' said the mullah. 'But given your present faculties, this is as near to a heavenly apple as you will ever get.' (P. 157)

The question about heaven depends on us. We have been assigned a positive role in co-creating cosmos, struggling with good and evil forces. It is up to us to frame heaven, as we frame the world. Can we detect goodness in others or in the environment if our own hearts move us toward evil? Life has little meaning under the guise of evil, and heaven even less. Can we imagine heaven through the wounded eye of suffering? The de Mello story expresses the limitations of human experience. For as long as we live, we are limited by the natural order and by our own tendencies toward it. Thus, our vision of heaven arises as the celebration of our richest moments and the rejection of our more unpleasant experiences. We need to celebrate the truths of this world before we can recognize the truths of heaven. On earth, for instance, we experience good things like love, compassion, honesty, fidelity, availability, justice, and truth. Heaven must be a place of moral virtue, not like the evil of the human heart. The critique of heaven is the celebration of evil.

Sacred texts such as the Holy Koran, the Biblical books of *Exodus* and *Deuteronomy*, the Aramaic text of the Lord's Prayer, and the Buddha's eightfold path toward enlightenment provide an indication of how we might frame reality in the afterlife. Beginning with *Exodus* (*Exodus, 20*:1-17) and *Deuteronomy* (*Deuteronomy, 5*: 6-21), God establishes the ten rules of the Mosaic law, or *Torah*. The first four commandments govern the behavior of the person as a being toward God, while the other six concern our associations with other human beings. The ten commandments are guidelines for the person as a being in relationships. The final decision of the dead judges the person's degree of holiness. In Christianity, the greater the conformity between the commandments and the person's way of framing reality, the greater the degree of holiness. For instance, the more the person celebrates the good within psyche rather than the false idols of the secular mentality, and the more the person respects the rights and freedoms of other human beings and the rights of the environment, then the greater the person's participation in the divinity. The Aramaic text of the Lord's Prayer suggests we cultivate insight or wisdom to move beyond the surface appearance of the secular level. As a consequence heaven and earth will merge in unity as a loving act of the Birther. The triumphant dead shall not be misled by the surface appearance of things, or strive toward a dualism of heaven and earth. They shall not be engaged in the struggle between good and evil. They shall not be tempted. The state of the dead is enlightened since, according to the teachings of the Buddha, they have been liberated from the false preoccupations with the self that lie at the heart of suffering.

The analogy between heaven and earth leads to the awareness that since we enter earth as infants we must likewise begin the infinite journey in God as infants. Harper's (1988) *Biblical Commentary on Matthew's Text of the Beatitudes*: "Happy the pure in heart: they shall see God. Happy the peacemakers: they shall be called the sons of God" (5:10), suggests that the blessed shall be like "angels," sons and daughters of God. The purity of heart announced in the Beatitudes is an invitation to become like children, trusting God, as Kierkegaard's *"den enkelte"*commitment celebrates.

The Biblical text of *Luke* on the resurrection of the dead adds:

> The children of this world take wives and husbands, but those who are judged worthy of a place in the other world and in the resurrection from the dead do not marry because they can no longer die, for they are the same as angels, and being children of the resurrection they are sons (and daughters) of God. (20:34-37)

The reference to the single state of persons in heaven connects with the Catholic belief (pre-Vatican II) that the primary purpose of marriage is the procreation and education of children (*Genesis,* 1:28). Since death comes to an end in the afterlife, we need not procreate. But a richer reading of the text raises the love between husband and wife to the level of the divinity. The love is wider, more inclusive than espousal love. Thus, the point is not that espousal love dissolves, but that it pales in comparison to divine love. The First Letter of John, "Live As God's Children," says: "My dear people, we are already the children of God but what we are to be in the future has not yet been revealed; we shall be like him because we shall see him as he really is" (2:2).

The "Second condition" specifies the importance of the law of love: "if you refuse to love you must remain dead" (2:15). We are instructed to love one another: "Whoever keeps this commandment lives in God and God lives in him (and her)" (2:24). Our "purity of heart" is expected to be childlike since it is unconditional love, based on trust.

If the blessed see God face-to-face (*John,* 22:4) it is because at the psychological level they already stand in the presence of the eternal. The habit of doing so is cultivated during our temporal existence whenever we live in the full immediacy of the present moment. The challenge before us is not to mistake the secular for the sacred level of existence. We usually run ahead of ourselves, planning the next step of a busy life rather than focusing on the present moment of experience. At times, we are struck by the presence of the eternal in the temporal as the manifestation of God in the present moment. The intuition arises whenever we move beyond the linear logic of reason to recognize the (yin) existence of intangible forces in the environment. Although these moments are fleeting, they provide a window on the eternal that can last a lifetime. The blessed stand in the presence of wisdom when they see God face-to-face. They manifest the gift of discernment, choosing the sacramental perspectives of reality. That distinction is the focal point around which the standing rights of being emerge to full unconcealment.

If the blessed see God face-to-face, they receive the reality of existence as blessing. The dead are fully aware of their own finitude. The acceptance of human limitation predisposes us to recognize being as blessing, to see in being, not only our presence in cosmos, but the unity, truth, goodness, and beauty of existence. That awareness generates a peace beyond understanding, or left-brain insight.

If the blessed see God face-to-face they stand in the presence of forgiveness and love. Although we do not attain spiritual perfection in the realm of finitude, enlightenment follows from seeing the other as an extension of self. Once we have rid ourselves of the ego, nothing threatens us since we become part of the All of existence. Nothing exists outside of us. We meet reality in an act of forgiveness and love because in meeting cosmos, we meet ourselves.

And how do we begin the infinite journey in God? If we as the blessed see God face to face it is because we begin the journey on earth. The ultimate reducibility of matter to mind (consciousness to personal identity), mind to being, being's unconcealment to the creator, and the creator to God is the logical outcome of a person-making process carved in the likeness of God. The human being joins cosmos in a panentheistic movement toward the All of creation, the alpha and omega of being in loving relationships. God becomes us so that we can become like God.

One of the major problems in theodicy concerns the plight of the damned. What becomes of individuals that, for a time, actually frustrate the divine telos? Are we free of evil in the afterlife? If so, how can that be us (or how can that be us in Hell, emptied of the tendency toward good)? The indeterminacy principle provides a possible response. Could the "damned" exist in the void as the no longer being of evil? The explanation of quantum physics suggests that under certain conditions, matter pops back into existence, as we saw. Thus, the divine observer, moving out of an act of infinite compassion, might give fresh life to evil through a panentheistic explosion of divine love, or Big Bang, thereby plunging the "damned" into another round of person-making processes. This is what reincarnationists have been saying all along. Rebirth is a plausible way of not remaining a rotten apple. The challenge is to conduct the observation within the range of divine justice.

6. Summary and Conclusion

I have argued that in dualism personal immortality does not get off the ground. But what is a person, if not body and soul? The person arises as the outcome of relationships or associations: I am nothing in the absence of divine patterns or laws; nothing in the absence of other human beings; and nothing in the absence of being's unconcealment. We can no more dissociate being human from relations than the part can dissociate itself from the whole. We might say, not, "I think, therefore, I am," but, "patterns exist, therefore, I am; other human beings exist, therefore, I am; being unconceals itself, therefore, I am." Relationships individuate me, giving birth to my physical, psychological, ethical, and metaphysical life. These characteristics of being human provide the horizon for a personal afterlife argument.

The evidence to support the case is seen from the perspective of wholes and their parts, as the part is the intrinsic limitation of the whole. Matter is ultimately reducible to mind, mind to being's unconcealment, and so on. My personal identity arises as the focal point of converging relationships. I know myself to be in dialogue with being's unconcealment. The truth-making character of being human suggests that embodied mind is the intrinsic limitation of being's unconcealment. The person does not stand outside being, but is a truth-disclosing entity engaged in the unfolding process of being's unconcealment. In addition, the "nothing" surrounding being's unconcealment is an intrinsic limitation of the creator. The creator is the ultimate sufficient reason of finitude, but is also bordered by a horizon, possibly God. The creator entering into personal relationship with us is another name for God. The relationship places us in the presence of the Almighty, providing an insight that sustains us in our person-making processes toward the divine.

The argument moves on three levels, beginning with the assurance, not only that God exists in our psyche, but that having entered into relationships with us, God will wish to maintain such relationships beyond our personal death. The first indication that this is the case results from the character of being's unconcealment, since it points beyond itself to the horizon bordering the nothing of being. Thus, the psyche's psychological addiction to God meets with the metaphysical promise that divine patterns cannot pass out of being without a radical shift in the divine essence. We have no evidence to suggest the possibility of such a shift. On the contrary, as panentheism suggests, the continued existence of our own social self beyond death means that God cannot rid God of the creator, or undo creation, without positing an act of God into non-being, which is manifestly impossible.

The person's social self executes a key role in the person- making process. It seems reasonable to suggest that it parallels the God-making process. This is to fulfill the covenant announced in *Genesis,* 1:26: And God made us in the likeness of God. Our person-making processes carry us into the afterlife where they continue to individuate us through a fixed commitment toward being good (or evil) by empowering (or dis-empowering) the manifold of our relationships. We not only arise out of the relationships of this life, but continue to carve fresh relationships in the afterlife as co-creative human beings.

What is the afterlife like? We can imagine an eschatology of relationships in which having become like God, or realized the divine telos, we naturally function in more divine fashion, namely, in the absence of moral evil. Yet, we cannot escape the condition of being created (physical evil). Perhaps our divine role occasions additional birthing, the emergence of new realities in the infinite world of divine possibilities. Will that still be we in the afterlife, acting more like supernatural entities than humans? Yes, of course. Given that the part is the intrinsic limitation of the whole, this view is not surprising.

The scientific evidence that we arise out of the nothing and the philosophic evidence that the nothing reclaims us at death assigns primacy to the existence of the nothing. It answers the question why something exists rather than nothing, thereby dismantling the illusion of relativism. We know that our nothing marks the place of a divine gift into the something of relationships, providing the sufficient and necessary condition of absolute truth. This truth provides ethics with the universal character required to move beyond relativism, although the exigencies of a locale cast human beings into an historical person-making process. The belief in the possibility of becoming more human in this world and in the afterlife is justified.

WORKS CITED

Anonymous. *Alcoholics*. (1980) 3rd ed. New York: Alcoholics Anonymous World Services.

Aquinas, Thomas. (1952) *Summa Theologica*. Translated by Fathers of the English Dominican Province. 2 vols. Chicago: Encyclopedia Britannica.

(1956) *Summa Contra Gentiles*. Book Two: Creation. Translated by James F. Anderson. New York: Doubleday.

(1956) *Summa Contra Gentiles*. Book 3: Providence. Part 1 & 2. Translated by Vernon J. Bourke. New York: Image Books.

(1958) *The Division and Method of the Sciences*. Translated by A. Maurer. Toronto: Pontifical Institute of Medieval Studies.

Aristotle. (1952) *The Works of Aristotle*. Translated by W. D. Ross. 2 vols. Chicago: Encyclopedia Britannica.

Ayer, A.J. (1992) "What I Saw When I Was Dead." In Edwards, ed., *Immortality*, pp. 269-275.

Badham, Paul. (1989) "Zen and Death: A Response to Cook" In Davis, ed., *Death and Afterlife*, pp. 172-176.

(1989) "God, the Soul, and the Future Life." In Davis, ed., *Death and Afterlife*, pp. 36-52

(1997) "Religion, Science, and Philosophy." Unpublished article.

Badham, Paul, and Linda Badham. (1982) *Immortality or Extinction*. London: Macmillan.

Berkeley, George. (1952) *The Principles of Human Knowledge*. A.C. Fraser, ed., vol. 35. *Locke, Berkeley, Hume*. Chicago: Encyclopedia Britannica.

Blackmore, Susan. (1993) *Dying to Live*. London: Grafton.

Boros, Ladislaus. (1965) *The Moment of Truth*. London: Burns and Oates.

Bruntland, Gro Harlem. (1987). *Our Common Future*. New York: Oxford University Press.

Bryson, Kenneth A. (1993) "The Metaphysical Foundations of Justice." In Choudhury, ed., *Humanomics*, pp. 74-85.

(1997) "Morality as Dialectical Process." In *Vera Lex*, vol. 15. Pleasantville, N.Y.: Pace University.

(1995) *Flowers and Death*. 3rd ed. North York, York University: University Press of Canada.

(1994) "Sue Rodriguez and the Argument for Assisted Suicide," *Policy Options*, 15:9 (November), pp. 41-44.

Butler, Joseph. (1975) "Of Personal Identity." In John Perry, ed., *Personal Identity*, pp. 99-105.

Canada. (1995) *Of Life and Death*. Report of the Special Senate Committee on Euthanasia and Assisted Suicide. Ottawa: Ministry of Supply and Services (June).

Capra, Fritjof. (1983) *The Tao of Physics*. London: Penguin Books.

Capra, Fritjof, T. Matus, and D. Steindl-Rast. (1992) *Belonging to the Universe*. London: Penguin Books.

Caputo, John. (1978) *Mystical Element in Heidegger's Thought*. Athens, Ohio: Ohio University Press.

Carlo, William. (1966) *The Ultimate Reducibility of Essence to Existence in Existential Metaphysics*. The Hague: Martinus Nijhoff.

Choudhury, Masud, ed., (1993) *Humanomics*. Kent, England: Barmarick Publications.

Cockburn, David. (1990) *Other Human Beings*. Basingstoke: Macmillan.

(1991) ed. *Human Beings*. Cambridge, England: Cambridge University Press. Royal Institute of Philosophy. Supplement: 29.

(1992) ed. *Death and the Value of Life*. Lampeter, U.K. Saint David's University: Trivium. No. 27.

Cohn-Sherbok, Dan, and Christopher Lewis, eds., (1995) *Beyond Death*. London: Macmillan.

Cook, Francis, H. (1989) "The Buddhist Thinks about Death." In Davis, ed., *Death and Afterlife*, pp. 154-171.

(1989) "Response to Badham's Response." In Davis, ed., *Death and Afterlife*, pp. 180-182.

Craig, W.L. (1994) "Scientific Confirmation of the Cosmological Argument." In Louis P. Pojman, ed., (1998) *Philosophy of Religion*. 3rd.ed. Belmont, Cal.: Wadsworth Publishing Company.

Craig, W. L., and Q. Smith. (1995) *Theism, Atheism, and Big Bang Cosmology*. Oxford: Clarendon.

Darling, David. (1996) *Zen Physics*. New York: Harper Collins.

Davies, Paul. (1992) *The Mind of God: Science and the Search for Ultimate Meaning*. London: Simon & Schuster.

Davis, Stephen, T. ed., (1989) *Death and After Life*. New York: St. Martin's Press.

(1989) "The Resurrection of the Dead." In Davis, ed., *Death and Afterlife*, pp. 119-144.

De Mello, Anthony. (1982) *The Song of the Bird*. Garden City, New York: Doubleday.

Descartes, René. (1968) *Philosophical Works of Descartes*. Translated by Elizabeth Haldane, and G.R.T. Ross. 2 vols. New York: Cambridge University Press.

Douglas, Mary. (1997) "An Anthropology of the Afterlife," The Ingersol Lecture on Immortality, *Harvard Divinity Bulletin*, 26:4

Douglas-Klotz, Neil. (1990) *Prayers of the Cosmos: Meditations on the Aramaic Words of Jesus*. New York: Harper Collins Publishers, Inc.

Durbin, Paul. (1992) *Social Responsibility in Science, Technology, and Medicine*. Bethlehem, Pa: Lehigh University Press.

Edwards, Paul, ed., (1992) *Immortality*. Toronto: Macmillan.

(1967) ed., *The Encyclopedia of Philosophy*. 8 vols. New York: Macmillan and The Free Press.

Ferré, Frederick. (1996) *Being and Value: Towards a Constructive Postmodern Metaphysics*. Albany: State University of New York Press.

Flew, Anthony. (1987) *The Logic of Mortality*. Oxford: Basil Blackwell.

Foster, John. (1991) *The Immaterial Self*. London: Routledge & Kegan Paul.

Fox, Matthew. (1983) *Original Blessing*. Santa Fe, N.M.: Bear & Company.

George, André. (1933) "Emile Meyerson 1859-1933," *Nouvelles Littéraires* (9 December).

Glorieux, R. P. (1932) "Endurcissement final et grâce dernières," *Nouvelle Revue Théologique*, No. 10 (December).

Griffin, David, Ray. (1989) "Life After Death, Parapsychology, and Post-Modern Animism." In Davis, ed., *Death and Afterlife*, pp. 88-107.

Hartle, Ann. (1986) *Death and the Disinterested Spectator*. Albany: State University of New York Press.

Hawking, Stephen. (1993) *Black Holes and Baby Universes*. London: Bantam.

(1988) *A Brief History of Time*. London: Bantam.

Heidegger, Martin. (1962) *Being and Time*. Translated by John Macquarrie and James Robinson. New York: Harper & Row.

(1977) *The Question Concerning Technology and Other Essays*. Translated by William Lovitt. New York: Harper and Row.

(1977) "The Turning." Translated by William Lovitt. In *The Question Concerning Technology and Other Essays*, pp. 36-49.

(1977) "On the Essence of Technicity." Translated by William Lovitt. In *The Question Concerning Technology and Other Essays*, pp. 226-249.

Hein, John (1989) "Global Economic Trends: What Lies Ahead for the '90's." New York: Conference Board, Inc. *Research Report No. 932.*

Heitler, Walter. (1963) *Man and Science*. New York: Basic Books.

Helm, Paul. (1988) *Eternal God*. Oxford: Clarendon Press.

Herbermann, C.G., E.A. Pace, C.B. Pallen, T.J. Shahan, and J.J. Wynne, eds., (1907) *The Catholic Encyclopedia*. New York: Robert Appleton Company.

Hick, John. (1966) *Faith and Knowledge*. New York: Cornell University Press.

(1976) *Death and Eternal Life*. London: Collins.

(1977) *Evil and the God of Love*, London: Macmillan.

(1989) "Response to Cook." In Davis, ed., *Death and Afterlife*, pp. 177-179.

(1989) "A Possible Conception of Life After Death." In Davis, ed., *Death and Afterlife*, pp. 183-196.

Hirvonen, Ari. (1995) "*Civitas Peregrina*: Augustine and the Possibility of Non-Violent Community," *International Journal for the Semiotics of Law*, 8:24.

Huchingson, James, ed., (1993) *Religion and the Natural Sciences*. New York: Harcourt Brace Jovanovich.

Hume, David. (1967) *A Treatise of Human Nature*. L.A. Selby-Bigge. ed., Oxford: Clarendon Press.

(1952) *An Enquiry Concerning Human Understanding*. L.A. Selby-Bigge. ed., Vol. 35. *Locke, Berkeley, Hume*. Chicago: Encyclopedia Britannica.

(1947) *Dialogues Concerning Natural Religion*. 2nd ed. Norman Kemp-Smith, ed., Edinburgh: Oxford University Press.

Humphrey, Robert L. (1994) "Human Nature's Natural Law," *Vera Lex*, 14:1&2, pp. 8-17.

James, William. (1983) *Talk to Teachers on Psychology*. Cambridge, Mass.: Harvard University Press.

Jerusalem Bible: Reader's Edition. (1968) New York: Doubleday & Co.

Jung, Carl G. (1959) "Aion." Translated by R.F.C. Hull. *The Collected Works of C.G. Jung*, Vol 9. London: Routledge & Kegan Paul.

(1992) *Answer to Job*. Translated by R.F.C. Hull. London: Ark Paperbacks.

Kant, Immanuel. (1952) "Refutation of the Argument of Mendelssohn for the Substantiality or Permanence of the Soul." *Critique of Pure Reason*. Translated by J.M.D. Meiklejohn. Vol. 42. *Kant*. Chicago: Encyclopedia Britannica.

Kelly, J.N.D. (1960) *Early Christian Creeds*. London: Longmans.

Kerr, Fergus. (1989) *Theology After Wittgenstein*. Oxford: Basil Blackwell.

(1991) "Getting the Subject Back Into the World." In Cockburn, ed., *Human Beings* Supplement: 29, pp. 173-190.

Kuhse, Helga, and Peter Singer. (1992) "Allocating Health Care Resources and the Problem of the Value of Life." In Cockburn, ed., *Death and the Value of Life.*

Küng, Hans. (1991) *Global Responsibility.* Translated by John Bowden. Munich: SCM Press.

Lackey, Douglas, P. (1993) "The Big Bang and the Cosmological Argument." In Huchingson, ed., *Religion and the Natural Sciences,* pp. 190-195.

Lamb, David. (1992) "Death and Personal Identity." In Cockburn, ed., *Death and the Value of Life,* pp. 43-56.

Lefevre, Frédéric. (1926) "Une heure avec M. Meyerson," *Nouvelles Littéraires* (6 November).

Leslie, John. (1989) *Universes.* London: Routledge.

Locke, John. (1952) *Essay Concerning Human Understanding.* A.C. Fraser, ed., Vol. 35. *Locke, Berkeley, Hume.* Chicago: Encyclopedia Britannica.

Lowenberg, Jacob. (1932) "Meyerson's Critique of Pure Reason," *The Philosophical Review,* 41 (July), pp. 351-367.

MacIntyre, Alasdair. (1981) *After Virtue.* London: Duckworth.

Maritain, Jacques. (1954) *Approaches to God.* New York: Harper.

Mays, James, L., and Joseph Blenkinsopp, eds., (1988) *Harper's Bible Commentary.* San Francisco: Harper and Row.

McKim, William A. (1997) *Drugs and Behavior.* 3rd ed. Upper Saddle River, N.J.: Prentice-Hall.

Meadows, D.H., D.L. Meadows, Jorgen Randers, and W.W. Behrens III. (1972) *The Limits to Growth.* New York: Signet.

Meyerson, Emile. (1962) *Identity and Reality.* Translated by Kate Lowenberg. New York: Dover.

⸻ (1991) *Explanation in the Sciences.* Translated by Mary-Alice and David A. Sipfle. Boston Studies in the Philosophy of Science, no. 128. Hingham, Mass: Kluwer Academic Publishers.

⸻ (1925) *La déduction relativiste.* Paris: Payot.

⸻ (1931) *Du cheminement de la pensée.* 3 vols. Paris: F. Alcan.

⸻ (1933) *Réel et déterminisme dans la physique quantique.* Paris: Hermann.

⸻ (1936) *Essais.* Paris: Vrin.

Moody, Robert. (1975) *Life After Life.* Toronto: Bantam Books.

Nef, George, Jokelee Vanderkop, and Henry Wiseman, eds., (1989) *Ethics and Technology.* Proceedings of the World Conference on Ethics and Technology. Toronto: Thompson Education Publishing.

Neuner, Josef, and Jacques Dupuis, eds., (1983) *The Christian Faith in the Doctrinal Documents of the Catholic Church.* London: Collins.

Nielsen, Kai. (1989) "The Faces of Immortality." In Davis, ed., *Death and Afterlife,* pp. 1-30.

Nietzsche, Friedrich. (1954) "The Gay Science." In Walter Kauffman, ed., *The Portable Nietzsche.* New York: Viking.

Parfit, Derek. (1984) *Reasons and Persons.* Oxford: Oxford University Press.

⸻ (1992) "Divided Minds and the Nature of Persons." In Edwards, ed., *Immortality,* pp. 308-315.

Paul II, Pope. (1983) "Man's Condition After Death." In Neuner, and Dupuis, eds., *The Christian Faith in the Doctrinal Documents of the Catholic Church.*

Perry, John, ed., (1975) *Personal Identity.* Berkeley: University of California Press.

Pierce, Christine, and Donald Van De Veer (1995) *People, Penguins, and Plastic Trees.* 2nd ed. Belmont, Cal.: Wadsworth Publishing Company.

Plato. (1952) *The Dialogues of Plato.* Translated by J. Harward. Vol. 7. *Plato.* Chicago: Encyclopedia Britannica.

Pojman, Louis P. (1998) *Philosophy of Religion.* 3rd ed. Belmont, Cal.: Wadsworth.

Polkinghorne, John (1993) "More to the World Than Meets the Eye." In Huchingson, ed., *Religion and the Natural Sciences,* pp. 235-248.

Postman, Neil. (1993) *Technopoly.* New York: Alfred A. Knopf.

Price, H. H. (1992) "What Kind of Next World?" In Edwards, ed., *Immortality,* pp. 213-219.

Reese, W.L. (1980) *Dictionary of Philosophy and Religion.* Atlantic Highlands, N.J.: Humanities Press.

Reid, Thomas. (1975) "Of Identity." In John Perry, ed., *Personal Identity,* pp. 107-112.
    (1975) "Of Mr. Locke's Account of Our Personal Identity." In John Perry, ed., *Personal Identity,* pp. 113-118.

Roy, David. (1989) "The Health and Life Sciences: Where Is the Ethics For Our Knowledge and Power?" In Nef, Vanderkop, and Wiseman, eds., *Ethics and Technology,* pp. 113-118.

Schumaker, E.F. (1973) *Small Is Beautiful: A Study of Economics as If People Mattered.* London: Blond and Briggs.

Siegel, Shepard. (1982) "The Mystery of Heroin Overdose." In William A. McKim, *Drugs and Behavior.* 3rd ed., pp. 44-45.

Swinburne, R. (1986) *The Evolution of the Soul.* Oxford: Clarendon Press.

Taylor, Paul, W. (1994) "The Ethics of Respect for Nature." In Westphal and Westphal, eds., *Planet in Peril,* pp. 15-37.

Vardy, Peter. (1995) "A Christian Approach to Eternal Life." In Cohn-Sherbok and Lewis, eds., *Beyond Death,* pp. 13-25.

Westphal, Dale, and Fred Westphal, eds., (1994) *Planet in Peril.* New York: Harcourt Brace College Publishers.

Williams, Alan. (1985) "The Value of QALY," *Health and Social Service Journal* (3 July).

Wolf, F. Alan. (1997) "Quantum Physics as Evidence of the Soul." Interviewed by Ronald S. Miller, *Science of Mind,* 70:2.

Woods, Roy. (1992) "Death and Ontology in Rilke, Heidegger, and Zen." In Cockburn, ed., *Death and the Value of Life,* pp. 108-142.

Yao, Xinzhong. (1996) "Self-Construction and Identity: The Confucian Self in Relation to Some of the Western Perceptions," *Asian Philosophy,* 6:3, pp. 179-195.

ABOUT THE AUTHOR

Kenneth A. Bryson is Professor of Philosophy at the University College of Cape Breton, where he has taught since 1970. He has held a teaching appointment at the University of Ottawa, and visiting appointments at l'Université de Moncton, Mount Saint Vincent University, Le CEGEP Régional de la Côte Nord, P.Q., and the University of Wales, Lampeter, U.K. He received his Ph.D. degree at the University of Ottawa, with a dissertation on the metaphysics of Emile Meyerson's philosophy of mind. He developed an interest in the philosophy of death and dying as a way of introducing students to philosophy. It has since become one of his primary research areas. He has published five books, including *Flowers and Death,* now in its tenth year and third edition. The central issue that animates his work is the belief that eternal truths exist.

INDEX

VIBS

The Value Inquiry Book Series is co-sponsored by:

American Maritain Association
American Society for Value Inquiry
Association for Personalist Studies
Association for Process Philosophy of Education
Center for East European Dialogue and Development, Rochester Institute
of Technology
Centre for Cultural Research, Aarhus University
College of Education and Allied Professions, Bowling Green State
University
Concerned Philosophers for Peace
Conference of Philosophical Societies
Institute of Philosophy of the High Council of Scientific Research, Spain
International Academy of Philosophy of the Principality of Liechtenstein
International Society for Universalism
Natural Law Society
Philosophical Society of Finland
Philosophy Born of Struggle Association
Philosophy Seminar, University of Mainz
R.S. Hartman Institute for Formal and Applied Axiology
Society for Iberian and Latin-American Thought
Society for the Philosophic Study of Genocide and the Holocaust
Society for the Philosophy of Sex and Love
Yves R. Simon Institute.

Titles Published

1. Noel Balzer, *The Human Being as a Logical Thinker.*

2. Archie J. Bahm, *Axiology: The Science of Values.*

3. H. P. P. (Hennie) Lotter, *Justice for an Unjust Society.*

4. H. G. Callaway, *Context for Meaning and Analysis: A Critical Study in the Philosophy of Language.*

5. Benjamin S. Llamzon, *A Humane Case for Moral Intuition.*

6. James R. Watson, *Between Auschwitz and Tradition: Postmodern Reflections on the Task of Thinking.* A volume in **Holocaust and Genocide Studies.**

7. Robert S. Hartman, *Freedom to Live: The Robert Hartman Story, edited by Arthur R. Ellis.* A volume in **Hartman Institute Axiology Studies.**

8. Archie J. Bahm, *Ethics: The Science of Oughtness.*

9. George David Miller, *An Idiosyncratic Ethics; Or, the Lauramachean Ethics.*

10. Joseph P. DeMarco, *A Coherence Theory in Ethics.*

11. Frank G. Forrest, *Valuemetrics*: The Science of Personal and Professional Ethics.* A volume in **Hartman Institute Axiology Studies.**

12. William Gerber, *The Meaning of Life: Insights of the World's Great Thinkers.*

13. Richard T. Hull, Editor, *A Quarter Century of Value Inquiry: Presidential Addresses of the American Society for Value Inquiry.* A volume in **Histories and Addresses of Philosophical Societies.**

14. William Gerber, *Nuggets of Wisdom from Great Jewish Thinkers: From Biblical Times to the Present.*

15. Sidney Axinn, *The Logic of Hope: Extensions of Kant's View of Religion.*

16. Messay Kebede, *Meaning and Development.*

17. Amihud Gilead, *The Platonic Odyssey: A Philosophical-Literary Inquiry into the Phaedo.*

18. Necip Fikri Alican, *Mill's Principle of Utility: A Defense of John Stuart Mill's Notorious Proof.* A volume in **Universal Justice**.

19. Michael H. Mitias, Editor, *Philosophy and Architecture.*

20. Roger T. Simonds, *Rational Individualism: The Perennial Philosophy of Legal Interpretation.* A volume in **Natural Law Studies**.

21. William Pencak, *The Conflict of Law and Justice in the Icelandic Sagas.*

22. Samuel M. Natale and Brian M. Rothschild, Editors, *Values, Work, Education: The Meanings of Work.*

23. N. Georgopoulos and Michael Heim, Editors, *Being Human in the Ultimate: Studies in the Thought of John M. Anderson.*

24. Robert Wesson and Patricia A. Williams, Editors, *Evolution and Human Values.*

25. Wim J. van der Steen, *Facts, Values, and Methodology: A New Approach to Ethics.*

26. Avi Sagi and Daniel Statman, *Religion and Morality.*

27. Albert William Levi, *The High Road of Humanity: The Seven Ethical Ages of Western Man*, edited by Donald Phillip Verene and Molly Black Verene.

28. Samuel M. Natale and Brian M. Rothschild, Editors, *Work Values: Education, Organization, and Religious Concerns.*

29. Laurence F. Bove and Laura Duhan Kaplan, Editors, *From the Eye of the Storm: Regional Conflicts and the Philosophy of Peace.* A volume in **Philosophy of Peace.**

30. Robin Attfield, *Value, Obligation, and Meta-Ethics.*

31. William Gerber, *The Deepest Questions You Can Ask About God: As Answered by the World's Great Thinkers.*

32. Daniel Statman, *Moral Dilemmas.*

33. Rem B. Edwards, Editor, *Formal Axiology and Its Critics.* A volume in **Hartman Institute Axiology Studies.**

34. George David Miller and Conrad P. Pritscher, *On Education and Values: In Praise of Pariahs and Nomads.* A volume in **Philosophy of Education.**

35. Paul S. Penner, *Altruistic Behavior: An Inquiry into Motivation.*

36. Corbin Fowler, *Morality for Moderns.*

37. Giambattista Vico, *The Art of Rhetoric (Institutiones Oratoriae,* 1711-1741), from the definitive Latin text and notes, Italian commentary and introduction by Giuliano Crifo, translated and edited by Giorgio A. Pinton and Arthur W. Shippee. A volume in **Values in Italian Philosophy.**

38. W. H. Werkmeister, *Martin Heidegger on the Way,* edited by Richard T. Hull. A volume in **Werkmeister Studies.**

39. Phillip Stambovsky, *Myth and the Limits of Reason.*

40. Samantha Brennan, Tracy Isaacs, and Michael Milde, Editors, *A Question of Values: New Canadian Perspectives in Ethics and Political Philosophy.*

41. Peter A. Redpath, *Cartes ian Nightmare: An Introduction to Transcendental Sophistry.* A volume in **Studies in the History of Western Philosophy.**

42. Clark Butler, *History as the Story of Freedom: Philosophy in Intercultural Context,* with Responses by sixteen scholars.

43. Dennis Rohatyn, *Philosophy History Sophistry.*

44. Leon Shaskolsky Sheleff, *Social Cohesion and Legal Coercion: A Critique of Weber, Durkheim, and Marx.* Afterword by Virginia Black.

45. Alan Soble, Editor, *Sex, Love, and Friendship: Studies of the Society for the Philosophy of Sex and Love, 1977-1992.* A volume in **Histories and Addresses of Philosophical Societies.**

46. Peter A. Redpath, *Wisdom's Odyssey: From Philosophy to Transcendental Sophistry.* A volume in **Studies in the History of Western Philosophy.**

47. Albert A. Anderson, *Universal Justice: A Dialectical Approach*. A volume in **Universal Justice.**

48. Pio Colonnello, *The Philosophy of Jose Gaos*. Translated from Italian by Peter Cocozzella. Edited by Myra Moss. Introduction by Giovanni Gullace. A volume in **Values in Italian Philosophy.**

49. Laura Duhan Kaplan and Laurence F. Bove, Editors, Philosophical Perspectives on Power and Domination: Theories and Practices. A volume in **Philosophy of Peace.**

50. Gregory F. Mellema, *Collective Responsibility.*

51. Josef Seifert, *What Is Life? The Originality, Irreducibility, and Value of Life.* A volume in **Central-European Value Studies.**

52. William Gerber, *Anatomy of What We Value Most.*

53. Armando Molina, *Our Ways: Values and Character*, edited by Rem B. Edwards. A volume in **Hartman Institute Axiology Studies.**

54. Kathleen J. Wininger, *Nietzsche's Reclamation of Philosophy*. A volume in **Central-European Value Studies.**

55. Thomas Magnell, Editor, *Explorations of Value.*

56. HPP (Hennie) Lotter, Injustice, *Violence, and Peace: The Case of South Africa*. A volume in **Philosophy of Peace.**

57. Lennart Nordenfelt, *Talking About Health: A Philosophical Dialogue*. A volume in **Nordic Value Studies.**

58. Jon Mills and Janusz A. Polanowski, *The Ontology of Prejudice*. A volume in **Philosophy and Psychology.**

59. Leena Vilkka, *The Intrinsic Value of Nature.*

60. Palmer Talbutt, Jr., *Rough Dialectics: Sorokin's Philosophy of Value*, with Contributions by Lawrence T. Nichols and Pitirim A. Sorokin.

61. C. L. Sheng, *A Utilitarian General Theory of Value.*

62. George David Miller, *Negotiating Toward Truth: The Extinction of Teachers and Students*. Epilogue by Mark Roelof Eleveld. A volume in **Philosophy of Education.**

63. William Gerber, *Love, Poetry, and Immortality: Luminous Insights of the World's Great Thinkers.*

64. Dane R. Gordon, Editor, *Philosophy in Post-Communist Europe.* A volume in **Post-Communist European Thought.**

65. Dane R. Gordon and Józef Ni_nik, Editors, Criticism and Defense of Rationality in Contemporary Philosophy. A volume in **Post-Communist European Thought.**

66. John R. Shook, *Pragmatism: An Annotated Bibliography, 1898-1940.* With Contributions by E. Paul Colella, Lesley Friedman, Frank X. Ryan, and Ignas K. Skrupskelis.

67. Lansana Keita, *The Human Project and the Temptations of Science.*

68. Michael M. Kazanjian, *Phenomenology and Education: Cosmology, Co-Being, and Core Curriculum.* A volume in **Philosophy of Education.**

69. James W. Vice, *The Reopening of the American Mind: On Skepticism and Constitutionalism.*

70. Sarah Bishop Merrill, *Defining Personhood: Toward the Ethics of Quality in Clinical Care.*

71. Dane R. Gordon, *Philosophy and Vision.*

72. Alan Milchman and Alan Rosenberg, Editors, *Postmodernism and the Holocaust.* A volume in **Holocaust and Genocide Studies.**

73. Peter A. Redpath, *Masquerade of the Dream Walkers: Prophetic Theology from the Cartesians to Hegel.* A volume in **Studies in the History of Western Philosophy.**

74. Malcolm D. Evans, *Whitehead and Philosophy of Education: The Seamless Coat of Learning.* A volume in **Philosophy of Education.**

75. Warren E. Steinkraus, *Taking Religious Claims Seriously: A Philosophy of Religion*, edited by Michael H. Mitias. A volume in **Universal Justice.**